AF540882

SELENIUM AND SILKWORMS

By

Dr. A.Vijaya Bhaskara Rao, *Ph.D.*
Associate Professor
Deptt. of Sericulture
Sri Krishnadevaraya University
Anantapur
(India)

&

Dr. S. Smitha
Reader
Deptt. of Sericulture
STSN Govt. Degree College
Kadiri
(India)

DISCOVERY PUBLISHING HOUSE PVT. LTD.
NEW DELHI-110 002

Published by:
Tilak Wasan

DISCOVERY PUBLISHING HOUSE PVT. LTD.
4383/4B, Ansari Road, Darya Ganj
New Delhi-110 002 (India)
Phone : +91-11-23279245, 43596064-65
Fax : +91-11-23253475
E-mail : parul.wasan@gmail.com
discoverypublishinghouse@gmail.com
web : www.discoverypublishinggroup.com

***First Edition:* 2012**

ISBN: 978-93-5056-118-8

Selenium and Silkworms

Printed at:
Shree Balaji Art Press
Delhi

Foreword

Success of Sericulture industry in general is depending on a wide range of techniques ranging from mulberry production and biological rearing. Keeping in view of this, the authors made an attempt on the nutritional aspects of silkworm by supplementing selenium as trace element. Selenium is known for its efficacy in improving the quality and quantity of muscle and wool in vertebrates especially sheep. However, the minimal information is available on insect herbivores. Hence the authors studied the biochemical, histological and cocoon commercial characters on exposure to selenium to explore the possibility of this element to enhance the cocoon production. The authors demonstrated that the selenium supplementation at lower doses is beneficial to the silkworm and for improving cocoon commercial qualities.

Each chapter of this book has a detailed introduction to fundamentals of biochemical, histological and cocoon commercial parameters and experimental methodology and results are discussed in the light of updated literature. It is unique and commendable experimental work of the recent times in seribiotechnology for enhancing the cocoon production and is useful for P.G. students, research scholars, teachers of life sciences and sericulturists.

Dr. K. NAGALAKSHMAMMA
Associate Professor
Head, Department of Sericulture,
Sri Padmavathy Women's University,
Tirupati-517 502
Andhra Pradesh
India

Preface

Sericulture or the commercial production of silk is an important industry in the developing countries like– China, India and Eastern Europe. The silkworm was domesticated by man for over 35 centuries, and now unable to survive in nature without his protection and assistance. Several other species of Bombyx that feed on mulberry as larvae have also been domesticated. Therefore, a particular methodology must be applied in order for growth of silkworms and to correlate the silk productivity to environmental and biotic factors. Since sericulture is practiced in diverse agro climatic zones of the country, there is a possibility of variations in the nutrients and the trace elements available in the mulberry leaves depending on the different soil constituents. The elements such as Fe, Mg, Na, K, S, Se and F can be acquired by the plants, is readily magnified in the food chain, and is known to influence the physiology and biochemical metabolism in wild life, domestic animals and man. For instance, higher than the usual amounts of certain trace elements are implicated as toxic agents. At the other extreme, low levels of essential elements cause deficiency diseases in flora and fauna.

Therefore it is imperative to study the possible role of different essential trace elements in plant and animals. Selenium is an essential trace nutrient important to humans and most other animals as an anti-oxidant, functioning as the metal co-factor for important enzymatic activity requiring glutathione peroxidase. Although the toxic effects of selenium have been recognized much earlier than the nutritional properties, the exact mechanism of the manifestation of selenium toxicity in animals is not yet understood. However research on the nutritional aspects of selenium and its interaction with other nutrients and/or environmental chemicals has been comprehensively reviewed. Metabolic disorders due to selenium inadequacy have been recognized practically in all the major livestock producing countries of the world. Some parts in China are associated with the selenium deficiency, where the selenium in the soil is low. In animals dietary selenium deficiency induces a number of pathological changes such as diminished growth and increased mortality in quail, pancreatic fibrosis and exudative diathesis in chicks, hepatic necrosis in rats and white muscle disease in cattle and sheep. Selenium supplementation improved the performance and meet quality in animals.

However, information on the effects of selenium on insect growth and survival is quite limited. Very little information is available on the effects of selenium in arthropods. Particularly, insects are considered to be the critical components of most terrestrial and fresh water eco-systems. They are key herbivores and recyclers and also become an important part of the food web for higher trophic levels. Selenium is toxic to mammals especially at higher doses and beneficial at lower doses. But, the information on the interaction of selenium with different doses of selenium in insects has not available. Hence, in the present investigation, a study has been made on the toxicity of selenium at different doses and at different exposure periods in silkworm *Bombyx mori L.* The study includes some biochemical and histological aspects in the organs of fat body, malpighian tubules and haemolymph of silkworms in relation to the accumulation of selenium. Further cocoon commercial characters have been studied in the silkworm *Bombyx mori L.* with reference to lethal and sub-lethal doses of selenium and changes have been correlated with histological changes in fat body and malpighian tubules of V instar silkworm.

This book comprises eight chapters dealing with various aspects of selenium and its impact on silkworm biology. The introductory chapter explains the nature and scope of selenium chemistry and biochemistry on flora and fauna. The second chapter deals with the methodologies to analyse various biochemical, histological and economic characters in silkworms. The third chapter deals with the nutritional parameters on supplementation of different doses of selenium. The fourth chapter provides information on the levels of bioaccumulation in different organs of silkworm at different periods. The fifth chapter deals with the metabolic aspects of carbohydrates in silkworm. The sixth chapter elucidates the protein catabolic and anabolic metabolisms in silkworm. The seventh chapter provides histomorphological studies in detail with precise photographic representations which will help the reader to correlate the molecular changes with cellular structural changes. As the quality of feed plays a remarkable role on the economic traits of cocoons, the eighth chapter discusses about these important parameters. An extensive list of references related to selenium and silkworm were given. This book makes an attempt to improve the silkworm cocoon productivity. However, the book also gives more prominence to some of the toxicological indices on exposure to lethal doses of selenium. This book will encourage readers to dig deeper into the selenium biochemistry in various organisms. Students and researchers of sericulture and life sciences should find this book valuable information on selenium as an essential trace element.

A.Vijaya Bhaskara Rao

S. Smitha

Contents

Chapter

1

General Introduction

The art of silk production is "Sericulture", an important cottage industry based on agro forestry earning foreign exchange worth about Rs. 1500 crores per annum. Presently sericulture is practiced in more than 60,000 villages providing gainful employment, economic development and improvement in the quality of life to the people approximately 58 lakhs, most of them being small and marginal farmers. India has the distinction of cultivating all the four commercially known varieties of silk, namely Mulberry, Tasar, Eri and Muga. The world raw silk production (Mulberry and non mulberry) about 125629 MT is mainly from two countries *i.e.*, China and India. China leads the world with silk production of 102560 MT or 81.6 per cent of the produce. India ranks second in respect of world raw silk production. It is this position, as one of only two major silk producers in the world, and from its employment potential, that sericulture and silk derive their importance in the Indian textile map. Policy decisions are defined mainly by these two considerations.

It is well known that the domestic production of raw silk is not adequate to meet the domestic and export demand. It is estimated that against the demand of around 26,000 tonne per annum the domestic production is around 16,500 tonnes. The gap of nearly 9500 tonnes in demand is mainly on account of the fact that high grade mulberry raw silk is not being produced in the country to the extent required by the industry. This quality of mulberry raw silk is basically required in the power loom industry, for export purposes, and to some extent in the hand loom industry for warp purposes. The present global production is fluctuating around 70,000 to 90,000 MT and the demand for silk is annually increasing by 5 per cent. With the increase in population and also with the increased demand for fashionable clothing items due to fast changing fashion designs in developed countries, the demand for silk is bound to increase even more.

For increasing the silk production, we require highly productive mulberry varieties and silkworm races and also races tolerant to adverse climatic conditions and diseases which can come mainly from the sericultural germplasm resources and also from the wild relatives of *Bombyx* available in the natural habitats. However the success of a silkworm crop depends on the quality and the quantity of the mulberry leaves. Since sericulture is practiced in diverse agro climatic zones of the country, there is a possibility of variations in the nutrients and the trace elements available in the mulberry leaves depending on the different soil constituents. The elements such as Fe, Mg, Na, K, S, Se and F can be acquired by the plants, is readily magnified in the food chain, and is known to influence the physiology and biochemical metabolism in wild life, domestic animals and man. For instance, higher than the usual amounts of certain trace elements are implicated as toxic agents. At the other extreme, low levels of essential elements cause deficiency diseases in flora and fauna. Therefore it is imperative to study the possible role of different essential trace elements in plant and animals. Selenium is an essential trace nutrient important to humans and most other animals as an anti-oxidant, functioning as the metal co-factor for important enzymatic activity requiring glutathione peroxidase (Mayland, 1994). Selenium was isolated by Berzilius in 1818. Much work is needed to clarify the chemistry of selenium in regard to dietary forms, their metabolic fate, and the forms in which selenium functions as an essential element. Comprehensive and systematic review of the various aspects of organic chemistry of selenium, was made by Campbell *et al.*, (1952). The nomenclature for organo-selenium compounds is similar to that of sulphur compounds. Selenium compounds exert their biological effects either directly or by being incorporated into enzymes and other bioactive proteins. The main inorganic dietary form of selenium is sodium selenite. In the organic forms selenomethionine and selenocysteine, where sulphur is replaced by selenium atom in the aminoacids methionine and cysteine.

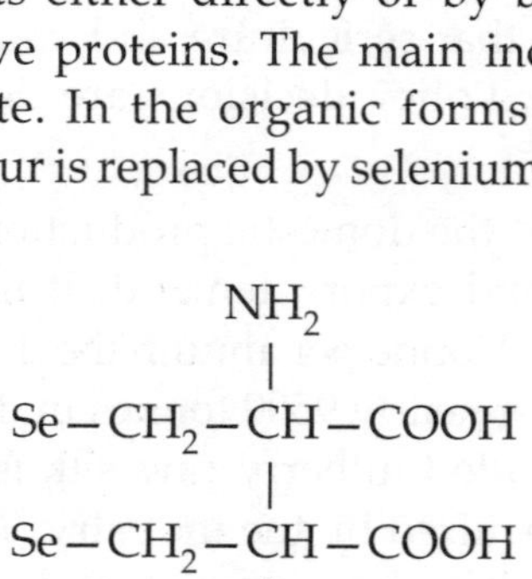

$$\begin{array}{c} NH_2 \\ | \\ Se-CH_2-CH-COOH \\ | \\ Se-CH_2-CH-COOH \\ | \\ NH_2 \end{array}$$

Selenocysteine

$$\begin{array}{c} H_2C-Se-CH_2-CH_2-CH-COOH \\ | \\ NH_2 \end{array}$$

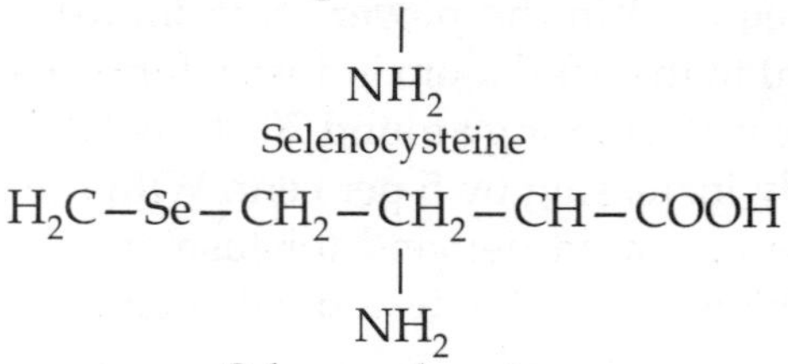

Selenometheonine

$$NaO-\overset{\overset{\displaystyle O}{\|}}{Se}-Ona$$

Sodium selenite

Considerable evidence has been presented to indicate that dimethylselenite is a metabolic product of inorganic selenium in biological system (Challenger, 1951).

$$Na_2Se + 2CH_3OSO_3Na\ (\ Se(CH_3)_2 + 2Na_2SO_4$$

Selenium analogs of antifungal bactereostatic and carcinostatic thiocompounds were synthesized and the biological effectiveness, was studied by a few investigators (Mautner *et al.*, 1956; Saw_cki and Carr, 1957; Carr *et al.*, 1958; Dingwall, 1962).

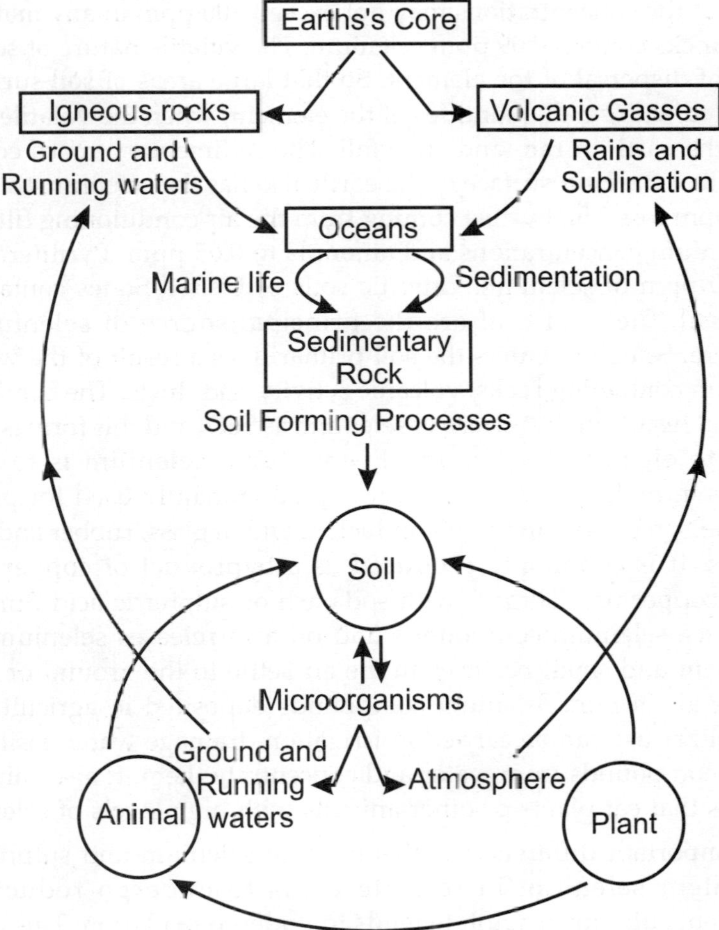

Fig. 1.1 : Biogeochemical Cycle of Selenium.

Selenium is found in man's natural environment (Figure 1.1) and under normal conditions, is present in the atmosphere, soils, igneous rocks, sedimentary rocks, volcanic gases, oceans, ground and running waters, in our food and body. It enters in the food chain by several routs but mainly through water much selenium in our environment comes from modern industry and commerce and the natural selenium chain is supplemented in selenium by man made chain. Phytoremediation programmes have been made for selenium contaminated soils, including a selection of agricultural and weed species (Nyberg, 1991; Parker and Paise, 1994; Wu *et al.*, 1996; Banuelos *et al.*, 1997).

Plant foods can be regarded as the major dietary sources of selenium in most countries through out the world. Food is the main source of selenium for the mammalian organism. The selenium is concentrated variably in varied sources but the concentrations may not exceed 100 ppm in any material. The ligneous rocks contain 0.09 ppm selenium. The volatile nature of selenium is a means of dispersal of the element. So that large areas of soil surfaces may be provided with small quantities of the element, when the volatile selenides come to the earth in rain and snowfall. The sedimentary rocks cover more than 3/4th of the land surface of the earth also has the selenium to the extent of 0.1–1 ppm fossil fuels, dust coming from the air conditioning filters varies in its selenium concentrations and amounts to 0.05 ppm. Pyritiferous shales have 1–10 ppm of selenium. Lateritic soils of United States contain 0.5–2.4 ppm. Fossil, fuel and coal are the principal source of selenium in the atmosphere. Selenium enters the soil primarily as a result of the weathering of selenium containing rocks, volcanic activity and dusts. The combustion of coal and oil results in the release of selenium as SeO_2 and this form is generally reduced to elemental selenium. Eventhough, selenium is toxic to the organisms in higher concentration, it is predominantly used for production of photocells, rectifiers and semiconductors and in glass, rubber and chemical industries. It is commonly produced as a byproduct of copper refining. Roasting copper ore "slimes" with soda ash or sulphuric acid Burning coal can produce selenium compounds and oil also releases selenium into the environment and small particles in the air settle to the ground or are taken out of the air in rain. Selenium compounds deposited in agriculture fields from fertilizer use can be carried in irrigation drainage water easily take up selenium compounds from water and concentrate them. It also can build up in animals that eat plants or other animals with high levels of selenium.

The important difference in chemistry of selenium and sulphur is that quadrivalent selenium in selenite tends to undergo reduction, but quadrivalent sulphur in sulphite tends to undergo oxidation. This difference in their chemistry results in having different roles in biological system (Levander, 1997). In 1957, it was discovered as an essential trace element for animals and human. Although the toxic effects of selenium have been recognized much earlier than the nutritional properties, the exact mechanism of the manifestation of selenium toxicity in animals is not yet understood. However, research on the nutritional aspects of selenium and its interaction with other nutrients and/or environmental chemicals has been comprehensively reviewed. Selenium is a semiconductor with photoconductivity *i.e.,* excitation with electromagnetic radiation can markedly increase by its conductivity. This property was made selenium compound to become useful in the production of photocells and xerography. Elemental selenium can exist as selenium dioxide (SeO_2), selenious acid (H_2SeO_3) or as selenite (SeO_3^{2-}).

Seleniferous soils were classified into two types with respect to the availability of selenium to plants. (1) Those that are alkaline and fairly any can support plant selenium concentration great enough to be toxic to animals; (2) Those acidic and moist are found to be non-toxic to plants. Widespread seleniferous vegetation has been found from Mexico through the United States into Canada Figure 1.2.

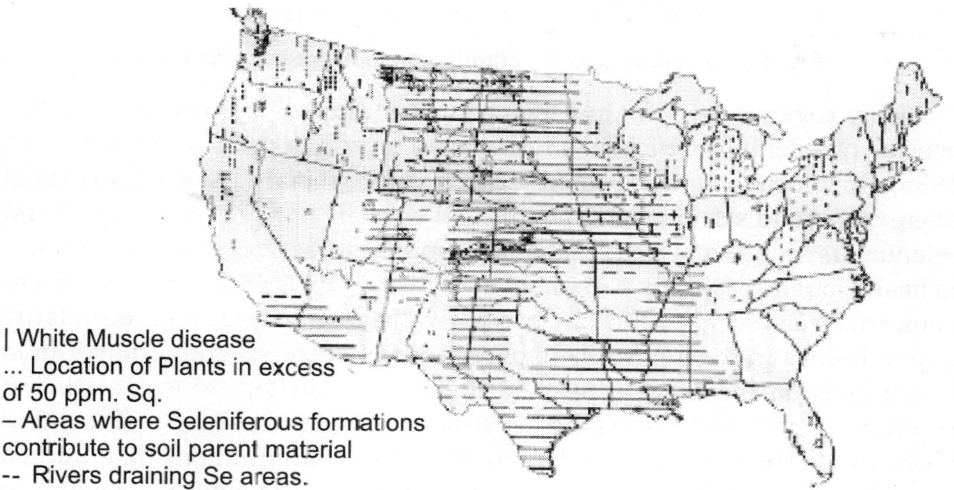

Fig. 1.2 : Map of the United States showing distribution of Seleniferous vegetation in regions considered to be seleniferous and distribution of white muscle disease of sheep in non-seleniferous regions (Muth and Allaway, 1963).

In other parts of the world seleniferous vegetation has also found in the countries like Australia, Ireland, Israel, South Africa and Venezuela. The accumulation of selenium is depends on specious and soil type. It is known that a South American tree *Leycylhis ollaria* bears a nut reported to contain as much as 18,000 ppm. of selenium; in Venezuela, ingestion of these nuts has caused severe toxicity symptoms and death in human beings. However, extremely small amounts of selenium ranging from 0.33, 1, 3 and 9 ppm. of selenium stimulated the growth in Astragalus racemosus (Trelease and Beath, 1949) (Fig. 1.3).

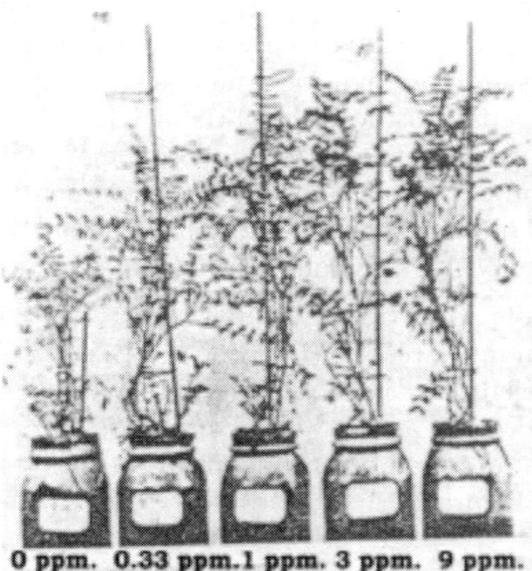

Fig. 1.3 : Selenium growth stimulation in Astragalus racemosus.

Most reviews on selenium biochemistry emphasize primarily on the aspects of selenium deficiency, rather than selenium toxicity (Shamberger, 1985). In recent years the toxic effects are associated with nutritional overexposure to selenium in humans and animals have been described and selenium is found to be an essential micronutrient that has major role to play in health and disease. The pathology in acute toxicity is wide spread necrosis, hemorrhage and death which are primarily due to hyporoxia and secondarily due to lesions in the lungs. The most serious effect of selenium intoxication in adults is on the nervous system. It acts as an irritant to eye, skin, and respiratory tract and also causes gastro intestinal disturbances (Frost and Hish, 1975). The presence of selenium in higher concentrations than normal may alter the metabolic functions. The dietary requirement of selenium to man was estimated to be 0.4 – 0.19 mg/kg food. The body develops defensive mechanism such as anti-oxidants to control levels of free radicals as they can damage cells and contribute to the development of some chronic diseases (Combs *et al.*, 1997). It is equally important for normal functioning of the immune system and thyroid gland or the human body (Levander, 1997; Arthur, 1991; Corvillain *et a*l. 1993).

Metabolic disorders due to selenium inadequacy have been recognized practically in all the major livestock producing countries of the world. Some parts in China are associated with the selenium deficiency, where the selenium in the soil is low. In animals dietary selenium deficiency induces a number of pathological changes such as diminished growth and increased mortality in quail, pancreatic fibrosis and exudative diathesis in chicks, hepatic necrosis in rats and white muscle disease in cattle and sheep (Martin and Gerlackh, 1969). Selenium is responsible for the cause of Keshan diseases under its deficiency (Levander and Beck, 1997). This condition in men arises when their dietary intake is less than 19 mcg and 13 mcg for women (Levander, 1991). Institute of Medicine Food and Nutrition Board, Washington (1996), revealed the recommended dietary allowances (RDA) for all ages as shown in Table 1.1.

Table 1.1 : Recommended dietary allowance for selenium for adults

Life Stages	Men	Women	Pregnancy	Lactation
Age 19 Years	55 mcg	55 mcg	—	—
All Ages	—	—	60 mcg	70 mcg

Source: Institute of Medicine, Food and Nutrition Board, Washington (1996).

Man is exposed to selenium through food, drinking water and by living near a selenium rich area. Higher doses of selenium could be fatal leading to chronic selenosis. The levels of selenium in food are enough to protect against diseases that may result from too little selenium. However, the food and drug administration recommends that adults take 55 mg of selenium a day and reported that selenium activates anti-oxidant enzymes and can boost the immune system and prevent cancer (Longtin, 2003; Broome, 2004). Arthur (1991) has proved the nutrient role of selenium in the active synthesis of thyroid hormone, where its deficiency leading to abnormality of thyroid functioning in human beings. Some reviews indicate that mortality from cancer, including lung colorectal and prostrate cancers (Russow *et al.*, 1997; Patterson and Levander, 1997) and incidence of osteo-arthritis (Kurz, 2002) is lower among the people with higher blood selenium levels or intake. Selenium is also known to protect against toxic metals such as mercury and arsenic (Yoneda, 1997; Zeng, 2005). A review on brain research reported that selenium deficiency can lead to epileptic seizures and may even contribute to Parkinson's disease. Selenium supplements for sheep were proved to be very effective in increasing the wool length and fibre diameter (Wilkins *et al.*, 1982). Considerably more information is available for selenium accumulation and elimination in mammals (Daniels, 1996), avians (Heinz *et al.*, 1990), and fish (Lemly, 1997).

Schwarz and Foltz, (1957) demonstrated that trace elements of Selenium protect against liver necrosis in vitamin-E deficient rats and thus the nutritional essentiality of Selenium was established. Rotruck *et al.*, (1973) reported the first known biological function of selenium as an important component of glutathione peroxidase, which can catalyze the reduction of peroxides that cause cellular damage. It is an established fact that meat quality is of increasing importance in commercial pork production. An attempt was made by Pehrson (1993) to improve meat quality and water holding capacity by adding anti-oxidants such as Vitamin-E and elements such as Selenium, which in combination with the enzyme Glutathione peraoxidase, prevented oxidative damage to cell membranes and improved their integrity which ultimately lead to reduced moisture loss from the cell. It was reported that the selenium is associated with proteins in animal tissues (Burk and Hill, 1993), and it nutritionally acts through its various selenoproteins to control the level of cellular hydrogen peroxides and redox tone of the cell organelle and DNA. It was also proved that the absence of selenoprotein of low molecular weight which can be compared to cytochrome, caused muscular dystrophy in selenium deficient sheep (M.P. Bansal and Parminder Kaur 2005). According to Clyburn *et. al.*, (2001), selenium supplementation improved the performance and meet quality in animals. It was reported that the supplementation of the diet with selenium normalizes the *Drosophila* life span by a process that may involve the newly identified proteins and experimentally proved that the number of eggs laid by *Drosophila* was reduced approximately in half in the chemically defined medium compared with the same medium supplemented with Selenium. (Javier *et. al.*, 2001).

Very little information is available on the effects of selenium in arthropods. Particularly, insects are considered to be the critical components of most terrestrial and fresh water eco-systems. They are key herbivores and recyclers and also become an important part of the food web for higher trophic levels. Despite these diverse roles, little is known about how some pollutants affect insects (Heliovera and Vaisemen, 1993). In particular, information on the effects of selenium on insect growth and survival is quite limited. Audas *et al.*, (1995), estimated the curves of newly emerged *Tenebrio molitor* feed reared on media containing different concentrations of selenium at different temperatures. An increased lethality was observed in controls when compared with the insects supplemented with diet containing selenium indicated the protective effect on survival for insects reared in media containing selenium. Selenium deficiency in the experimental models, *coturnix* and *corcyra* resulted in impaired mitochondrial substrate oxidations and lowered thiol levels (Knekt *et al.*, 1998; Fleet, 1997). It is evident that the involvement of selenium in structural and functional efficiency of mitochondria (Rani and Lalitha 1996). Carla *et al.*, (2006) investigated interactive effects of dietary selenium on growth and survival of house crickets *Acheta domesticus L.* and described improved survival and increased weight gain on the diet supplemented with selenium.

The above information clearly states that selenium is toxic to mammals especially at higher doses and beneficial at lower doses. But, the information on the interaction of selenium with different doses of selenium in insects has not available. Hence, in the present investigation, a study has been made on the toxicity of selenium at different doses and at different exposure periods in silkworm *Bombyx mori L.* The study includes some biochemical and histological aspects in the organs of fat body, malpighian tubules and haemolymph of silkworms in relation to the accumulation of selenium. There are many reasons to select the above organs for studies. The fat body of an insect is an organ with multiple metabolic functions including carbohydrates, lipids and nitrogenous compounds, the storage of glycogen, fatty acid synthesis and regulation of blood sugar and the synthesis of major haemolymph proteins (Dean *et al.*, 1985; Keeley, 1985). A number of observations demonstrated that the insect fat body functional homology with mammalian liver (Abel *et al.*, 1992; Sondergaard, 1993). Further, fat bodies played a role in the detoxification of metabolic environmental stimuli (Abel *et al.*, 1992; Tae *et al.*, 2002).

Insect malpighian (renal) tubules perform jobs analogous to the human kidney. They purify the blood (haemolymph) of waste materials, excrete and adjust a primary urine, and thus play a major role in ion and water homeostasis (Gullan and Cranston 2000). Malpighian tubules are also major immune tissues, and they also detoxify many compounds, like human liver (Dow and Davies, 2003).

The circulatory system in silkworm is an open system, haemolymph (blood) spends much of its time flowing freely within body cavities where it makes direct contact with all internal tissues and organs (Miller, 1985). About 90 per cent of haemolymph is plasma; a watery fluid which is clear, but some times greenish or yellowish in colour. Compared to vertebrate blood, it contains relatively high concentrations of aminoacids, proteins, sugars and inorganic ions (Mullins, 1985). Over wintering insects, often, sequester enough ribulose, trehalose or glycerol in the plasma to prevent it from freezing during coldest winter (Worland and Block, 2003; Worland *et al.*, 2004). The remaining 10 per cent of haemolymph volume is made up of various cell types, which are also called as haemocytes. They are involved in the clotting reaction, phagocytosis, and/or encapsulation of foreign bodies. These are free floating cells and play a role in the insect immune system (Schmid-Hempel, 2005). Therefore involvement and participation of the enzymes of the above organs in this new approach of toxicity of selenium stress is yet to be established in silkworms. Hence an attempt is made in this study to also estimate the carbohydrate, protein, accumulation and histological profiles in different tissues of silkworm *Bombyx mori L.* on exposure to lethal and sub lethal doses of selenium.

CHAPTER

2

Materials and Methods

Silkworm as Test Material

The mulberry silkworm, *Bombyx mori L. (Linnaeus)* belongs to phylum *Arthropoda* and class *Insecta* which has been under the patronage of man for its economic value and has been an ideal organism of research next only to *Drosophila melanogastar*. The morphology, physiology and genetical aspects of silkworms have been investigated with full application and as such great progress has been made in the field of sericulture.

The silkworm, *Bombyx mori L.* is basically an insect of temperate belt but the contribution made by many researchers, particularly with respect to temperate breeds has not been compiled at one place in India. Apart from its wide availability and commercial value, this insect is known for its adaptability to toxic tests, hence it is proved to be an important tool for toxicity testing of toxicants and this study is ecophysiological, nutritional in nature and realizing its economic importance and expanding scope of sericulture, the need for comprehensive review of silkworm biology can provide a suitable information.

In the present investigation the crossbreed V Instar silkworm, *Bombyx mori L.*, larvae from the parentage of $PMXNB_4D_2$ used as test insects. They were obtained from the Government grainage, Anantapur District, A. P. The silkworm, *Bombyx mori L.* is a holometabolous insect and pass through 4 distinct stages of life cycle, *viz.*, 'Egg', 'Larva', 'Pupa' and 'Moth'. The duration of life cycle may range from 6–8 weeks depending on racial characteristics and climatic conditions. The "Silkworm eggs" are tiny and weigh around 2000 eggs/gm. They are oval in shape with a micropyle at its anterior pole. Egg stage is of 9–12 days. The "Larvae" alone are the real feeders and the larval duration ranges from 24–28 days. The various chemicals found in the mulberry leaf especially, the Morin that attracts the silkworm to feed on mulberry leaves. In view of the 4 intervening moults the larval life is divided into 5 distinct instars namely I, II, III, IV and V. The entire body is covered with a thin, elastic chitinous cuticle, which is capable of being extended considerably to permit rapid growth of the larvae during V instar. This is real feeding active stage and accumulates the nutrients required for physiological growth. At the end of the larval life, the silkworm builds a silken abode, the "Cocoon" and the larva transforms itself into "Chrysalis" (Pupa) inside the cocoon, which can be regarded as transitional phase and during this period silkworm is incapable of feeding and appears dormant and the duration of pupal period lasts for 10–12 days. The pupa develops the adult organs and emerges as a moth and this is incapable of flight due to domestication and meant for reproducing the generations. This stage lasts for 3–5 days. The duration of life cycle of the silkworm *Bombyx mori L.* is presented in Figure 2.4.

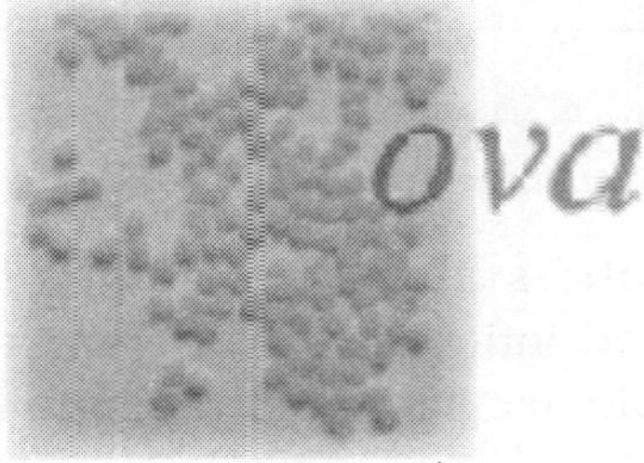

Life Cycle

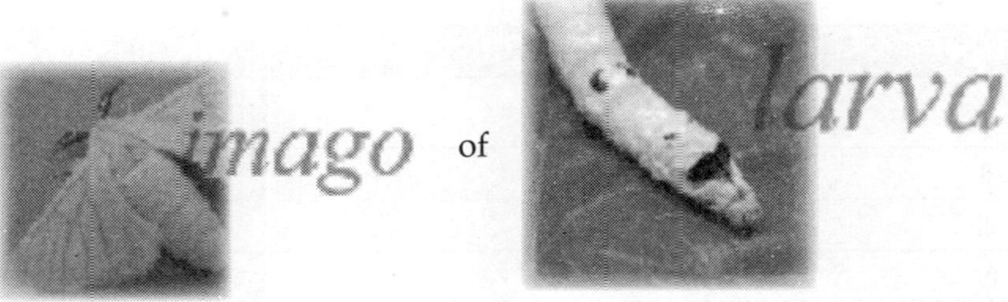

Bombyx mori.L.

Fig. 2.4 : Life Cycle of Silkworm Bombyx mori L.

Tremendous increase in size and weight has been recorded during the larval period of 25 days alone. Silkworm puts an increase 10000 times in weight and 7000 times increase in size. Under the ideal conditions of temperature (23 – 25°C $\pm$ 1°C) and 70 per cent relative humidity, days required for each larval stadium to different larvae changes under our laboratory conditions are given in Table 2.2.

Table 2.2 : Duration of larval period and moulting period for different larval Instars of the silkworm *Bombyx mori L.*

Instars	No. of Days	Moult	Moult Duration
I	3-4	I	20 Hrs.
II	2-3	II	20 Hrs.
III	3-4	III	24 Hrs.
IV	4-5	IV	24 Hrs
V	7-9	—	—

Source: FAO Manual on Sericulture.

In the tropical countries like India, abiotic factor temperature and humidity exert a profound influence on different larval forms of silkworm. The optimum temperature and humidity required for the health or growth of different silkworm larvae are as given below (Table 2.3)..

Table 2.3 : Temperature and humidity requirements of different larval instars of the silkworm *Bombyx mori L.*

Stage	Opt. Temp. (°C)	Opt. Humidity (%)
I	26-28	75-85
II	26-27	75-85
III	24-26	70-75
IV	24-25	70-75
V	23-24	65-70

Source: FAO Manual on Sericulture.

Chemical Used

Selenium is known as a *double-edged sword*. At higher dose it acts as a toxicant whereas at lower concentration it acts as an essential micronutrient. Since sodium selenite is readily soluble in water, a pure salt with molecular formula of Na_2SeO_3 and molecular weight 172.94 is selected. Every 2.19 g of sodium selenite contains 1g of selenium.

Maintenance of Silkworm

The disease free laying of the crossbreed silkworm from the parentage of $PMXNB_4D_2$ were procured from the Government Grainage, Anantapur, Andhra Pradesh and brought to the laboratory where the present investigation was carried out. The method of incubation of disease free layings (DFLs) and silkworm rearing was followed as advocated by Krishnaswamy (1978).

The freshly hatched larvae were collected from the egg sheet into pre-disinfected rearing trays, where they were fed 4 times (6.00, 10.00, 16.00 and 22.00 hrs) on fresh Morus species Mulberry leaves, (Variety V-I). A strict hygiene was maintained through bed cleaning during all the instars as per the schedule. The larvae at moult were kept undistributed. The temperature and relative humidity and 12 hours moderate light are maintained as mentioned in Table 2.3.

Maintenance of V Instar Silkworms for Experimentation

The silkworm larvae of V instar 1st day were collected from the rearing tray and divided into batches. Each batch is consisting of 20 larvae. They were maintained at a temperature 23.5 ± 1°C. Mulberry leaves collected from the garden are sprayed with selenium solutions of various concentrations prepared for the experimentation and dried under shade at room temperature. A batch of silkworms was fed without selenium treated leaves as "Controls". The silkworm larvae resumed from the 4th moult are very active and V instar larvae were fed with selenium treated leaves at different intervals of 6.00; 10.00; 16.00; and 22.00 hrs. Three batches of V instar larvae are maintained separately where Batch I treated as controls. Batch II treated with lethal dose of Se and Batch III fed on leaves sprayed with sub lethal dose of selenium. The static bioassay is followed for the selenium toxicity evaluation and LD_{50} was determined as dissected by Finney (1971).

In the present study the 24 hrs LD_{50} obtained for V instar of *Bombyx mori L.* is 32.39 μgms/kg b.wt. and 1/5th of 24 hr LD_{50} *i.e.,* 6.47 μg/kg b.w for silkworm *Bombyx mori L.* was taken as sub lethal dose of selenium for study of estimating the carbohydrates and proteins.

Treatment of Silkworm with Selenium

For experimentation the silkworms are divided into 12 groups according to Smitha (2002), the LD_{50} of 24 hours was estimated as 32.39 μ gm/kg body wt. Thus the present investigation is started with the assessing of food consumption and excretion on exposure to lethal (32.39 μ gm/kg body wt.) and sub lethal (1/5th of LD_{50} 6.47 μ gm/kg body wt.) doses of selenium. Silkworm of V instar with an average weight of 1.2 grams was used for the study. The silkworms divided into three groups of 50 silkworms each and were reared in rearing trays, one group in each tray and were maintained at temperature 23 ± 1°C and relative humidity 70 – 75 per cent, and silkworms are kept at 16 hours light and 8 hours dark and allowed free access to mulberry leaves of V-1 variety. Silkworms were fed on selenium treated leaves for a period of 4 days, in order to analyze the impact of lethal and sub lethal doses of selenium toxicity. Control silkworms were received equivalent amounts of distilled water and were treated in the similar way. After scheduled exposure, the silkworms were sacrificed. Haemolymph samples were collected from silkworm body and fat bodies and malpighian tubules were isolated at 15±1°C to carry out further work.

The following are the groups used for the present investigation

Groups	Selenium dosage		Exposure period in V Instar
Group-1	Control	Distilled water	3 day
Group-2	Lethal	32.39 μ gm/kg body wt.	3 day
Group-3	Sub lethal	6.47 μ gm/kg body wt.	3 day
Group-4	Control	Distilled water	4 day
Group-5	Lethal	32.39 μ gm/kg body wt.	4 day
Group-6	Sub lethal	6.47 μ gm/kg body wt.	4 day
Group-7	Control	Distilled water	5 day
Group-8	Lethal	32.39 μ gm/kg body wt.	5 day
Group-9	Sub lethal	6.47 μ gm/kg body wt.	5 day
Group-10	Control	Distilled water	6 day
Group-11	Lethal	32.39 μ gm/kg body wt.	6 day
Group-12	Sub lethal	6.47 μ gm/kg body wt.	6 day

METHODS

Larval and Cocoon Characters

Under the larval characters, wet and dry weight of the larvae, wet and dry weight of the dry matter food ingesta, digesta and excreta and haemolymph volume were measured in selenium treated and untreated (control) silkworms.

Wet and Dry Weight of the Larvae

As described by Venkatarami Reddy *et al.*, (1991), six selenium treated and untreated (control) silkworms were taken immediately before the first feed of day 3, 4, 5 and 6 of fifth instar, as the case may be, with 24 hrs interval between each day, and their wet weights were measured separately in an electrical balance. They represent the wet weights of the 3rd, 4th, 5th and 6th day silkworms of the fifth instar. Similarly, for dry weight, a random of another six selenium treated and untreated (control) silkworms from each variety at each day were taken and kept in hot air oven at 80°C for 24 hours. After that, weights of these worms were measured separately in an electrical balance. Wet and dry weights of the larvae are expressed in g/larva and mg/larva respectively.

Dry Matter Food Ingesta, Digesta and Excreta

Waldbauer (1968) gravimetric methods were followed to calculate the dry matter food ingesta, digesta and excreta. Hundred silkworms from each untreated (control) and selenium treated batches were reared separately to determine dry matter food ingesta from day 3 to day 6 of the fifth instar of all the three types. A known quantity of mulberry leaf was supplied to silkworms. The same quantity of leaves was kept in the oven at 80°C for 24 hours and measured the dry leaf weight. Next day, the left over leaf was collected from the rearing tray, kept in the oven at 80°C for 24 hours and measured the dry left over leaf weight. This value was substracted from the dry leaf weight supplied, which gave the dry matter food ingesta. Alongside the left over leaf and excreta of the worms were also collected separately and kept in the oven at 80°C for 24 hours and measured its dry weight. This gave the dry matter excreta. For measuring the dry matter food digesta, the dry matter excreta was substracted from the dry matter food ingesta. The weights of the dry matter food ingesta, digesta and excreta are expressed in mg/larva.

Under the cocoon characters, cocoon weight, shell weight, cocoon–shell ratio, floss percentage, cocoon length, cocoon width, filament length, filament weight and denier of untreated (control) and selenium treated cocoons were measured as described by Prasad (1990).

Measurement of Cocoon Weight

A random of six cocoons was taken from each batch spinned by untreated (control) and selenium treated silkworm larvae. Accurate weight of cocoons was measured with the help of electrical balance. Cocoon weight is expressed in g/cocoon.

Measurement of Shell Weight

A random of six cocoons was taken from each variety spinned by untreated (control) and selenium treated silkworm larvae The pupae and exuvium were removed from the cocoons. Accurate weight of the shell was measured with the help of electrical balance. Shell weight is expressed in g/cocoon.

Measurement of Cocoon Shell Ratio

A random of six cocoons was taken from each batch spinned by untreated (control) and selenium treated silkworm larvae. Calculated the weights of cocoon and shell separately. Using these weights the cocoon shell ratio was measured by the formula.

$$\frac{\text{Shell weight}}{\text{Cocoon weight}} \times 100$$

Cocoon shell ratio is expressed in percentages.

Measurement of Floss Percentage

A random of six cocoons was taken from each batch spinned by untreated (control) and selenium treated silkworm larvae. The floss layer was removed completely from the cocoons and weighed separately. The pupae and exuvium were removed from the cocoons and the shell was weighed accurately with the help of electrical balance. Using these weights floss percentage (with reference to weight of shell) was calculated by the formula.

$$\frac{\text{Total weight of floss}}{\text{Total weight of shell}} \times 100$$

Measurement of Cocoon Length and Weight

A random of six cocoons was taken from each batch spinned by untreated (control) and selenium treated silkworm larvae. Their length and width were measured with the help of Vernier calipers. Cocoon length and width are expressed in mm/cocoon.

Measurement of Filament Length and Width

A random of six cocoons was taken from each variety spinned by untreated (control) and selenium treated silkworm larvae. Length of the single cocoon filament reeled was measured with the help of epprouvette. Filament length is expressed in mts./cocoon. Its weight was taken with the help of electrical balance and is expressed in mg/filament.

Measurement of Filament Denier

Denier is the thickness of the filament. For its measurement a random of six cocoons was taken from each variety spinned by untreated (control) and selenium treated silkworm larvae. Length and weight of each cocoon filament reeled was measured, and the denier was calculated using the following formula.

$$\text{Denier} = \frac{\text{Weight of reeled silk in grams}}{\text{Length of reeled silk in meters}} \times 9000$$

Wherein, 9000 is the standard length of thread in meters per gram weight of the reeled silk.

GENERAL EXPERIMENTAL PROCEDURE FOR FURTHER STUDIES

The further studies in this investigation were made in the haemolymph, fat bodies and malpighian tubules of untreated (control) and selenium treated silkworms. In *Bombyx mori L.*, like other insects, fat bodies are the major tissue for the synthesis and storage of various biochemical constituents (Steele, 1983). Abel *et al.*, (1992) and Tae *et al.*, (2002) described the role of fat body in detoxification of the various metabolic stimuli. Haemolymph, which is in intimate contact with the fat bodies and malpighian tubules, acts as the medium for the interchange of metabolites. Insect Malpighian tubules play a major role in maintenance of ion and water homeostasis (Gullan and Cranston, 2000) and perform the detoxification of many compounds (Dow and Davies, 2003). So, it is possible that any changes in the metabolic profiles of the haemolymph on selenium exposure exhibit corresponding influence on fat bodies and malpighian tubules.

Mode of Isolation of Haemolymph, Fat Bodies and Malpighian Tubules for Experimentation

The haemolymph was drawn out from the larvae by puncturing the pro leg. The haemolymph was collected in small ice-cooled test tubes rinsed with phenylthiourea solution (1% w/v). Dissection of fat bodies and malpighian tubules was made in cold condition (4°C) after making a longitudinal mid-ventral incision along the entire body length and carefully pinning back the cuticle. The fat bodies, freed from adhering connective tissues, were carefully taken with the help of forceps and washed with physiological saline (0.9% NaCl). The excess water was removed with the filter paper. The required weight of the tissue was weighed nearest to 0.1 mg and used for biochemical analysis.

Some Aspects of Carbohydrate Metabolism

The levels of total carbohydrates, glucose, glycogen, trehalose, pyruvate and lactate and the activities of total phosphorylase, succinate dehydrogenase (SDH) and lactate dehydrogenase (LDH) were estimated in the haemolymph and fat bodies of untreated (control) and selenium treated silkworm larvae under this study.

Estimation of Glucose

Glucose in the samples was determined by the method as described by Nelson and Somogyi (1952). 1 per cent homogenate of fat bodies was prepared in pure distilled water. To 0.5 ml of homogenate, 4.5 ml of 10 per cent TCA solution was added and the mixture was centrifuged at 3000 rpm for 10 minutes. To 0.5 ml of haemolymph, 3.9 ml of deproteinizing solution (5% zinc sulphate and 0.3 N sodium hydroxide in 1:1 ratio) was added and the mixture was centrifuged at 3000 rpm for 10 minutes. To 1.0 ml of the filtrate from each of these mixtures 1.0 ml of alkaline copper reagent was added, shaken vigorously and heated in a boiling water bath exactly for 20 minutes. Then it was cooled and added 1.0 ml of arsenomolybdate colour reagent. Entire solution was made up to 10 ml with distilled water and the density of the colour developed was measured in a spectrophotometer at a wavelength of 540 nm. A blank and glucose standards were also run simultaneously. Glucose content was expressed in mg glucose/100 ml of haemolymph and mg glucose/g wet of tissue.

Estimation of Glycogen

The glycogen content was estimated by the method followed by Caroll *et al.*, (1956). 1 per cent homogenate of fat bodies was prepared in 10 per cent Tri-chloro-acetic acid (TCA). The tissue contents were centrifuged at 6000 rpm for 15 minutes. To 0.5 ml of fat body TCA filtrate, 2.5 ml ethanol was added and allowed to stand overnight in a refrigerator. After the precipitation was complete, the tube was again centrifuged at 6000 rpm for 15 minutes. The supernatant was decanted and the tube was allowed to drain in an inverted position for 10 minutes. The residue was dissolved in 0.5 ml distilled water, to it 5 ml of 2 per cent anthrone reagent dissolved in 72 per cent concentrated sulphuric acid was added. A reagent blank and a standard were prepared in the same way. The tube was kept in boiling water bath for 15 minutes and later cooled to room temperature. The density of the colour developed was measured in a spectrophotometer at 620 nm against blank. The glycogen content is expressed as mg glycogen/g wet wt. of tissue.

Estimation of Trehalose

Since glucose, glycogen and trehalose were the only sugars present either in haemolymph or fat bodies of silkworms, the trehalose concentration was determined by the substraction of glucose plus glycogen values from the total carbohydrates present in them (Schmidt and Platzer, 1980). The trehalose content is expressed as mg/100 ml and mg/g wet wt. of haemolymph and fat bodies respectively.

Estimation of Glucose-6-phosphatase (E.C.3.1.3.9)

Glucose-6-phosphatase activity in the fat body was estimated by using the method of Yeung *et al.*, 1968. A 5 per cent homogenate (w/v) was prepared in 0.25 M ice-cold sucrose solution. 0.5 ml of 0.2 M Tris malate buffer, 0.2 ml of 0.05 M glucose-6-phosphate and 0.2 ml of distilled water were incubated at 37°C for 5 minutes and to this 0.1 ml of homogenate was added and incubated exactly for 10 minutes. The reaction was stopped, by adding 1.0 ml of 10 per cent trichloroacetic acid. A blank was also run similarly. Finally, the inorganic phosphates liberated were estimated by the method of Fiske and Subba Row (1925) at a wavelength of 660 nm and the activity is expressed as ug Pi liberated/mg protein/h.

Estimation of Total Phosphorylase Activity

Phosphorylase activity in fat bodies was estimated using the method described by Sutherland (1955). A 5 per cent homogenate (w/v) was prepared in 0.1 M sodium fluoride solution (P^{H}6.5). It was centrifuged at 1500 rpm for 15 minutes. Thus extracting the enzyme into the supernatant. The supernatant was diluted four times with the cold sodium fluoride solution. The phosphorylase activity in it was estimated with the co-factor AMP (Adenosine-5-monophosphate). For this, incubation mixture was prepared, consisting of 0.2 ml of 2 per cent glycogen and 0.4 ml of diluted enzyme. This was incubated at 37°C and the reaction was started, by adding 0.2 ml of 0.016 M glucose-1-phosphate and 0.004 M adenosine-5-monophosphate (1:1 ratio) to the incubation mixture. The reaction was stopped after 30 minutes by adding 5 ml of 10 per cent TCA. A blank was also run similarly. Finally, the inorganic phosphates liberated were estimated by the method of Fiske and Subba Row (1925). For this, to an aliquate of the above reaction mixture 4.5 ml of 0.44 per cent ammonium molybdate and 0.2 ml of 1-amino-2-naphthol-4-sulphonic acid (ANSA) were added. The contents were mixed well and heated in a boiling water bath for 10 minutes. After cooling, the volume was made to 10 ml with distilled water and the colour developed was measured in a spectrophotometer at a wavelength of 660 nm. The activity is expressed as μM Pi liberated/mg protein/h., using the phosphate standards.

Estimation of Pyruvate

Pyruvate in the tissues was estimated using the method of Friedman and Hangen (1942). A 5 per cent homogenate (w/v) of the fat bodies was prepared in 10 per cent trichloroacetic acid. To 1 ml of haemolymph 4 ml of 10 per cent trichloroacetic acid was added. Both the mixtures were centrifuged at 3000 rpm for 15 minutes. The supernatant was used for the estimation of pyruvate. 1.0 ml of supernatant was taken and to it 1.0 ml of 0.001 M 2, 4-dinitro phenylhydrazine and 3 ml of 0.4 N sodium hydroxide were added. After 10 minutes, the optical density of the colour developed was measured in a spectrophotometer at a wavelengths of 540 nm against the reagent blank. Pyruvate standards were prepared alongside for comparison. The pyruvate content is expressed as mg/ml and mg/g wet wt. of haemolymph and fat bodies respectively.

Estimation of Lactate

Lactate in the tissues was estimated using the method of Barker and Summerson (1941) as modified by Huckabee (1961). A 5 per cent homogenate (w/v) of the fat bodies was prepared in cold 10 per cent TCA. To 1 ml of haemolymph 4 ml of 10 per cent TCA was added. Both mixtures were centrifuged at 3000 rpm for 15 minutes. The supernatant was used for the estimation of lactate. To 1.0 ml of supernatant, 1.0 ml of 20 per cent copper sulphate was added and the mixture was made to 10.0 ml with distilled water. Then 1.0 g of powdered calcium hydroxide was added, shaken vigorously and kept for an hour at room temperature with intermittent shaking. The contents were centrifuged at 3000 rpm for 10 minutes and to 1.0 ml of the supernatant 0.5 ml of 4 per cent copper sulphate was added followed by 6.0 ml of concentrated sulphuric acid. The contents were mixed by lateral shaking, kept in boiling water bath for exactly 6.5 minutes and cooled. When the contents were sufficiently cooled, 0.1 ml of 1.5 per cent p-Hydrophenyl (prepared in 0.5 per cent of sodium hydroxide) was added and the precipitate formed was kept at laboratory temperature for 30 minutes. Then the contents were placed in a boiling water bath for 90 seconds, cooled and the optical density of the colour developed was measured in a spectrophotometer at a wavelength of 560 nm against reagent blank. Lactate standards were prepared alongside for comparison. The lactate content is expressed as mg/ml and mg/g wet wt. of haemolymph and fat bodies respectively.

Estimation of Succinate Dehydrogenase (SDH) (Succinate : Acceptor oxido-reductase, EC 1.3.99.1) Activity

Succinate dehydrogenase activity in the tissues was estimated using the colorimetric method of Nachlas *et al.*, (1960). A 5 per cent homogenate (w/v) of the fat bodies was prepared in 0.25 M ice cold sucrose solution. To 1 ml of haemolymph 4 ml of 0.25 M ice cold sucrose solution was added. Both mixtures were centrifuged at 3000 rpm for 10 minutes and the supernatant was taken as the source of enzyme. The incubation mixture consisted of 0.2 ml of 0.4 M phosphate buffer (pH 7.7), 0.2 ml of 0.2 M sodium succinate, 1.0 ml of 0.004 M 2-(P-indophenol)-3-p-nitrophenyl-5-phenyltetrazolium chloride (INT), 0.1 ml of 0.005 M phenazine methosulphate and 0.5 ml of 5 per cent enzyme preparation. The mixture was incubated at 37°C for 30 minutes and the reaction was stopped, by adding 6.0 ml of glacial acetic acid. The formazon formed was extracted into 6.0 ml of toluene overnight at 0°C and the optical density of the colour developed was measured in a spectrophotometer at a wavelength of 495 nm. A blank taking 0.5 ml of distilled water and control taking 0.5 ml of boiled enzyme were also run similarly. INT standards were prepared alongside for comparison. The activity is expressed as µM formazon/ mg protein/h.

Estimation of Lactate Dehydrogenase (LDH) (L-lactate NAD oxido-Reductase, Ec 1.127) Activity

Lactate dehydrogenase activity, in the tissues was estimated using the method of Srikantan and Krishnamoorthi (1955) as modified by Govindappa and Swami (1965). A 5 per cent homogenate (w/v) of the fat bodies was prepared in 0.25 M ice-cold sucrose solution. To 1 ml of haemolymph 4 ml of 0.25 M ice-cold sucrose solution was added. Both mixtures were centrifuged at 2500 rpm for 15 minutes and the supernatant was taken as the source of enzyme. The incubation mixture consisted of 1.0 ml of 0.4 M phosphate buffer (pH 7.4), 0.5 ml of 0.1 M lithium lactate, 0.1 ml of 0.0001 M nicotinamide adenine dinucleotide (NAD), 1.0 ml of 0.0004 M 2 – (p- indophenol) – 3 – p – nitrophenyl – 5 – phenyltetrazolium chloride and 0.5 ml 5 per cent enzyme preparation. The mixture was incubated at 37°C for 30 minutes and then the reaction was stopped, by adding 6.0 ml of glacial acetic acid. The formazon formed was extracted into 6.0 ml of toluene overnight at 0°C. The optical density of the colour developed was measured in a spectrophotometer at a wavelength of 495 nm. A blank using 0.5 ml of distilled water and a control by taking 0.5 ml of boiled enzyme were also run similarly. INT standards were prepared alongside for comparison. The enzyme activity is expressed as µM formazon/ mg protein/h.

Some Aspects of Protein Metabolism

The levels of total proteins and free amino acids in fat bodies and malpighian tubules, the levels of ammonia and urea in haemolymph, fat bodies and malpighian tubules, the activities of protease, alanine and aspartate aminotransferases and glutamate dehydrogenase in the fat bodies and malpighian tubules of untreated (control) and selenium treated silkworm larvae were estimated under this study.

Estimation of Total Proteins

Total protein content was estimated by the method of Lowry *et al.*, (1951). A 1 per cent homogenates of fat bodies and malpighian tubules were prepared with 10 per cent TCA. Both fat body and malpighian tubules TCA extracts were centrifuged at 6000 rpm for 15 minutes individually and the residues were dissolved in 15 ml of 1 N sodium hydroxide for fat bodies and malpighian tubules. To 1 ml of fat body and malpighian tubules solutions, 4 ml of alkaline copper solution (a mixture of 2 per cent sodium carbonate and 0.5 per cent copper sulphate in 50 : 1 ratio) was added. The samples were allowed to stay for 10 minutes. At the end of which 0.4 ml folin phenol reagent (diluted with distilled water in 1:1 ratio before use) was added and the resultant colour was read at 600 nm in a spectrophotometer against reagent blank. Bovine serum albumin was used for the preparation of protein standards. The total protein content in fat bodies and malpighian tubules is expressed as mg protein/g wet wt. tissue.

Estimation of Free Amino Acids

Free amino acid levels were estimated by the method followed by Moore and Stein (1954). A 1 per cent homogenates of fat bodies and malpighian tubules were prepared in 10 per cent TCA. The contents were centrifuged at 6000 rpm for 15 minutes. To 0.5 ml of fat bodies supernatant and malpighian tubules supernatant 2 ml of ninhydrin reagent was added and kept in boiling water bath for exactly 6½ minutes and immediately cooled. The solution was made up to 10 ml with distilled water, and the colour was read at 570 nm in a spectrophotometer against reagent blank. Tyrosine was used for the preparation of standards. The free amino acid levels in fat bodies and malpighian tubules are expressed as mg of tyrosine equivalents/g wet wt. tissue.

Estimation of Protease Activity

Protease activity in the tissues was estimated using the ninhydrin method as described by Davis and Smith (1955). A 1 per cent homogenates (w/v) of fat bodies and malpighian tubules were prepared in cold distilled water. Both mixtures were centrifuged at 1000 rpm for 20 minutes and the supernatants were used for enzyme assay. The incubation mixture contained the following, 1 ml of 1 per cent casein solution, 2 ml of 0.1 – M phosphate buffer (pH 5.0) and 0.2 ml of enzyme. The contents were mixed well and incubated at 30°C for 30 minutes, then the reaction was stopped by adding 2 ml of 2 per cent ninhydrin reagent. Again the contents were mixed thoroughly and boiled at 100°C for 10 minutes, cooled and made up to 10 ml with dilutent (distilled water and n-propanol in 1:1 ratio). The optical density of the colour developed was measured in a spectrophotometer at a wavelength of 570 nm. A blank taking distilled water and control taking boiled enzyme were also run similarly. Amino acid standards were prepared alongside for comparison. The protease activity is expressed as µ moles tyrosine equivalents formed/mg protein/h.

Estimation of Alanine (DL-alanine : 2-oxoglutarate, EC 2.6.1.2) and Aspartate (L-aspartate : 2-oxoglutarate, EC2.6.1.1) Aminotransferase Activities

Activities of alanine and aspartate aminotransferases in the tissues were estimated using the method of Reitman and Frankel (1957). A 5 per cent homogenates (w/v) of fat bodies and malpighian tubules were prepared in 0.25 M ice-cold sucrose. Both contents were centrifuged at 3000 rpm for 10 minutes and the supernatants were used as the source of enzyme. Two sets of incubation mixtures were prepared, the first set (for alanine aminotransferase activity) consisted of 0.5 ml of 0.2 M alanine, 0.5 ml of 0.0005 M α - Ketoglutaric acid (which was prepared in M/15 phosphate buffer and adjusted with 10% sodium hydroxide to 7.4 pH) and 0.1 ml of enzyme. The second set (for aspartate aminotransfarase activity) consisted of 0.5 ml of 0.2 M aspartic acid, 0.5 ml of 0.005 M α - ketoglutaric acid (which was prepared in M/15 phosphate buffer and adjusted with 10 per cent sodium hydroxide to 7.5 pH) and 0.1 ml of enzyme. The mixtures were incubated at 37°C for 30 minutes and then the reaction was stopped by the addition of 1 ml of 0.001 M 2, 4 – dinitrophenylhydrazine (Ketone reagent). Finally, the reaction mixtures were made to 10.0 ml with, 0.4 N sodium hydroxide and the optical density of the colour developed was measured in a spectro-photometer at a wavelength of 545 nm. A blank taking 0.1 ml of distilled water and control taking 0.1 ml of distilled water and control taking 0.1 ml of boiled enzyme were also run similarly. Pyruvate standards were prepared along side for comparison. The alanine and aspartate aminotransferase activities are expressed as µM pyruvate formed/mg protein/h.

Estimation of Glutamate Dehydrogenase (GDH) (L. glutamate : NAD oxalo – reductase EC 1.4.13) Activity

GDH activity was estimated in the tissues using the method of Lee and Lardy (1965) with slight modification. A 5 per cent homogenates (w/v) of fat bodies and malpighian tubules were prepared in 0.25 M ice-cold sucrose solution. Both mixtures were centrifuged at 2500 rpm for 20 minutes at 2°C to remove cell debris. The clear cell-free extract was subjected to dialysis against 0.25 M sucrose at 2°C to 4°C for 24 hours. The incubation mixture in a final volume of 2.0 ml contained 40 µM of sodium glutamate, 100 µM of sodium phosphate buffer (pH 7.4), 0.1 µM of NAD (nicotinamide adenine dinucleotide) and 4.0 µM of INT (2-p-indophenol-3-p-nitrophenyl-5-phenyltetrazolium chloride). The reaction was initiated by the addition of 0.5 ml of the enzyme preparation. The mixture was incubated at 37°C for 30 minutes in a thermostatic water bath, and then the reaction was stopped by the addition of 5.0 ml of glacial acetic acid. The formazon formed was extracted into 5.0 ml of toluene overnight at 5°C. The optical density of the colour developed was measured in a spectrophotometer at a wavelength of 495 nm. A blank by taking 0.5 ml of distilled water and control by taking of 0.5 ml of boiled enzyme were also run similarly. INT standards were prepared alongside for comparison. The enzyme activity is expressed as µM formazon formed/mg protein/h.

Estimation of Ammonia

Ammonia was estimated in fat bodies, malpighian tubules and haemolymph of silkworm *Bombyx mori L.* by a method of Bergmeyer (1965). To 1.0 ml. of haemolymph 2 ml of 15 per cent perchloric acid was added and centrifuged at 2000 rpm for 15 minutes. 5 per cent tissue homogenates (w/v) were prepared in cold distilled water and centrifuged at 2000 rpm for 15 minutes. To 1.0 ml of supernatant, 2 ml of 15 per cent perchloric acid was added and centrifuged at 2000 rpm for 15 minutes. The supernatant was neutralized with 2.0 ml of 15 per cent sodium hydroxide. To this, 0.5 ml of Nessler's reagent was added and the colour developed was read immediately in a spectrophotometer at 495 nm against a reagent blank. Ammonium sulphate standards were run alongside for comparison. The ammonia content is expressed as µM/gm wet wt. tissue and µM/100 ml.

Estimation of Urea

Urea was estimated in the haemolymph, fat bodies and malpighian tubules by diacetylmonoxime method as described by Natelson (1971). To 1.0 ml of haemolymph, 3.4 ml of distilled water, 0.3 ml of 10 per cent sodium tungstate and 0.3 ml of 2/3 N sulphuric acids were added. The contents were centrifuged at 2000 rpm for 15 minutes. 1.0 ml of supernatant was taken and to this 1 ml of distilled water, 0.4 ml of 2 per cent diacetylmonoxime and 1.6 ml of 1:3 sulphuric acid and orthophosphoric acid mixture were added. Then the mixture was boiled for 30 minutes, cooled and the colour developed was read against reagent blank at 480 nm in a spectrophotometer. Standards of urea in different concentrations were run simultaneously. The urea content is expressed as µM/100 ml of haemolymph.

Urea in fat bodies and malpighian tubules was also estimated by taking 10 per cent tissue homogenates (w/v) in 15 per cent perchloric acid and centrifuged at 2000 rpm for 15 minutes. To 1.5 ml of supernatant, 1.0 ml of acid mix (3:1 Orthophosphoric acid and conc. sulphuric acid) was added and the contents were shaken well. To this 0.5 ml of 2 per cent diacetylmonoxyme was added and heated at 100°C in boiling water bath for 30 minutes. The tubes were cooled and the colour developed was read against a reagent blank at 480 nm in spectrophotometer. Standards of urea in different concentrations were run simultaneously. The urea content is expressed as μM/gm wet wt. tissue.

Estimation of Nutritional Parameters

Food budget involves the various nutritional parameters such as food ingestion, faeces defaecated, total food assimilated, total food oxidised and total food converted. These nutritional parameters were estimated by the method followed by Waldbauer (1968) and Delvi and Pandian (1972).

The food and faeces defaecated by the silkworm were weighed in an electronic single pan balance (Metler) to an accuracy of 0.01 mg. Faeces and foods were dried in an oven at 90°C till the weight constancy was attained.

Consumption was determined by substracting the dry weight of uneaten food from the dry weight of the food provided (Waldbauer, 1968). All faeces were separated daily at 6 a.m. from the rearing tray prior to first feeding and its dry weight was taken as measurement for excretion.

Dry food assimilated by the test individuals during the final instars was calculated substracting the dry weight of the faeces produced from the dry food consumed. Assimilation of food was calculated by the method followed by Delvi and Pandian, (1972.

The total amount of food converted into body substance was calculated by substracting the dry weight of the individual before the experiment from the dry weight of the individual after the experiment. Food oxidised was calculated by substracting the food converted from the food assimilated. Food utilization Budget of silkworms was studied using IBP terminology (Petrusewiez and Mac.Fayden, 1970).

$$I = B + M + F,$$

Where I = Ingested food

F = Faeces (Undigested food + Excretory products)

M = Metabolized food (Assimilated food metabolized)

I-F = Assimilated food (Expressed in mg. dry weight except growth which is expressed in wet weight)

B = (I-F) Assimilated food used for growth (Bio mass gained = Conversion, cc, 1972; Scriber and Slansky, 1981).

Estimation of Selenium in Biological Materials

Selenium was estimated according to the method of Alfthan, (1984). 100 mg of tissue samples, standards and blanks were transferred to the test tubes. A 1 ml portion of nitric acid was added to each tube and left at room temperature for overnight for sample digestion. A few anti bumping granules were added to each tube followed by 0.4 ml of 1:20 sulfuric: perchloric acids (v/v) as digestion mixture which results in complete recovery of resistant selenium spices present in biological samples. The tubes were transferred to the heating block of ambient temperature in a fume hood. The temperature of the block was set to 120°C, which has reached in 40 minutes and maintained for 20 minutes. 0.5 ml of nitric acid was added to prevent the charring of the sample and temperature was next set to 150°C for 1 hour followed by 180°C for 1 hour the cessation of boiling and the evolution of perchloric acid fumes were taken as signs of complete digestion, which occurred between 60-90 min. Aluminum foils around the test tubes during heating at 180°C was used to avoid condensation of vapours. At the end of the digestion the digest was cooled. The test tubes were cooled and a few drops of 30 per cent hydrogen peroxide were added to each tube and heated for 10 minutes at 150°C. This step was repeated because fumes of nitrogen dioxide were observed. To each cooled tube 1 ml of 6 M HCl was added and the tubes heated at 110°C for 10 minutes. They were removed from heating block, 1 ml of 6 M formic acid as buffer and 1.5 ml of EDTA reagent were added to each tube and the contents mixed well. The P.H was adjusted to 7.5 with 4 M ammonia. Here after the tubes were protected from direct sun light. A 1 ml of 0.1 per cent DAN reagent was added mixed well and the tubes were stoppered and extracted vigorously, manually for 30 sec. The cyclohexane layer was transferred to 1 cm cuvette with a Pasteur pipette and the fluorescence was measured at excitation and absorption wavelengths of 369 and 518 nm respectively using cyclohexane as the blank in fluorescence spectrophotometer. The amount of selenium is expressed in µg/g wet wt. tissue.

HISTOLOGICAL SECTIONING

The control and experimental silkworms were preserved in aqueous Bouin's fluid for nearly 24 hrs (helps to immobilize the cell structures, while maintaining their morphology). Afterwards the routine procedure for preparation of biological material for the purpose of histological sectioning was used. The fixed tissue was then dehydrated by the graded dehydrating agent (ethyl alcohol). The grades used for dehydration are 30 per cent, 50 per cent, 70 per cent, 90 per cent and 100 per cent alcohol respectively.

The dehydrated tissue was then kept in clearing agent xylene for 3 hrs. After the process of clearing the material was then embedded in paraffin wax and made into blocks. The blocks after trimming were subjected to sectioning process. Rotary microtome was used in the present work and sections of 6-micron thickness were taken. The sections were then spread on the slide by using Mayer's albumen, then flooded with water and kept on a hot plate for one or two minutes. After words the slides were stained. This was done 48 hrs after the drying of sections, which is in the form of ribbon pieces on the slide. By staining, the material was made sharply visible when observed under microscope.

Before staining the paraffin sections, the slides were deparaffinized by keeping it in xylene for nearly 30 minutes. Then the deparaffinized sections were passed through a downgraded series of alcohol (hydration or running down slide to water). The grades used for hydration are 100 per cent, 90 per cent, 80 per cent, 70 per cent, 50 per cent & 30 per cent alcohol respectively and finally in distilled water.

The slides were then stained in Ehrlich's haematoxyline by keeping it for nearly 2-5 minutes in the stain and then washed in water. Then the slides were passed through graded series of alcohol in acceding order up to 70 per cent alcohol then the slides were taken out and then counter stained in Eosin by giving a quick dip and then washed in 70 per cent alcohol. Then the slides were dehydrated by passing through 80 per cent, 90 per cent alcohol, rectified spirit, absolute alcohol-I and alcohol-II for 5 minutes. After dehydrating the slides were transferred to Xylene-I and Xylene-II, and then mounted in DPX mountant. The slides thus prepared were photographed by the Photo-micrographic technique. The magnification was 450 X.

Statistical Analysis

All the results obtained in this investigation were subjected to statistical analysis. The data obtained for each parameter was analyzed for their significance, according to the method of Duncan's multiple range test (Duncan, 1955). The significance was calculated at 5 per cent level ($P < 0.05$).

CHAPTER

3

Nutritional Studies

Introduction

Nutrition comprises various chemical, physiological and biochemical activities, which transform food elements into body elements. Nutrients are the main components of the food that leads to weight gain and increase in body volume. Hence food plays major role in growth, fattening, silk secretion, or other reproductive functions, however, a substantial part of its food is used for supporting body processes, which must go on whether or not any new tissue or product is being formed.

This demand for food is referred to as the maintenance requirement, as it comprises the amount needed to keep intact the tissues of an animal which is not growing, working, or yielding any product. If this need is not met, which is commonly revealed by a loss in weight and which leads to various undesirable consequences. This destruction of body tissue is referred to as the fastening metabolism, and it can be measured in terms of the waste product eliminated through the various parts of excretion. Most of the breakdown is for energy, which occurs in response to the demand of the fasting organism. An animal, which is receiving sufficient protein and energy to permit growth of its tissues and organs, show an increase in size and weight.

The growth of the body as a whole is most commonly measured as an increase in weight. An animal may increase in weight through the deposition of fat without any increase in the structural tissues and organs, which characterize growth. An animal, which receives insufficient protein and energy to permit growth of its organs and tissues, may still show an increase in size due to skeletal growth. In nutritional studies normal growth is referred to as the state of nutrition and health and in descending growth and reproductive performance. Growth retardation is reduced by malnutrition, either in calories or in some specific essential nutrients. The nature and extent of the effect on growth are dependent upon the character and severity of the deficiency and upon the period involved. A deficiency of energy for example, will immediately check growth in mass while lack of calcium may not, as it's primary effect is upon bone structure rather than its size. A deficiency of certain other nutrients such as phosphorus or Vitamin-B exerts an indirect influence on increase in size by decreasing appetite, as well as causing direct physiological effects. Restriction in diet upto 800 days of age in rats resulted in much learner animals with somewhat less skeletal size, but improved health, female fertility and longevity and delayed the onset of degenerative disease (Benjamin, 1960; Benjamin and Simms, 1960). Tonge and McCance (1965) exhibited that growth retardation is due to food restriction in pigs.

Study of various nutritional parameters such as food consumption, excretion, food assimilation and oxidization give an idea regarding growth and energy. The silkworm, *Bombyx mori L.* feeds on the food mulberry leaves from which it ingests various nutrients to support physiological activities. The nutrients include protein, carbohydrate, fat, vitamin, inorganic salt and water. Food preference of silkworm largely depends upon the physical and chemical components of the food. It was reported that the appetizing factors, biting factors, swallowing factors and repellent substances play a key role in accepting the diet (Hanamura *et al.*, 1962). The appetizing factors include many volatile substances such as alcohol, citric aldehyde and linalol influence the larval appetite and feeding reaction. Whereas biting factors like beta sito sterol, isoquercertrin and flavinin cause the larval biting motion. Continuous feeding of the larvae is kept by the swallowing factors such as cellulose, sucrose, inositol, phosphate, silicate, Vitamin-C and sulphur amino acids etc.

Food ingestion by the larvae of *Bombyx mori L.* varies during its different instars. The intake of mulberry leaves into oral cavity is "Ingestion". Active feeding occurs only during IV and V instars and 97 per cent accounts for of total ingestion. The larval feeding is discontinuous, and initial feeding time is different among various instars. This quiscentrest before feeding helps the newly moulted larvae in hardening of new cuticle and the continuous developing of internal organs (Naik 1985; Radhakrishna, 1989). The duration of feeding is only about 27 per cent of the larval feeding period. Each time of feeding lasts for 12-16 minutes. Delvi (1972) described the cessation of appetite considerably 20-30 hours prior to moult in many insects as pre-moult starvation period. The complex organic nutrients in mulberry leaves are covered by cell wall of cellulose hence are insoluble, impermeable and are not utilized by the silkworm directly and silkworm needs to convert the macro, complex insoluble and impermeable substances into simple, permeable products, those actions are called "Digestion".

Food in the buccal cavity is digested primarily by the saliva and lubricated and expelled to midgut, which is the main region for digestion and assimilation. The goblet cells of midgut play a key role in digestion by secreting digestive juices and absorb nutrients into the haemolymph through cylindrical cells of midgut. The remains are combined with the secretions by the Malpighian tubules, the mixtures are pressed by the colon into the hexagonal excrements and then expelled into rectum. Water in the excrements is reabsorbed and the faecal matter is pressed further and excreted the undigested matter as solid faecal pellets.

Eventhough the literature available on selenium nutritional aspects of vertebrates is abundant, a little is available in lower organisms such as arthropods. Hence the author is made an attempt to study various nutritional parameters such as food consumption, excretion, assimilation, food combustion and total food converted under lethal and sub lethal doses of selenium at 3, 4, 5, and 6 days of V instar silkworm of PM X NB_4D_2 perentage.

RESULTS

The data on the various nutritional parameters such as food consumption, faecal excretion, assimilation, food conversion and oxidation of V instar silkworm *Bombyx mori L* (groups 2, 5, 8, and 11) exposed to lethal and groups 3, 6, 9, and 12 to sub lethal doses of selenium at 3, 4, 5 and 6 days of exposure period besides controls are presented in Table 3.1. For comparative assessment, the differences obtained in relation to controls in nutritional parameter at the said exposure periods of lethal and sub lethal doses were converted as percentage of the corresponding controls (groups 1, 4, 7, and 10) and these per cent change values were also given in the Table 3.1 and plotted against exposure periods in Figure 3.1.

Food Consumption

From the data presented in the Table 3.1 and Figure 3.1 a, it is observed that, relative to controls, the total amount of food consumed at 3, 4, 5 and 6 days exposure of V instar silkworms (groups 2, 5, 8 and 11) to lethal dose of selenium was significantly ($P < 0.05$) decreased. Based on per cent values, the percent decrease in the food consumption in the lethal dose was progressed gradually from the 3 day to 6 days of exposure period studied and was in the order 3 < 4 < 5 < 6 days. In the sub lethal dose (groups 3, 6, 9, and 12), however, the amount of food consumed gradually increased in all days of exposure periods studied and this increase was significant ($P < 0.05$). The per cent increase also found high at 6 day when compared to that of 3 day.

Table 3.1 : Estimation of Nutritional Parameters (mg/kg. body weight/day/larva) at 3, 4,5, & 6 days in V instar of Silkworm fed on Mulberry leaves treated with Lethal and Sub-lethal doses of Selenium

Days exposure	Dosage	Consumption	Excretion	Assimilation	Conversion	Oxidization
3 days	Control	510 **b**	254 **c**	256 **b**	21.24 **b**	234.76 **b**
	Lethal	400 **a** (-21.56)	216 **a** (-14.9)	184 **a** (-23.1)	16.0 **a** (-24.6)	168 **a** (-28.4)
	Sub-lethal	**560 c (+9.8)**	**221.2 b (-12.9)**	**338 8 c (+32.3)**	**29.47 c (+38.7)**	**309.33 c (+31.7)**
4 days	Control	605 **b**	302 **c**	303 **b**	24.24 **b**	278.75 **b**
	Lethal	470 **a** (-22.31)	253.8 **a** (-16.2)	216.2 **a** (-23.7)	18.7 **a** (-22.8)	197.5 **a** (-29.14)
	Sub-lethal	**685 c (+13.2)**	**270.5 b (-10.4)**	**414.5 c (+36.6)**	**36.0 c (+48.5)**	**378.5 c (+35.7)**
5 days	Control	720 **b**	359 **c**	361 **b**	29.7 **b**	331 **b**
	Lethal	515 **a** (- 28.47)	278 **a** (-22.5)	237 **a** (-34.3)	20.61 **a** (-30.6)	216.3 **a** (-34.6)
	Sub-lethal	**810 c (+12.5)**	**319.95 b (-10.8)**	**490.05 c (+35.7)**	**42.6 c (+43.4)**	**447.45 c (+35.1)**
6 days	Control	940 **b**	469 **c**	471 **b**	38.8 **b**	432.18 **b**
	Lethal	600 **a** (-36.17)	324 **a** (-30.9)	276 **a** (-41)	24.01 **a** (-38.14)	251.9 **a** (-41.7)
	Sub-lethal	**1115.0 c (+18.6)**	**440 b (-6.2)**	**675 c (+43.3)**	**58.7 c (+51.2)**	**616.3 c (+42.6)**

* Each value is a mean of eight estimates.

** Per cent decrease over control is given in parenthesis.

*** Mean with in a column followed by the same method are not significantly different (P > 0.05) from each other according to Duncan's Multiple Range Test.

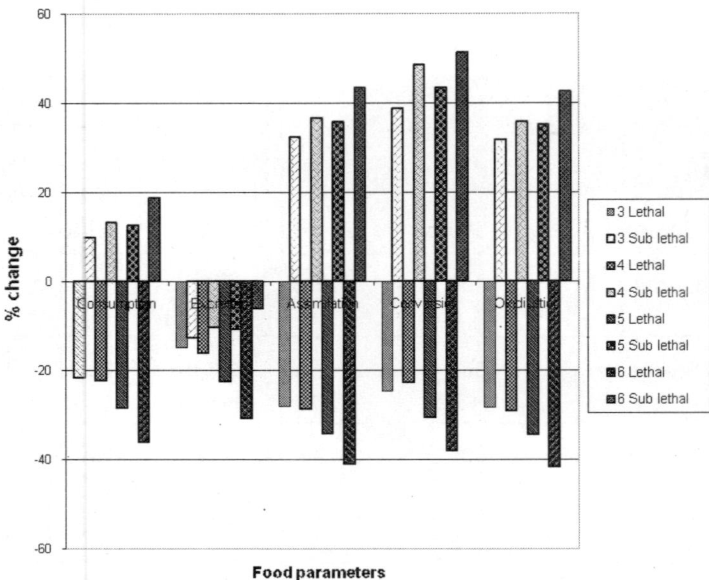

Fig. 3.1 : Estimation of Nutritional Parameters (mg /kg. body weight/day/ larva) at 3,4,5, & 6 days in V instar of Silkworm fed on Mulberry leaves treated with Lethal and Sub-lethal doses of Selenium.

Faecal Output

Corresponding to the decrease in food consumption in lethal dose of selenium (groups 2, 5, 8 and 11), the excretion of faecal matter also decreased significantly ($P < 0.05$) in relation to controls (groups 1, 4, 7, and 10) on all exposure periods studied and followed the trend 3 < 4 < 5 < 6. Based on per cent change values, it is seen that the per cent decrease in faecal output of silkworm exposed to lethal dose progressed gradually from 3 day to 6 days and was in the order 3 < 4 < 5 < 6.

Even in sub lethal dose (groups 3, 6, 9, and 12), a significant decrease in faecal output was observed at 3, 4, 5 and 6 days of exposure periods studied indicating the enhanced food assimilation due to increased oxidation.

Food Assimilation, Oxidation and Conversion

Corresponding to the decrease in food consumption and faecal output of the V instar silkworm exposed to lethal dose of selenium (groups 2, 5, 8 and 11), the other nutritional parameters such as food assimilation, conversion and oxidation registered a significant ($P<0.05$) decrease at 3, 4, 5 and 6 days of exposure periods studied. Based on per cent values, the per cent decrease in these parameters is less at 3 day of exposure and this decrease progressed gradually and was in order 3 < 4 < 5 < 6. In sub lethal dose of selenium (groups 3, 6, 9, and 12), however, all the above nutritional parameters registered an elevation at 3, 4, 5 and 6 days of exposure.

Discussion

The parameters like food consumption, digestion and utilization in insects are of immense importance to understand the nutritional aspects in insects (Waldbauer, 1964). It is well known that fluctuations in food intake in the silkworm *Bombyx mori L.* were clearly evident during its different instars. The results presented on food consumption, digestion, utilization and excretion bring out many significant and interesting aspects with regard to the lethal and sub lethal doses of selenium at different days. The literature on food utilization budgets related to selenium effects on animals is very scanty (Harrison and Conrad, 1984). The food intake in selenium treated silkworms was significantly reduced at lethal intoxication, whereas sub lethal dose enhanced the food intake significantly when compared to the controls. Here the lethal dose acted as inhibitor and sub lethal dose acted as attractant. However these changes in the food intake may be attributed to food assimilation efficiency when fed with selenium may not be entirely due to the decrease in the consumption, but it may also be due to the action of selenium, which enhances the digestibility by increase in enzyme secretion rate/activity at least in the sub lethal selenium exposed silkworm. It has been suggested that selenium acts as an oxidant functioning as the metal co-factor for important enzymatic activity requiring glutathione peroxidase (Mayland, 1994). Lethal dose of an insecticide when fed to *Philosamia ricini* resulted in inhibition of Acetyl Choline activity and the inhibited esterase, may induce the toxicity that results in the lack of appetite in Silkworm (Pant *et al.*, 1982). The decrease in food assimilation at lethal intoxication is reportedly due to lack of enzymatic mechanism, due to breakdown of proteins into amino acids and peptones and also may be due to the malfunction of mid intestine for transport of amino acids and peptones to respective organs. The results coincide with the reports of Lemly (1998), who observed that high concentration of selenium that substituted for sulphur in sulphur-to-sulphur linkages of proteins. This results in inability to form a helical structure leading to non-functioning of malformed proteins. Such an inhibitory activity in the digestive process might also have brought in the silkworm of the present study during the lethal dose exposure of selenium.

The total food assimilation and oxidation in silkworm treated with lethal selenium dose are suppressed and silkworm treated with sub lethal dose of selenium are enhanced. The results are in agreement with Deka *et al.*, (1999) as in non-mulberry silkworms. The enhanced assimilation and oxidation of food is probably due to the better consumption of food and enhanced transaminases activity of the intestine and the haemolymph of the silkworm as suggested by Shyamala and Bhatt, (1956), with reference to toxicity of chloromycetin. The lepidopteran larvae are able to adopt and express in different ways in various environmental conditions by altering one or more parameters of food utilization. The efficiency increases during toxicant supplement is in agreement with the homolygosis hypothesis which credits that sub lethal dose of any stressing agent may be stimulatory to the organism by providing it increased sensitivity or respond to change in its environment and increased efficiency for coping with sub optimum environment (Lucky, 1968). Cholinesterase inhibition may induce the toxicity by killing the larva reflecting on their lack of appetite and under nourishment. This further leads to the lysis of all nutrients such as carbohydrates, glycogen, proteins and lipids and also an increase in lipolytic, proteolytic phosphorylase and amino transferase activities (Pant *et al.*, 1982; Pant and Katiyar, 1983). From the present study it is evident that the findings of the present are in agreement with earlier reports.

In the present study, the selenium at lethal doses could decrease the parameters like food consumption assimilation efficiencies and food conversion rate. However the sub-lethal dose of selenium particularly at 6 days of exposure, silkworm could exhibit significant increased levels of the above parameters leading to better survival and normal life by suppressing toxic action by detoxification mechanisms.

CHAPTER

4

Bioaccumulation and Excretion

Introduction

The distribution and subsequent accumulation of selenium occurs mainly through the circulatory system to the various organs of the body. The extent of its accumulation varies with the types of tissues, the level of selenium administered and the individual susceptibility to selenium intoxication. The liver is the primary organ for detoxification of any toxicant in vertebrates (Hutterer *et al.*, 1969). Hence it is logical that toxicants reach this organ in abundant quantities for detoxification and disposal. Highest quantities of selenium are reported, in the liver, followed in the decreasing order by the kidneys, spleen and lungs. (Dudley, 1936, Glenn *et al.*, 1964). Myocardium, skeletal muscle and brain accumulate trace amounts of selenium and fat has practically no selenium. Usually in animals, Chronic selenosis is expected when their blood selenium levels reach 2-4 ppm (Miller and Williams, 1940; Maag *et al.*, 1960; Rosenfield and Beath, 1964). In acutely poisoned animals, blood selenium levels reach 25 ppm (Dudley, 1936). Hair also accumulates selenium and is a good indicator for routine diagnosis of chronic selenium toxicity in cattle and as reported by Olson (1969), hair accumulates up to 10 ppm. Values obtained by Glenn *et al.*, (1964), on eight sheep lethally poisoned by sodium selenate are presented as representative values. Mean values are presented per million on a wet weight basis are as follows :

Liver	-	28 ppm
Kidney	-	6.9 ppm
Lung	-	3 ppm
Spleen	-	2.4 ppm
Myocardium	-	4.0 ppm
Skeletal muscle	-	0.6 ppm
Brain	-	0.8 ppm

It was also observed that selenium toxicosis affects the kidney where its concentration is higher than dose the liver. Klug *et. al.*, (1950), Levander (1991) and Levander and Argrett (1969) reported a much higher percentage of radio selenium in the liver of rats, after 12 hours injection of radio selenite than in the kidneys of the same animal.

It has been found that animals on very low levels of selenium concentrate more selenium in their kidneys than in any other organ. Allaway *et al.*, (1966) made an observation on selenium content of sheep fed with alfa alfa that had a selenium content of less than 0.01 ppm and it was found that the accumulated selenium in kidney of these sheep was 0.52 ppm. The quantity of selenium accumulated in tissues also depends on the chemical form in which the element is administered. Smith *et al.*, (1938) reported that the concentrations of selenium in various tissues of rabbits fed seleniferous Oats were many times those found in the tissues of rabbits fed comparable amount of selenium as selenite. The deposition of selenium in tissues also depends upon the exposure of the animal to this element. Jaffe and Mondragon (1969) observed that the young rats born to mothers fed a moderately high selenium diet and after weaning they showed a steady decrease in selenium content in liver. Hopkins *et al.*, 1966 demonstrated that the distribution of selenium in tissues can be influenced by the previous selenium intake. Aquatic organisms accumulate selenium (Se) from inorganic and organic selenium species via aqueous and food-chain exposure routes. Generally plants have been classified based on the amount of selenium accumulated as high, moderate or non-accumulators (Rosenfield and Beath, 1964). The high accumulator group may accumulate hundreds to thousands of $\mu g\ g^{-1}$ selenium (dry weight of plant tissue) while the moderate accumulators develop concentration of 50-100 $\mu g\ g^{-1}$ plant tissues. Several reports described the uptake and fate of selenium in plants. Plants can accumulate selenium as either sodium selenate, sodium selenite in organic forms such as selenomethionine or selenocystine. The most common soluble form of selenium in agricultural drainage converted into sodium selenite by plants. The selenite in sodium selenite is substituted for sulphur in certain amino acids commonly producing selenomethionine selenocystine (Presser *et al.*, 1994). This selenium containing amino acids may account for 10 per cent (Wu *et al.*, 1997) or more than 50 per cent (Ge *et al.*, 1996) of the total selenium in plants. All these form have been found in leaves, stems and roots (Terry and Zayed, 1994; Ge *et al.*, 1996).

The available data provide insight into individual and population level responses to selenium for insects attacking living plants, most of which accumulate selenium at concentrations below 100 $\mu g\ g^{-1}$ (Banuelos *at al.*, 1997). Previous studies where insects were fed with selenium, focused on the peroxidation responses of houseflies to low levels of selenium in their drinking water (Simmons *et al.*, 1989). These reports utilized insects as a model system for measuring metabolic activity, rather than examining potential population responses to selenium contaminations. Hogan and Razniak (1991) reported that beetles infesting grain and other dried stored products suffered additional mortality when exposed to diets containing 0.125–1.00 per cent sodium selenite. These relatively high rates correspond to concentrations of 1250 to 10000 $\mu g\ g^{-1}$. Such information may become essential as effects increase to produce sustainable remediation programmes using plants. Selenium homeostasis is regulated primarily through excretion. Selenium is excreted via urinary path (50-67%) and through fecal matter. (40–50%) (Groff *et al.*, 1995). Within certain physiological limits trace amounts of selenium is retained in the body while excessive amounts are excreted (Hammond and Beliles, 1980).

Extremely high intakes of selenium can lead to ventilatory elimination of the mineral in the form of dimethyl selenide. Studies on rats, have shown that the urinary path way is the dominant route for selenium excretion, as long as the dietary selenium exceeds a certain critical threshold level. Hawkes *et al.*, (2003) studied the selenium absorption and excretion in human beings and reported that selenium levels in urine and plasma changes with the change in food intake. Only a small fraction of the amount absorbed through the gastro intestinal tract is excreted in faeces. According to. Bopp *et al.*, 1982, urinary excretion after ingestion of trace amounts seldom exceeds 10-15 per cent. Burk *et al.*, (1972) reported that selenium excreted in urine of rats with selenium-supplemented diet, than that in faeces.

RESULTS

From the data presented in Tables 4.1, 4.2, and 4.3 and Figures 4.1a, 4.2a and 4.3a, it is seen that selenium administration in silkworm resulted in a significant increase of it in malpighian tubules, fat body and haemolymph. The bioaccumulation of selenium in fat body and malpighian tubules, however, increased with increase in selenium dose and also increased with period of exposure. So the per cent increase in bioaccumulation and rate of accumulation were greater in group 8 (5 day), group 11 (6 day) than in group 2 (3 day) and group 5 (4 day) in lethal dose. The bioaccumulation in haemolymph also showed a significant increase in-group 8 (5 day), group 11 (6 day) than in group 2 (3 day) and group 5 (4 day) in lethal dose. The bioaccumulation of selenium in haemolymph increased with selenium dose and period of exposure, thus the per cent increase in rate were greater in group 11 (6 day), group 8 (5 day) than in group 2 (3 day) and group 5 (4 day) in lethal dose. Among the tissues, the concentration of Selenium was in the order Malpighian tubule > fat body > haemolymph.

From the data presented in Tables 4.1, 4.2 and 4.3, it is seen that in silkworm, which received the sub lethal dose of selenium, the levels of selenium were significantly less compared to the silkworm treated to lethal dose with selenium. The bioaccumulation of selenium in fat body and malpighian tubules increased with the increase in Selenium dose and also increased with the period of exposure. So the percentage and rate of accumulation is greater in group 9 (5 day), group 12 (6 day) than in group 3 (3 day) and group 6 (4 day). The bioaccumulation of selenium in haemolymph showed steep increase in group 12 (6 day), group 9 (5 day), group 6 (4 day), group 3 (3 day). The bioaccumulation of selenium in haemolymph at lethal dose increased with increase of period of exposure. In sub-lethal dose groups, it increased with increase of period of exposure. So the percentage of increase and rate of accumulation were greater in group 9 (5 day), group 12 (6 day) than in group 3 (3 day) and group 6 (4 day). The levels of selenium in the tissues was in the order malpighian tubules > fat bodies > haemolymph.

Excretion

From the data presented in Table 4.4 and Figure 4.4, it is seen that relative to controls, selenium excretion through faeces significantly increased in group 2 (3 day), group 5 (4 day), group 8 (6 day) and group 11 (6 day). The excretion of selenium however increased with increase in selenium dose and period of exposure in lethal dose. So the percentage and rate of elimination of selenium was greater in group 8 (5 day), group 11 (6 day) than in group 2 (3 day) and group 5 (4 day) in lethal dose. In the sub-lethal dose of selenium treated silkworms the excretion of selenium was significantly less than that in lethal dose treated silkworms. The percentage and rate of elimination of selenium was more in group 9 (5 day), group 12 (6 day) than in group 3 (3 day) and group 6 (4 day). The rate of elimination increased with period of exposure.

Discussion

For toxicological evaluation it is important to measure the highest concentration of selenium reached in the organs of silkworm on its continuous exposure. The dominant factor that determines the highest concentrations, in addition to the period of exposure, is the rate of elimination of selenium from the body, and in particular from the individual organs. A low elimination rate leads more accumulation of any element in the critical organs even at short duration of exposure.

In the present study, significant amounts of accumulation of selenium in the organs of silkworm on exposure to lethal and sub-lethal doses of selenium indicates the potentiality of these elements for bioaccumulation and persistence. However the amount and rate of accumulation are dose and time dependent. In addition, the significant differences observed in the amount and rate of accumulation of selenium in different organs of Silkworm (Malpighian tubules, fat body and haemolymph) reflect the dependency of selenium accumulation on a number of factors.

The fat body is the primary organ for the detoxication of any toxicant. And hence it is logical that toxicants reach this organ in abundant quantities for detoxification and disposal. As the fat body is one of the important target organs for selenium, a significant amount of selenium is absorbed in it in the silkworm exposed to both lethal and sub-lethal doses of selenium. However in the silkworms treated with sub-lethal doses of selenium, the percentage of bioaccumulation of this trace element is less than in silkworm treated with lethal dose of selenium. Greater accumulation of Selenium in the fat bodies of silkworm exposed to selenium especially in group 8 (5 day) and group 11 (6 day) could cause structural and functional damage leading to the inhibition of all its metabolic activities. Burk *et al.*, (1972) reported that Selenium is readily absorbed from the intestine and excreted through urine. The present study has shown that malpighian tubules retained more selenium than the fat bodies. A direct correlation between the Selenium intake and excretion was reported (Hawkes *et al.*, 2003) and nearby 50–70 per cent of the ingested Selenium is bound to be excreted and retention a part of it in malpighian tubules. Selenium removal (clearance) through malpighian tubules might be the cause of greater degree of bioaccumulation. It is reported that malpighian tubules were affected more than the fat bodies in selenium toxicity. The haemolymph is the transport medium. It usually carries O_2 to the tissues and CO_2, Nitrogenous wastes and other substances from the tissues. The haemolymph acts as a transporting medium for selenium.

In the present study, the haemolymph selenium level increased following selenium ingestion. The increase in selenium content is proportionate to the duration and dose of selenium administration. The haemolymph selenium content is a reflection of balance between selenium absorption, excretion transfer to, release from, storage depots. Usually in animals, chronic selenosis is expected when their blood selenium levels reach 2-4 ppm (Miller and Williams, 1940; Magg *et al.*, 1960; Rosenfield and Beath, 1964. In acutely poisoned animals, blood selenium levels reach 25 ppm. (Dudely, 1936). Hopkins *et al.*, (1966) demonstrated that the distribution of selenium in tissues can be influenced by the previous selenium intake. Selenium concentrations in circulating haemolymph are the resultant of several processes such as absorption of selenium from alimentary canal and removal of it from haemolymph by malpighian tubules through urine. The importance of these processes results in a magnitude of the circulating haemolymph selenium elevation. Spagnolo *et al.*, (1991) who observed that serum selenium levels were slightly higher in males 83.1 ± 10.1 µg/1) than in females (1.7 ± 11.0 µg/1). The results in the selenium treated silkworms indicated that the selenium bioaccumulation is dose and time dependent in haemolymph. It has been postulated that the concentration of selenium in haemolymph and other tissues will increases with period and that this increase will be associated with an increased severity of selenium induced effects in the silkworms.

Selenium present in faeces results from two sources : the ingested selenium that is not absorbed and the absorbed selenium that is reabsorbed into the alimentary canal. The present study has shown that considerable amount of selenium is excreted through faeces in all groups of selenium treated silkworms. The results indicated that the excretion of selenium through faeces is dependent on dose and period of exposure. This supports the view of Hammond and Beliles (1980) who reported that with in certain physiological limits the trace amounts of selenium are retained in the body while excessive amounts are excreted. Bioaccumulation models were reported by many authors in herbivorous bivalves (Wang *et al.*, 1996), copepods (Wang *et al.*, 1996; Wang and Fisher, 1998), deposit feeding polychaetes (Wang and Stupakoff, 1999) and larval fish (Reinfelder and Fisher, 1994; Baines *et al.*, 2002).

Urinary selenium and plasma selenium responded most rapidly to changes in selenium intake (Hawkes *et al.*, 2003). Faecal excretion decreased by half, representing an important but previously under appreciating adaptation to selenium restriction. Increased dietary selenium in improved survival and increased weight gains in *Acheta domesticus* and signs of deficiency were evident from diminished biomass in groups fed lower concentrations (Carla *et al.*, 2006).

Table 4.1 : Selenium accumulations (µ gms/g. wet wt.) in the Haemolymph of V instar Silkworm *Bombyx mori.L.* on exposure to different doses of Selenium at 3, 4, 5 and 6 days

Dose	3 day	4 day	5 day	6 day
Control	0.0880 [a]	0.09 [a]	0.0930 [a]	0.14 [a]
Lethal	1.2187 [c] (+ 1284.88) r: 1307	1.813 [c] (+1915.21) r: 1.7131	2.096 [c] (+2154.44) r: 2.003	3.936[c] (+2711.82) r: 3.796
Sub-lethal	0.7417 [b] (+742.84) r: 0.6537	0.8340 [b] (+826.66) r: 0.744	0.9203 [b] (+889.156) r: 0.8273	1.501 [b] (+971.1) r: 1.361

* Each value is a mean of eight estimates.

** Per cent decrease over control is given in parenthesis.

*** Means with in a column followed by the same letter are not significantly different ($p > 0.05$) from each other according to Duncan's multiple range tests.

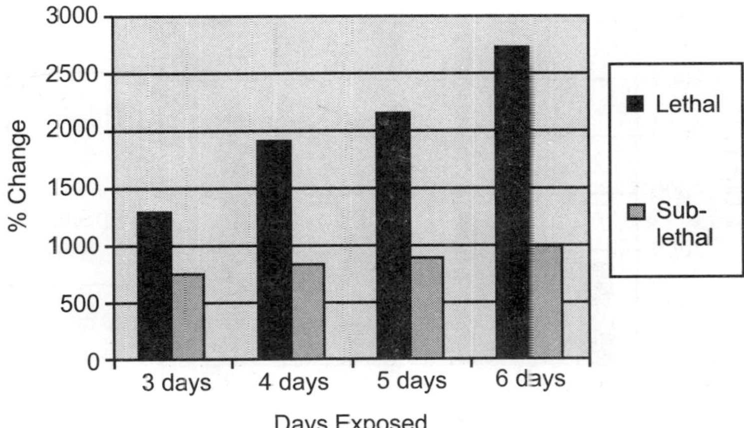

Fig. 4.1: Per cent change over control in the Selenium accumulations (µ gms/ g.wet wt.) in the Haemolymph of V Instar Silkworm *Bombyx mori.L.* on exposure to different doses of Selenium at 3, 4, 5 and 6 days.

Table 4.2 : Selenium accumulations (µ gms/ g wet wt.) in the Fat body of V instar Silkworm *Bombyx mori.L.* on exposure to different doses of Selenium at 3, 4, 5 and 6 days

Dose	3 day	4 day	5 day	6 day
Control	0.0780 [a]	0.0823 [a]	0.0870 [a]	0.0907 [a]
Lethal	0.7647 [c] (+880.38) r: 0.6867	1.12 [c] (+1260.87) r:1.0377	1.1907 [c] (+1268.62) r: 1.1037	2.1227 [c] (+2240.35) r: 2.032
Sub-lethal	0.53 [b] (+579.48) r: 0.452	0.7140 [b] (+767.55) r: 0.6317	0.8020 [b] (+821.83) r: 0.908	1.0019 [b] (+1004.6) r: 0.9112

* Each value is a mean of eight estimates.

** Per cent decrease over control is given in parenthesis.

*** Means with in a column followed by the same letter are not significantly different ($p > 0.05$) from each other according to Duncan's Multiple range test.

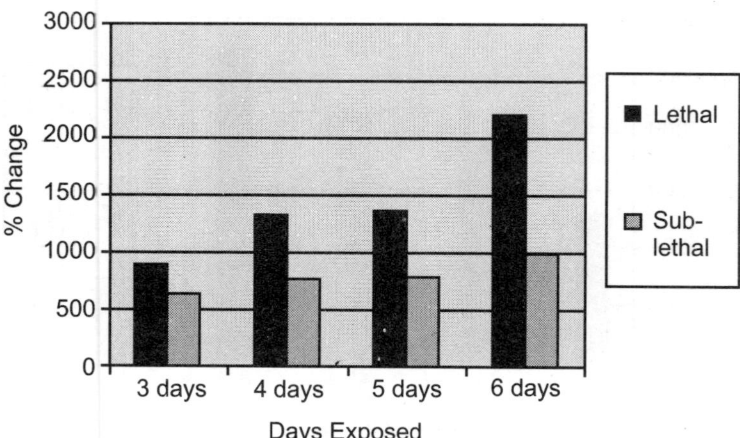

Fig. 4.2 : Per cent change over control in the Selenium accumulations (μ gms/ g wet wt.) in the Fat body of V Instar Silkworm *Bombyx mori.L.* on exposure to different doses of Selenium at 3, 4, 5 and 6 days.

Table 4.3 : Selenium accumulations (μ gms/ g wet wt.) in the malpighian tubules of V instar Silkworm *Bombyx mori.L.* on exposure to different doses of Selenium at 3, 4, 5 and 6 days

Dose	3 day	4 day	5 day	6 day
Control	0.0230[a]	0.0413[a]	0.0613[a]	0.0673[a]
Lethal	0.619[c] (+ 2592) r: 0.596	1.2413[c] (+ 2905) r: 1.200	2.5503[c] (+4060.47) r:2.489	3.1880[c] (+4737) r:3.1207
Sub lethal	0.5737[b] (+2394.34) r:0.05507	1.1000[b] (+2563.4) r:1.0587	1.7210[b] (+2705.8) r: 1.6597	1.9870[b] (2852.45) r: 1.91

* Each value is a mean of eight estimates.

** Per cent decrease over control is given in parenthesis.

*** Means with in a column followed by the same letter are not significantly different ($p > 0.05$) from each other according to Duncan's multiple range tests.

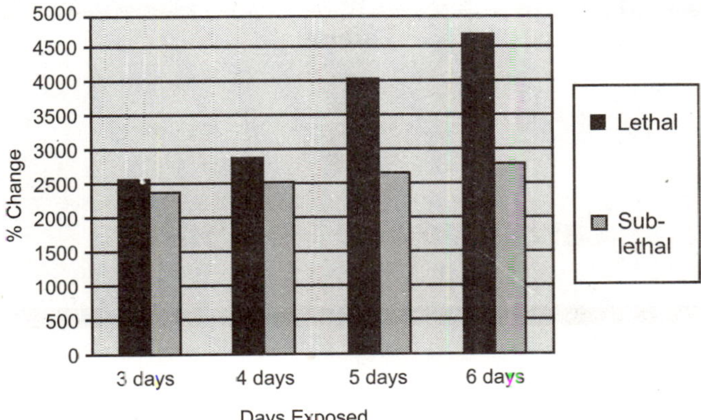

Fig. 4.3 : Per cent change over control Selenium accumulations (μ gms/ g wet wt.) in the malpighian tubules of V Instar Silkworm *Bombyx mori.L.* on exposure to different doses of Selenium at 3, 4, 5 and 6 days.

Table 4.4 : Faecal Selenium Excretion (μgms/g wet weight/day) by the V Instar Silkworm *Bombyx mori. L.* on exposure to different doses of Selenium at 3, 4, 5 and 6 days

Dose	3 day	4 day	5 day	6 day
Control	0.153a	0.32 a	0.5063 a	0.7303 a
Lethal	23.74c +15416	52.0c +16150	90.35c +17970	135.0c +18393
Sub-lethal	2.082 +1361.6	5.8368 +1724	10.742 +2021.8	17.94 +2357.5

* Each value is a mean of eight estimates.

** Per cent decrease over control is given in parenthesis.

*** Means with in a column followed by the same letter are not significantly different ($p > 0.5$) from each other according to Duncan's multiple range tests.

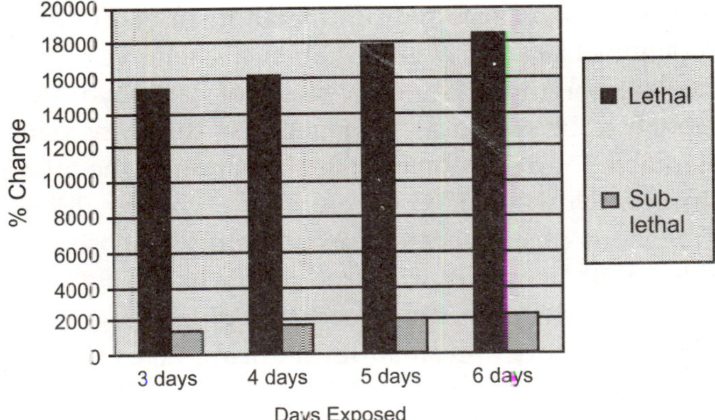

Fig. 4.4 : Per cent change over control of Faecal Selenium Excretion (μgms/g wet wt. /day) by the V Instar Silkworm *Bombyx mori L.* on exposure to different doses of Selenium at 3, 4, 5 and 6 days.

Chapter

5

Carbohydrate Metabolism

Introduction

Carbohydrates are the chief complex organic constituents, the breakdown of which facilitates the liberation of the 'Energy' required for the biological reactions to occur rapidly through well defined pathways. Trehalose and Glucose are the most common in the caterpillars and probably also in other insects body whereas glycogen is the storage carbohydrate which is built up by the fat body during periods of active feeding. This store becomes depleted during sustained activity over a moult, when the insect is not feeding of if it is starved. Significance of glucose lies in its participation in energy-storage and energy-release systems. Glycogen is composed of many glucose units, it is readily hydrolysed in a stepwise manner to glucose. Most of the glucose contained in food is absorbed via the alimentary canal and converted to glycogen in the fat body. The concentration of glucose in the haemolymph is normally be regulated by conversion of glycogen to glucose. Fat body plays an important role in the carbohydrate metabolism of the insect organism. One of the functions of fat body is to maintain a relatively constant level of glucose in the haemolymph. The conversion of carbohydrates to fat when there is too much to be stored as glycogen and the conversion of fats into compounds suitable for oxidation during starvation in the fat body has been reported in insects (Downer, 1985; Steele, 1985; Wheeler, 1989). Even in the absence of exogenous carbohydrate, the circulating glucose which continues to be available to all tissues by its production in the fat body from non-carbohydrate source through the process of gluconeogenesis. Gluconeogenesis maintains haemolymph sugar level during times when food intake is restricted or glycogen stores are depleted. It also contributes significantly to the utilization of amino acids, which are either absorbed from the alimentary tract or released during protein breakdown. When conditions of metabolic acidosis exist such as prolonged starvation, the renal gluconeogenesis contributes about 50 per cent of glucose production (Owen *et al.*, 1969). At low PH the conversion of glutamate and α- Ketoglutarate to glucose enhances, this in turn leads to an increase in ammonia production, which is used to counteract the acidosis (Good man *et al.*, 1966; Steiner *et al.*, 1968).

Importance of glucose lies in its participation in energy storage and energy release systems. Chitra and Sridhara (1973) reviewed the role of glucose in the intermediate metabolism of silkworm and Kilby (1963) stated the correlation of blood glucose levels with that of metabolism and it is comparable with the mammalian blood glucose. The Lepidopteron insects maintain relatively higher amounts of blood sugar when compared with other insects (Roeder, 1953). Haemolymph sugar level, in the silkworm larvae has been worked out by many entomologists (Hemmingsen, 1924; Kuwana, 1937; Morris, 1962; Thompson and Sikoroshiki, 1980).

Glycogen is composed of mainly glucose units, it is readily hydrolyzed in stepwise manner to glucose. Maintenance of glycogen reserves is an important feature of the normal metabolism, adult differentiation, reproductive process and flight as in many insects (Wyatt, 1967; Turner and Mancheslei, 1972; Steele, 1980; Chandrasekhar and Geetha Bali, 1987). In the insect fat body and haemolymph the glycogen levels always vary depending upon its life cycle and the requirement of energy. It was reported that in silkworm fat body glycogen amounts to 52.5 mg/g dry weight at the beginning of the V instar rising to 215 mg/g at the end, but had fallen to 35.6 mg/g by the 2nd day of the pupal stage (Shigematsu, 1956). Some apparent glycogen has been reported in the haemolymph of *Bombyx mori L.* and in some other insects (Shigematsu, 1956; Wyatt and Kalf, 1957).

The main haemolymph sugar, trehalose, a non-reducing disaccharide is maintained at a steady state in insects through homeostatic regulation at all stages of the life cycle (Wyatt, 1967). In the normal state of silkworm larvae, the haemolymph trehalose levels vary little during a certain limited period of development, and then a mechanism of homeostatic regulation is maintained (Horie, 1961 and Saito, 1963). There are at least two distinctive components of trehalases in the muscle and midgut of the silkworm and their enzymatic properties have been clarified (Yanagawa, 1971). The amount of trehalose in the silkworm blood has been reported to correspond to 20-35 per cent of the total storage carbohydrates of 5th instar larvae (Yanagawa, 1973). Though the trehalose levels vary in different sps. 100 mg/ 100 ml is common (Duchateau and Florkin, 1959). In silkworm *Bombyx mori L.* trehalose content in haemolymph declines to half or even less at the transformation of larva to pupa, due to the decrease of its synthesis, but not due to the increased utilization by the tissues (Sakamoto and Horie, 1979). The enzyme trehalase, has an important function through out the life cycle, and hydrolyses trehalose into 2 molecules of glucose (Yamashita *et al.*, 1972). Yamashita and Hasegawa (1974) and Horie (1963) studied that the trehalose levels in the haemolymph and glycogen in the fat body on the silkworm *Bombyx mori L.* Under stress conditions, the changes in the haemolymph trehalose were observed by Bhosale and Kallapur (1985). Wyatt (1961) studied the effects of experimental injury on carbohydrate metabolism in pupal and silk moth. In female, silkworm *Bombyx mori L.*, during its metamorphosis, the mobilization of carbohydrates, in the tissues, has been studied by Yamashita and Hasegawa (1974).

A study on the comparative quantitative estimation of glycogen and trehalose was made during starvation in silkworm *Bombyx mori L.* by Band (1977). Trehalose (α-D-glucose pyranosyl-α-D-glucopyranoside), a non reducing disaccharide is known to occur in the haemolymph and to a limited extent, in the fat body of a variety of insects. Wyatt and Kalf G. (1956) first isolated and identified trehalose from the haemolymph of the larval and pupal Antheraea polyphemus. Later, Howden G. and Kilby B. (1956), reported about trehalose levels in the haemolymph of *Schistocerca gregaria.*

Saito (1963) reported that the fat bodies of silkworm are the main site for the synthesis of trehalose from glucose. The amount of trehalose in the fat bodies and haemolymph vary from one insect group to another. The biosynthetic pathway of trehalose, has been studied in cell free homogenate of *Hyalophora cercopia* fat body by Murphy and Wyatt (1965). It was discovered that Trehalases can be isolated as membrane bound or soluble enzymes from the gut tissues of *Hyalophora cercopia* (Gussin, A. and Wyatt G., 1965) and in *Bombyx mori L.* cocoon floss (Shimada *et al.*, 1980). Insects need carbohydrates as major fuel for their growth and development, being derived mostly from the diet. The Silkworm *Bombyx mori L.* conserves sufficient quantity of energy reserves during larval stage to be utilized during pupal and adult stages. Trehalose is the major and metabolically active, non reducing disaccharide in the insect blood. (Wyatt and Kalf, 1956; Wyatt and Kalf, 1957) which is synthesized in the fat body, (Candy and Kilby, 1959; Candy and Kilby, 1961; Clegg and Evans, 1961) and utilized during spinning, flight and starvation of insects. (Saito.1963; Horie, 1961). It is well known that haemolymph; the only extra cellular fluid in insect is having diverse functions. (Pawar and Ramakrishnan, 1977).

It has been reported that the haemolymph trehalose level in insects is maintained by the absorption of digested sugars through the gut (Horie, 1959) and or by the breakdown of the fat body glycogen to glucose, which serves as precursor for the synthesis of trehalose (Candy and Kilby, 1959; Candy and Kilby, 1961; James *et al.*, 1961).

A key control step in glycogenolysis of insects is catalyzed by "glycogen phosphorylase", the enzyme responsible for the primary cleavage of glycogen. The phosphorylase enzyme exists in two forms, the active, tetrameric phosphorylase "a" form and the inactive dimeric phosphorylase "b". The main difference between these two is that phosphorylase "a" is active even in the absence of cyclic-5-AMP, while phosphorylase "b" requires cyclic-5-AMP for its activity (Cori and Cori 1945; Cori *et al.*, 1955). The inter conversion of these forms regulates the rate of glycolysis (Steele, 1982). As it is the enzyme needed for the metabolic breakdown of glycogen, estimation of glycogen phosphorylase activity assumes considerable importance. Increase in glycogen phosphorylase activity confirms glycogen breakdown, a cause for the lowered glycogen level, which may even be caused by a decrease in its synthesis rate. In *Schistocerca gregaria* flight muscle, the glycogen levels were reported to be decreased by 64% within 10 seconds of flight (Rowan and Newsholme, 1979), indicating the glycogen phosphorylase activity during flight to generate energy in amounts upto 100-fold greater than that produced at rest (Davis and Fraenkel, 1940) and *Locusta migratoria* fat body, the amount of glycogen levels declined by 75 per cent in two hours of flight (Van Marrewijk *et al.*, 1980). This enzyme, is known to be controlled by both direct and indirect effectors. A decrease in phosphorylase activity facilitates the synthesis of glycogen from glucose (Glycogenesis). It is a known fact that under stress, shifts in glucose and glycogen levels also alter the activity of glycogen phosphorylase. In silkmoth fat body also, phosphorylase exists in active and inactive forms which are called fat body phosphorylase "a" and "b" (Stevenson and Wyatt, 1964; Yanagawa and Horie, 1977a and b; Yanagawa and Horie, 1978). Glycogen Phosphorylase catalyses the sequential removal of glycosyl residues from the non reducing end of the glycogen molecule, phosphorylated glucose, in contrast to glucose, can not readily diffuse out of cells. The fat body contains a hydrolytic enzyme glucose 6-phosphotase that enables glucose to leave that organ. This enzyme is essential for gluconeogenesis. Glucose-6-Phosphotase is also present in the malpighian tubules and alimentary canal, but is absent in the muscle and brain, impairment of carbohydrate metabolism was observed in a variety of physiological and pathological conditions (Latner, 1975; Harper *et al.*, 1979). This could prove to be negative survival value for the affected organisms. Investigations were conducted earlier on carbohydrate metabolism during pathological conditions in different animals following exposure to selenium. Wayne *et al.*, 2004, reported that an increase in selenium concentration increases the blood glucose levels. Many studies were made to achieve superior quality silk and greater output. The dietary administration of several vertebrate hormones and prostaglandins enhanced both developmental and metabolic processes of silkworm *Bombyx mori L.* (Bharathi and Miao, 2002).

Present study is aimed at understanding the role of selenium on the haemolymph glucose level of silkworm at different doses and exposure periods, and the possible effects of it on carbohydrate metabolism.

RESULTS

Glucose Levels

The results pertaining to the glucose content in haemolymph (mg/100 ml), in fat body (mg/gm. wet wt.) of V instar silkworm in respect of control (groups 1, 4, 7, and 10), lethal (groups 2, 5, 8, and 11) and sub-lethal (groups 3, 6, 9 and 12) exposure to selenium at 3, 4, 5 and 6 days are presented in Table 5.1, 5.2 and Figures 5.1 and 5.2 respectively. Relative to controls, the glucose

Table 5.1 : Levels of Glucose (mg/100 ml) in Haemolymph of Silkworm *Bombyx mori.L.* (PM X NB_4D_2) on exposure to lethal and sub lethal doses of Selenium

Dose	3 days	4 days	5 days	6 days
Control	28.9^{a}	30.1^{a}	30.86^{a}	32.50^{a}
Lethal	32.01^{c} (+10.76)	32.20^{b} (+6.97)	33.33^{b} (+8.0)	35.24^{b} (+8.4)
Sub-Lethal	29.9^{b} (+3.77)	30.30^{a} (+0.6)	31.08^{a} (+0.71)	32.95^{a} (+1.3)

* Each value is a mean of eight estimates.

** Per cent decrease over control is given in parenthesis.

*** Mean within a column followed by the same letter are not significantly different ($p > 0.05$) from each other according to Duncan's Multiple Range Test.

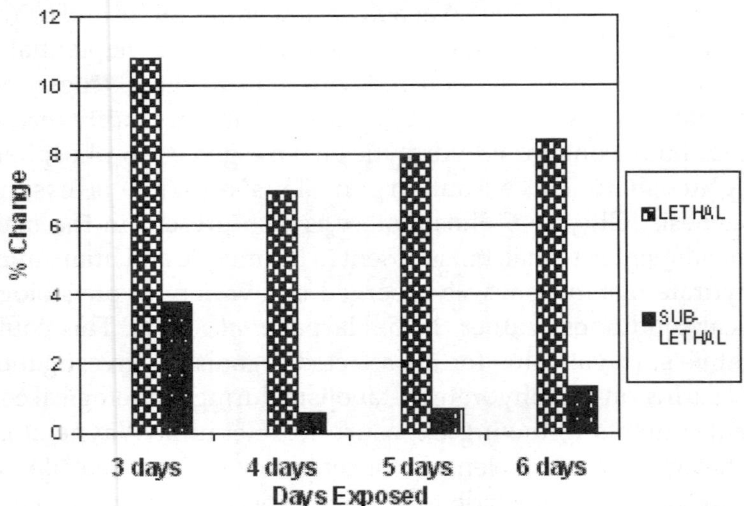

Fig. 5.1 : Per cent change over control over control in Glucose (mg/100 ml) in Haemolymph of Silkworm *Bombyx mori.L.* (PM X NB_4D_2) on exposure to lethal and sub-lethal doses of Selenium.

Table 5.2 : Levels of Glucose (mg/gm wet wt.) in Fat body of Silkworm *Bombyx mori.L.* (PMX NB_4D_2) on exposure to lethal and sub-lethal doses of Selenium

Dose	3 days	4 days	5 days	6 days
Control	0.6993[a]	0.7320[a]	0.8813[a]	0.9193[a]
Lethal	0.7417[c] (+7.6)	0.7925[b] (+8.19)	0.9564[b] (+8.521)	1.001[b] (+8.9)
Sub-lethal	0.7064[b] (+1.05)	0.7393[a] (+1.01)	0.9007[a] (+2.13)	0.944[a] (+2.74)

* Each value is a mean of eight estimates.

** Per cent decrease over control is given in parenthesis.

*** Mean within a column followed by the same letter are not significantly different (p > 0.05) from each other according to Duncan's Multiple Range test.

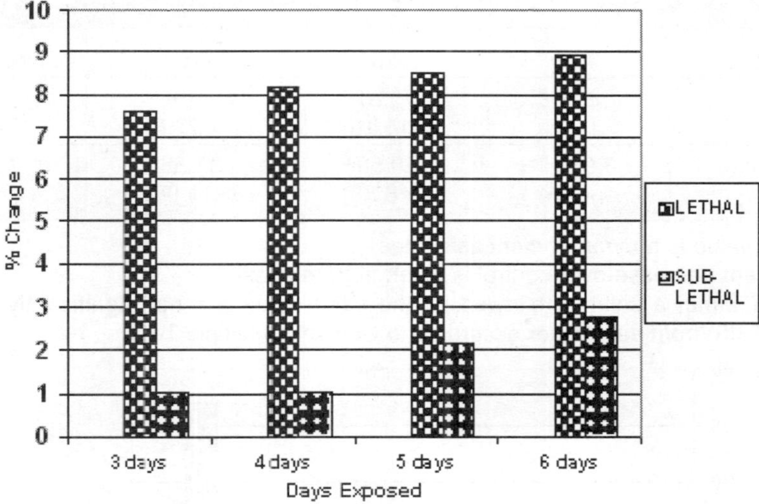

Fig. 5.2 : Per cent change over control over control in Glucose (mg/gm wet wt.) in Fat body of Silkworm *Bombyx mori.L.* (PMX NB_4D_2) on exposure to lethal and sub-lethal doses of Selenium.

level increased in the lethal dose at 3 day of exposure was high than the increase at 4, 5 and 6 days of exposures, and this increase was significant ($P<0.05$). However, the increase in glucose level at 4, 5, and 6 days of exposure was progressed gradually and followed the trend $3<4<5<6$ in haemolymph of silkworm exposed to lethal dose. Whereas in fat body, the haemolymph glucose level of silkworm exposed to lethal dose of selenium gradually increased from 3 day to 6 days and followed the trend $3<4<5<6$, and this increase was significant ($p < 0.5$). In sub-lethal dose of selenium also, the glucose level could exhibit an increase in all the organs on all exposure days studied. However this increase in glucose level was significant ($p < 0.5$) at 3 day of exposure, but insignificant ($p > 0.05$) on further exposure at 4, 5 and 6 days of exposure period studied. This followed the trend of 3 < 4 < 5 < 6 days. Among the exposure periods, the accumulated glucose was more in the haemolymph than in fat body at sub-lethal dose. Based on per cent values, the per cent increase in glucose level was progressed gradually at 4, 5, and 6 days of exposure periods studied in all organs of silkworm.

Glycogen Levels

In agreement with the changes in the glucose levels, a decrease was observed in glycogen content of Silkworm fat body exposed to lethal dose of selenium (groups 2, 5, 8, and 11) and presented in Table 5.3 and Figures 5.3. This

Table 5.3 : Levels of Glycogen (mg/gm wet wt.) in Fat body of Silkworm *Bombyx mori.L.* (PMX NB_4D_2) on exposure to lethal and sub-lethal doses of Selenium

Dose	3 days	4 days	5 days	6 days
Control	9.22 c	9.67 b	10.61 b	11.10 b
Lethal	8.80 a (-4.5)	8.31 a (-14.16)	7.66 a (-27.8)	6.98 a (-37.1)
Sub-lethal	8.989 b (- 2.5)	10.50 c (+8.58)	11.68 c (+10.08)	12.39 c (+10.9)

* Each value is a mean of eight estimates.

** Per cent decrease over control is given in parenthesis.

*** Mean within a column followed by the same letter are not significantly different ($p > 0.05$) from each other according to Duncan's Multiple Test.

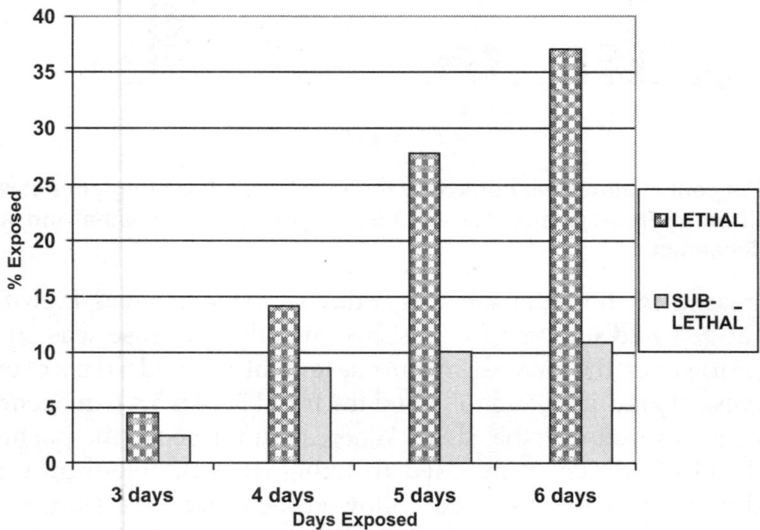

Fig. 5.3 : Percent change over control in Glycogen (mg/gm wet wt.) in Fat body of Silkworm *Bombyx mori.L.* (PMX NB_4D_2) on exposure to lethal and sub-lethal doses of Selenium.

decrease was significant ($p < 0.05$) in fat body of silkworm at lethal dose of all exposure periods studied. The decrease in the per cent values in the lethal dose at 3 day was less, but progressed gradually at 4, 5 and 6 days of further exposure and followed the trend, 3 < 4 < 5 < 6 days. Eventhough a significant decrease was observed initially at 3 day of exposure period in sub-lethal dose of selenium (groups 3, 6, 9 and 12), a significant increase in glycogen levels was observed at 4, 5 and 6 days of exposure period. The results also revealed that the per cent increase in glycogen level in fat body of silkworm exposed to sub-lethal dose was progressed gradually at 4, 5, and 6 days and in the order 4 < 5 < 6 days.

Trehalose Levels

The results pertaining to the trehalose levels in the haemolymph and fat body are presented in Table 5.4, 5.5 and Figures 5.4, 5.5 respectively. Relative to controls (groups 1, 4, 7 and 10), the trehalose content in haemolymph has registered an elevation in V instar silkworm haemolymph and fat body exposed to lethal dose of selenium (groups 2, 5, 8, and 11) at 3, 4, 5, and 6 days of exposure period studied. This increase was significant ($p < 0.05$) and followed the trend 3 < 4 < 5 < 6. Even in sub-lethal dose (groups 3, 6, 9 and 12), though the trehalose levels increased significantly at 3 day of exposure, this increase was insignificant on further exposure at 4, 5 and 6 days of exposure period studied. However the per cent increase in sub-lethal dose was less than the increase in lethal dose in fat body and haemolymph.

Table 5.4 : Activity of Glucose-6-Phosphotase (µM.PI/mg. Protein/hr) in Fat body of Silkworm *Bombyx mori. L.* (PMX NB_4D_2) on exposure to lethal and sub-lethal doses of Selenium

Dose	3 days	4 days	5 days	6 days
Control	0.130 [a]	0.177 [a]	0.194 [a]	0.255 [a]
Lethal	0.133 [b] (+3.0)	0.182 [b] (+3.9)	0.204 [b] (+5.5)	0.272 [b] (+6.9)
Sub-lethal	0.139 [c] (+7.21)	0.179 [a] (+1.2)	0.197 [a] (+2.0)	0.260 [a] (+2.2)

* Each value is a mean of eight estimates.

** Per cent decrease over control is given in parenthesis.

*** Mean within a column followed by the same letter are not significantly different ($p > 0.05$) from each other according to Duncan's Multiple Range test.

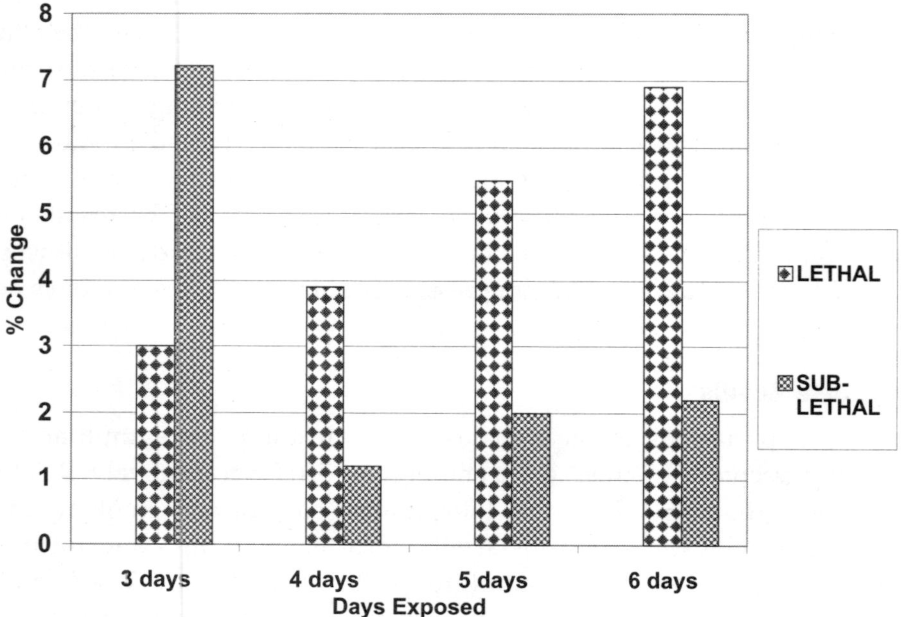

Fig. 5.4 : Percent change over control in Glucose- 6-Phosphotase (µM.PI/mg. Protein/hr) in Fat body of Silkworm *Bombyx mori. L.* (PMX NB_4D_2) on exposure to lethal and sub-lethal doses of Selenium.

Table 5.5 : Activities of Phosphorylase (µM.PI/mg.Protein/hr) in Fat body of Silkworm *Bombyx mori.L.* (PMX NB_4D_2) on exposure to lethal and sub-lethal doses of Selenium

Dose	3 days	4 days	5 days	6 days
Control	0.176 [a]	0.223 [a]	0.24 [a]	0.301 [a]
Lethal	0.182 [b] (+3.40)	0.231 [b] (+3.59)	0.255 [b] (+6.25)	0.325 [b] (+7.9)
Sub-lethal	0.193 [c] (+9.6)	0.229 [a] (+2.69)	0.249 [a] (+3.75)	0.316 [a] (+4.98)

* Each value is a mean of eight estimates.

** Per cent decrease over control is given in parenthesis.

*** Mean within a column followed by the same letter are not significantly different ($p > 0.05$) from each other according to Duncan's Multiple Range test.

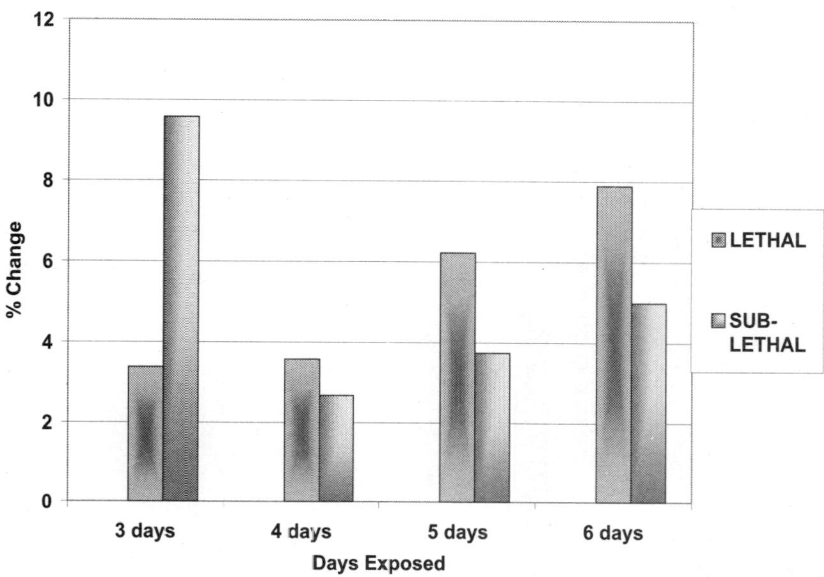

Fig. 5.5 : Per cent change over control in Phosphorylase (µM.PI/mg.Protein/hr) in Fat body of Silkworm *Bombyx mori.L.* (PMX NB_4D_2) on exposure to lethal and sub-lethal doses of Selenium.

Phosphorylase Activity

From the data presented in the Table 5.6 and Figure 5.6 , it was observed that the activity of phosphorylase was increased significantly ($p < 0.05$) in the fat body of silkworm exposed to lethal dose of selenium (groups 2, 5, 8, and 11) at 3, 4, 5 and 6 days exposure periods studied. The increase in phosphorylase activity in lethal dose corresponds with the decrease in

Table 5.6 : Levels of Trehalose (mg/100 ml) in Haemolymph of Silkworm *Bombyx mori.L.* (PMX NB_4D_2) on exposure to lethal and sub-lethal doses of Selenium

Dose	3 days	4 days	5 days	6 days
Control	155.07 [a]	157.02 [a]	157.95 [a]	159.7 [a]
Lethal	156.93 [b] (+1.19)	161.2 [b] (+2.66)	164.2 [b] (+3.9)	166.020 [b] (+3.95)
Sub-lethal	162.8 [c] (+5.00)	157.96 [a] (+0.6)	159.37 [a] (+0.9)	161.77 [a] (+1.2)

* Each value is a mean of eight estimates.

** Per cent decrease over control is given in parenthesis.

*** Mean within a column followed by the same letter are not significantly different ($p > 0.05$) from each other according to Duncan's Multiple Range test.

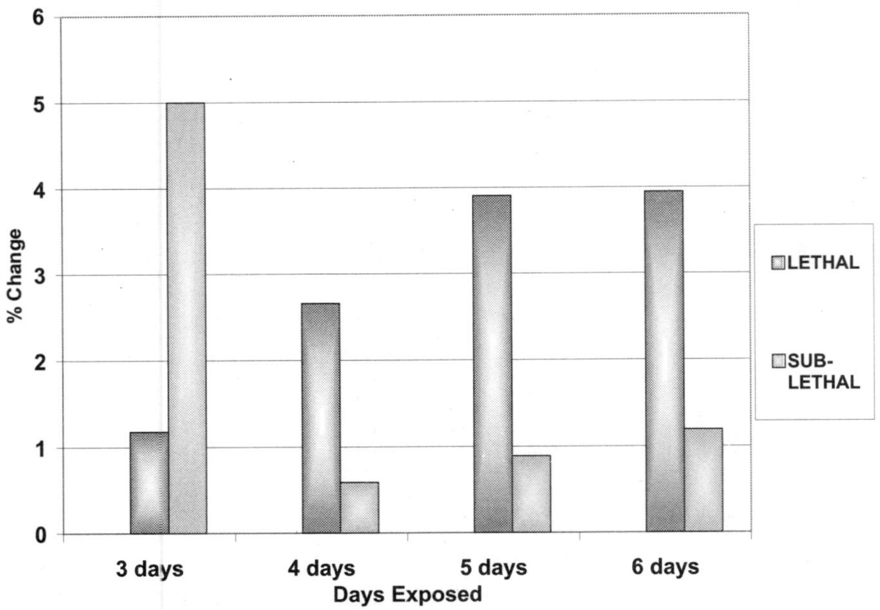

Fig. 5.6 : Per cent change over control in Trehalose (mg/100 ml) in Haemolymph of Silkworm *Bombyx mori.L.* (PMX NB_4D_2) on exposure to lethal and sub-lethal doses of Selenium.

glycogen content. The increase in the activity of phosphorylase was progressed gradually from 3 days to 6 days. In sub-lethal dose (groups 3, 6, 9 and 11), the activity of phosphorylase exhibited an increase significantly ($p < 0.05$) at 3 day and insignificant elevation at 4, 5 and 6 days of periods studied.

Pyruvate Levels

The data on the levels of pyruvate in haemolymph, fat body of V instar silkworm on exposure to lethal (groups 2, 5, 8, and 11) and sub-lethal doses of selenium (groups 3, 6, 9, and 12) at 3, 4, 5, and 6 days besides control (groups 1, 4, 7, and 10) are presented in Tables 5.7, 5.8 and Figures 5.7, 5.8 respectively. From the data, it is seen that the pyruvate levels increased significantly ($P < 0.05$) in haemolymph and fat body of V instar silkworm exposed to lethal dose of selenium at 3, 4, 5 and 6 days and followed the trend of 3 < 4 < 5 < 6 days. Though elevation in pyruvate levels in sub-lethal dose increased, it is significant at 3 days of exposure and insignificant ($P > 0.05$) at 4, 5 and 6 days. Based on per cent values, it is seen that the pyruvate accumulation was more in haemolymph than in fat body of silkworm exposed to sub-lethal dose selenium and in the order of haemolymph > fat body.

Table 5.7 : Levels of Trehalose (mg/gm wet wt.) in Fat body of Silkworm *Bombyx mori.L.* (PMX NB_4D_2) on exposure to lethal and sub-lethal doses of Selenium

Dose	3 days	4 days	5 days	6 days
Control	5.13 [a]	6.06 [a]	6.24 [a]	6.6 [a]
Lethal	5.41[b] (+5.45)	6.72 [b] (+10.89)	7.01 [b] (+12.3)	7.23 [b] (+9.54)
Sub-lethal	5.59 [c] (+5.0)	6.08 [a] (+0.3)	6.29 [a] (+0.9)	6.68 [a] (+1.2)

* Each value is a mean of eight estimates.

** Per cent decrease over control is given in parenthesis.

*** Mean within a column followed by the same letter are not significantly different ($p > 0.05$) from each other according to Duncan's Multiple Range test.

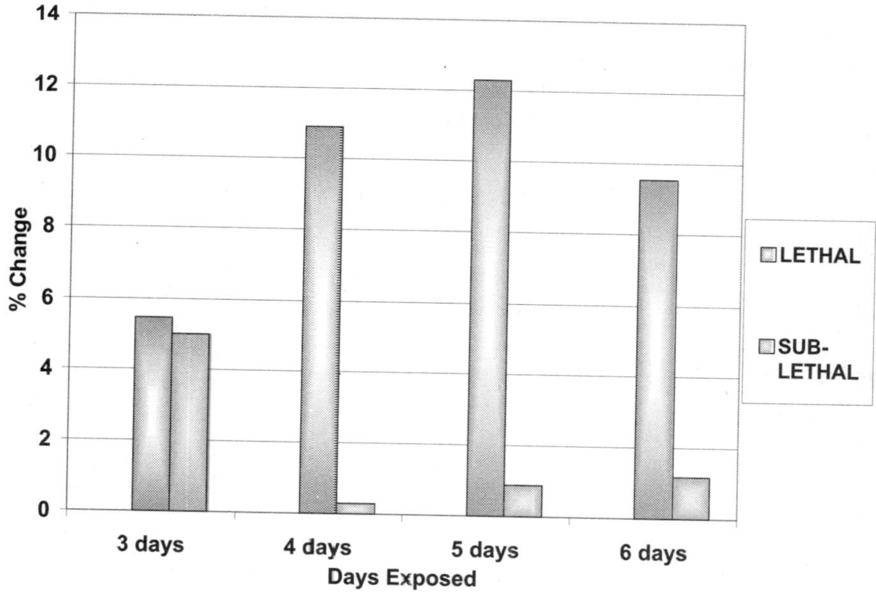

Fig. 5.7 : Per cent change over control in Trehalose (mg/gm wet wt.) in Fat body of Silkworm *Bombyx mori.L.* (PMX NB_4D_2) on exposure to lethal and sub-lethal doses of Selenium.

Lactate Levels

From the data presented in Table 5.9, 5.10 and Figures 5.9, 5.10, it is revealed that relative to controls (groups 1, 4, 7, and 10) the lactate levels in haemolymph and fat body increased at lethal dose of selenium (groups 2, 5, 8, and 11) and this increase was significant ($p < 0.05$) at all days of exposure period studied. In sub-lethal dose of selenium exposure (groups 3, 6, 9, and 12), the lactate levels decreased significantly at 4, 5 and 6 days. However this decrease was insignificant at 3 day of exposure in haemolymph and fat body. Based on per cent values, this decrease in lactate levels at sub-lethal dose progressed gradually from 3 day to 6 days and was in the order of 3 < 4 < 5 < 6 days.

Table 5.8 : Levels of Pyruvate (mg/ ml) in Haemolymph of Silkworm *Bombyx mori.L.* (PMX NB_4D_2) on exposure to lethal and sub-lethal doses of Selenium

Dose	3 days	4 days	5 days	6 days
Control	0.990 [a]	1.06 [a]	1.08 [a]	1.19 [a]
Lethal	1.10 [b] (+11.1)	1.24 [b] (+16.98)	1.32 [b] (+22.2)	1.63 [a] (+36.97)
Sub-lethal	1.05 [b] (+6.6)	1.081 [a] (+2.0)	1.11 [a] (+2.2)	1.21 [a] (+2.3)

* Each value is a mean of eight estimates.

** Per cent decrease over control is given in parenthesis.

** Mean within a column followed by the same letter are not significantly different ($p > 0.05$) from each other according to Duncan's Multiple Range test.

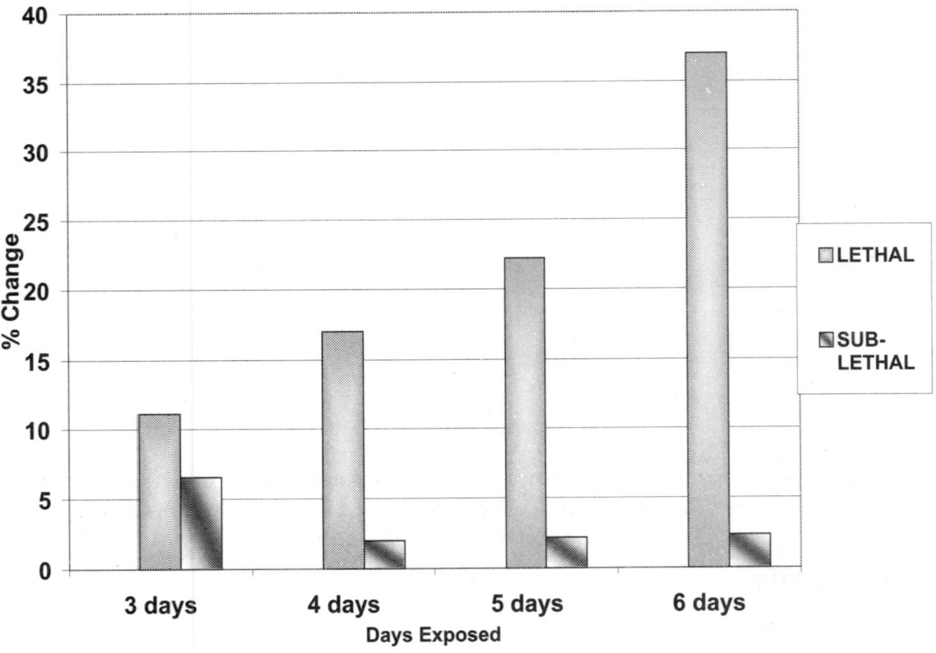

Fig. 5.8 : Per cent change over control in Pyruvate (mg/ ml) in Haemolymph of Silkworm *Bombyx mori.L.* (PMX NB_4D_2) on exposure to lethal and sub-lethal doses of Selenium.

Table 5.9 : Levels of Pyruvate (mg/gm wet wt.) in Fat body of Silkworm *Bombyx mori.L.* (PM X NB_4D_2) on exposure to lethal and sub-lethal doses of Selenium

Dose	3 days	4 days	5 days	6 days
Control	0.271 [a]	0.290 [a]	0.294 [a]	0.34 [a]
Lethal	0.441 [c] (+62.7)	0.361 [b] (+24.48)	0.321 [b] (+9.18)	0.298 [b] (+12.3)
Sub-lethal	0.31 [b] (+14.31)	0.299 [a] (+3.44)	0.304 [a] (+3.46)	0.353 [a] (+3.78)

* Each value is a mean of eight estimates.

** Per cent decrease over control is given in parenthesis.

*** Mean within a column followed by the same letter are not significantly different (p > 0.05) from each other according to Duncan s Multiple Range test.

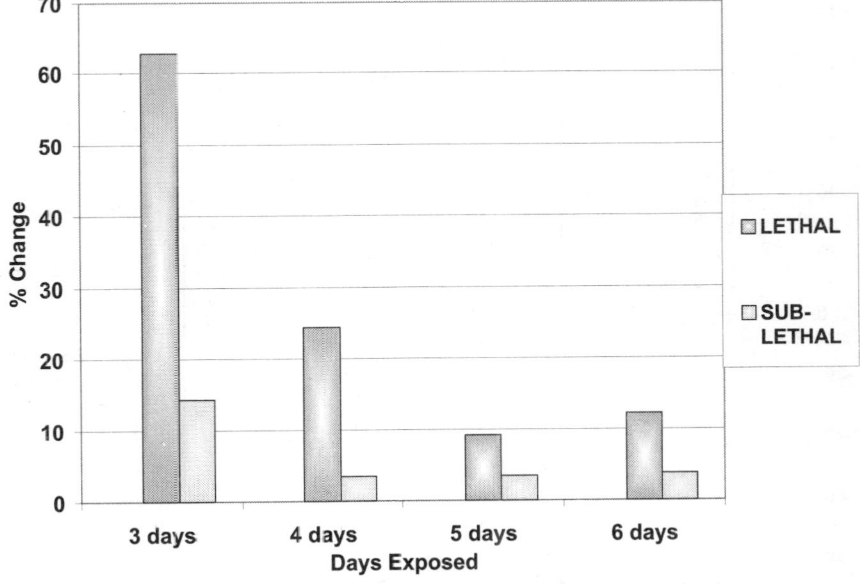

Fig. 5.9 : Per cent change over control in Pyruvate (mg/gm wet wt.) in Fat body of Silkworm *Bombyx mori.L.* (PM X NB_4D_2) on exposure to lethal and sub-lethal doses of Selenium.

Activity of SDH

From the data presented in Table 5.11, 5.12 and Figures 5.11, 5.12, the activity of SDH decreased significantly ($p < 0.05$) in haemolymph and fat body of silkworm at all exposure periods studied in the lethal dose of selenium. In lethal concentration (groups 2, 5, 8, and 11), an insignificant decrease was observed ($P>0.05$) in haemolymph at 3, 4 day of exposure but in the remaining exposure periods, the decrease in SDH activity showed a significant decrease at 5 and 6 day of exposure. In sub-lethal dose of selenium (groups 3, 6, 9,

Table 5.10 : Levels of Lactate (mg/ ml) in Haemolymph of Silkworm *Bombyx mori.L.* (PM X NB_4D_2) on exposure to lethal and sub-lethal doses of Selenium

Dose	3 days	4 days	5 days	6 days
Control	0.947 [a]	0.961 [b]	0.981 [b]	1.09 [b]
Lethal	1.81 [b] (+91.1)	1.59 [c] (+65.4)	1.26 [c] (+28.4)	1.42 [c] (+30.2)
Sub-lethal	0.926 [a] (-2.2)	0.71 [a] (-26.1)	0.53 [a] (-45.9)	0.50 [a] (-54.12)

* Each value is a mean of eight estimates.

** Per cent decrease over control is given in parenthesis.

** Mean within a column followed by the same letter are not significantly different ($p > 0.05$) from each other according to Duncan's Multiple Range test.

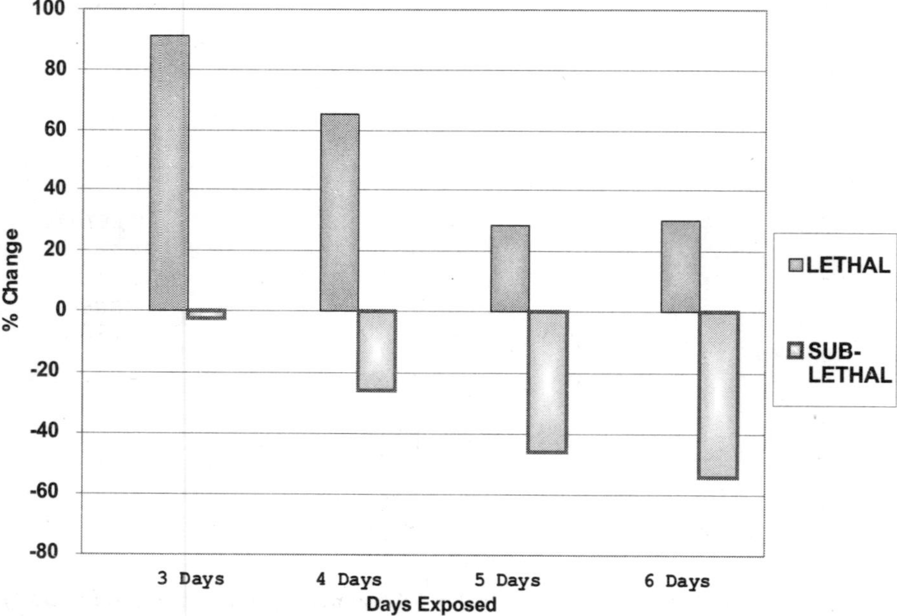

Fig. 5.10 : Per cent change over control in Lactate (mg/ ml) in Haemolymph of Silkworm *Bombyx mori.L.* (PM X NB_4D_2) on exposure to lethal and sub-lethal doses of Selenium

and 12), a significant ($p < 0.05$) increase was observed in the parameters at 3 day where as 4, 5 and 6 days exhibited insignificant decrease. The per cent decrease at sub-lethal dose of selenium in the fat body appeared insignificant at 3 day and insignificant decrease was observed in 4, 5 and 6 days of selenium exposure. Based on per cent values, it was seen that the SDH activity was more in fat body than in haemolymph of silkworm exposed to lethal and sub-lethal dose of selenium and in the order fat body > haemolymph.

Table 5.11 : Levels of Lactate (mg/gm wet wt.) in Fat body of Silkworm *Bombyx mori.L.* (PMX NB_4D_2) on exposure to lethal and sub-lethal doses of Selenium

Dose	3 days	4 days	5 days	6 days
Control	0.988 [a]	1.056 [c]	1.18 [c]	1.39 [c]
Lethal	1.10 [b] (+11.3)	1.426 [c] (+35.03)	1.733 [c] (+46.6)	2.1 [c] (+51.0)
Sub-lethal	0.96 [a] (-2.8)	0.72 [a] (-31.8)	0.64 [a] (-45.76)	0.52 [a] (-62.58)

* Each value is a mean of eight estimates.

** Per cent decrease over control is given in parenthesis.

*** Mean within a column followed by the same letter are not significantly different ($p > 0.05$) from each other according to Duncan's Multiple Range test.

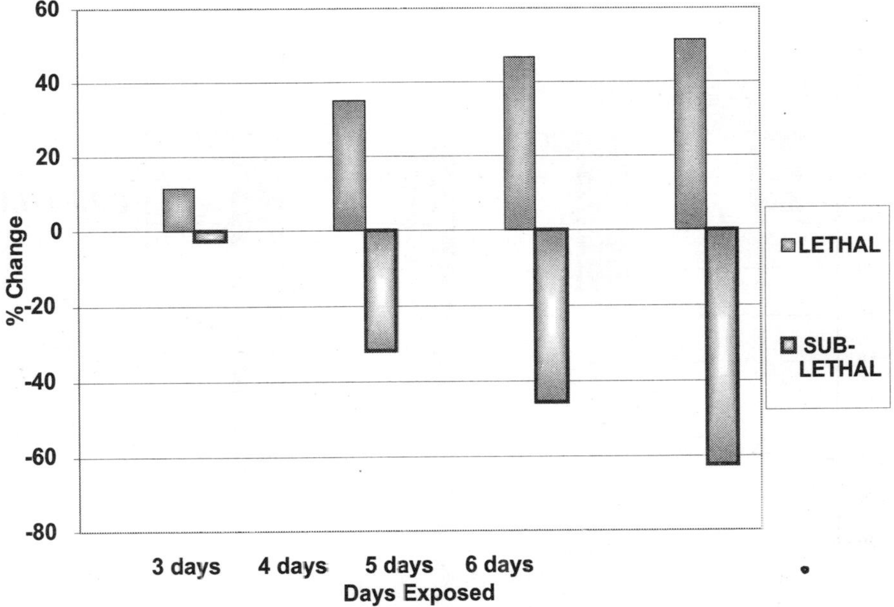

Fig. 5.11a : Per cent change over control in Lactate (mg/gm wet wt.) in Fat body of Silkworm *Bombyx mori.L.* (PMX NB_4D_2) on exposure to lethal and sub-lethal doses of Selenium.

Activity of LDH

From the data presented in Tables 5.13, 5.14 and Figures 5.13, 5.14, it is seen that the LDH activity increased in haemolymph and fat body of silkworms at 3, 4, 5 and 6 days of exposure to the lethal dose of selenium (groups 2, 5, 8, and 11) with a significant ($p < 0.05$) change and followed the trend of $3 < 4 < 5 < 6$.

Table 5.12 : Activity of SDH (μ M formozan/mg. Protein/hr) in Haemolymph of Silkworm *Bombyx mori.L.* (PMX NB_4D_2) on exposure to lethal and sub-lethal doses of Selenium

Dose	3 days	4 days	5 days	6 days
Control	0.04 [b]	0.051 [b]	0.062 [b]	0.09 [b]
Lethal	0.033 [a] (-17.5)	0.030 [a] (-34.11)	0.0206 [a] (-66.77)	0.016 [a] (-82.2)
Sub-lethal	0.043 [c] (+7.5)	0.049 [b] (-3.9)	0.059 [b] (-4.8)	0.085 [b] (-5.5)

* Each value is a mean of eight estimates.

** Per cent decrease over control is given in parenthesis.

*** Mean within a column followed by the same letter are not significantly different ($p > 0.05$) from each other according to Duncan's Multiple Range test.

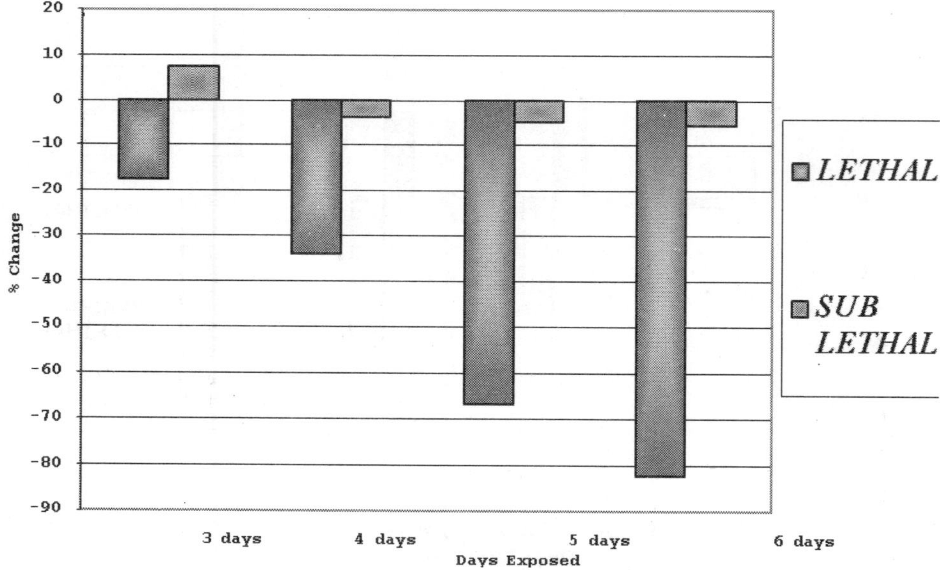

Fig. 5.12 : Per cent change over control in SDH (μ M formozan/mg.Protein/hr) in Haemolymph of Silkworm *Bombyx mori.L.* (PMX NB_4D_2) on exposure to lethal and sub-lethal doses of Selenium.

The enzyme activity in lethal dose is tissues dependent. In sub-lethal dose (groups 3, 6, 9, and 12), the LDH activity in haemolymph and fat body increased, but the observed change was insignificant at all exposure periods studied and followed the trend of 4 < 5 < 6. The results also revealed that LDH activity is more in haemolymph than in fat body, in the order of haemolymph > fat body.

Table 5.13 : Activity of SDH (µ M formozan/mg. Protein/hr) in Fat body of Silkworm *Bombyx mori.L.* (PMX NB_4D_2) on exposure to lethal and sub-lethal doses of Selenium

Dose	3 days	4 days	5 days	6 days
Control	0.135 [b]	0.141 [b]	0.19 [b]	0.203 [b]
Lethal	0.129 [a] (-4.4)	0.092 [a] (-34.7)	0.074 [a] (-61.05)	0.043 [a] (-78.81)
Sub-lethal	0.120 [c] (-11.1)	0.134 [c] (-4.2)	0.181 [b] (-4.7)	0.193 [b] (-4.9)

* Each value is a mean of eight estimates.

** Per cent decrease over control is given in parenthesis.

*** Mean within a column followed by the same letter are not significantly different ($p > 0.05$) from each other according to Duncan's Multiple Range test.

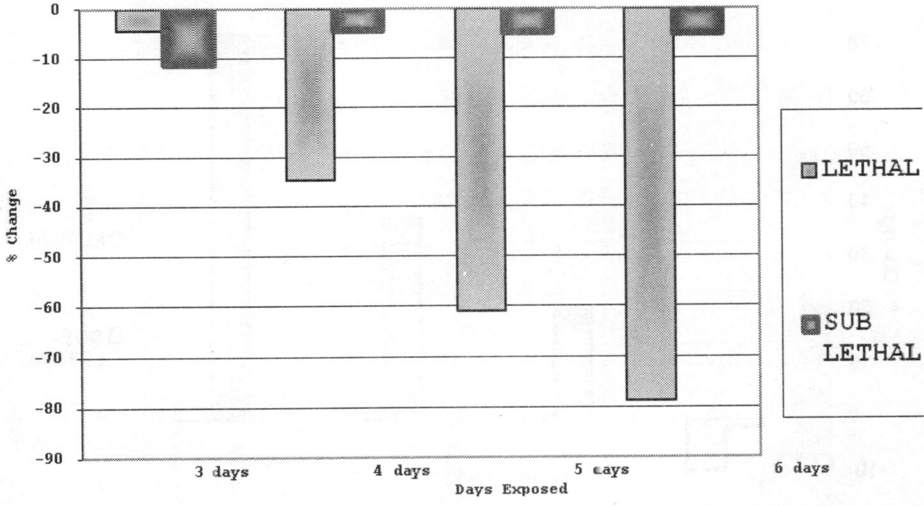

Fig. 5.13 : Per cent change over control in SDH (µ M formozan/mg. Protein/hr) in Fat body of Silkworm *Bombyx mori.L.* (PMX NB_4D_2) on exposure to lethal and sub-lethal doses of Selenium.

Discussion

Glucose, glycogen, and trehalose play important roles in the organization and metabolic activity in the Lepidopteron insects. The levels of glucose, glycogen and trehalose in haemolymph are the result of inter play of certain neurosecretory hormonal phenomena existing in the system. The substances secreted by neurosecretory cells of the brain, which are comparable to the pituitary glands of vertebrates are involved in their homeostasis. According to Steele (1976), corpora cardiaca is an important source of neurohormones

Table 5.14 : Activity of LDH (μ M formozan/mg. Protein/hr) in Haemolymph tubules of silkworm *Bombyx mori.L.* (PMX NB_4D_2) on exposure to lethal and sub-lethal doses of Selenium

Dose	3 days	4 days	5 days	6 days
Control	0.144 [b]	0.151 [a]	0.159 [a]	0.168 [a]
Lethal	0.142 [b] (-1.38)	0.182 [b] (+20.5)	0.219 [b] (+37.7)	0.29 [b] (+72.61)
Sub-lethal	0.13 [a] (-9.7)	0.152 [a] (+1.0)	0.161 [a] (+1.3)	0.175 [a] (+2.17)

* Each value is a mean of eight estimates.

** Per cent decrease over control is given in parenthesis.

*** Mean within a column followed by the same letter are not significantly different ($p > 0.05$) from each other according to Duncan's Multiple Range test.

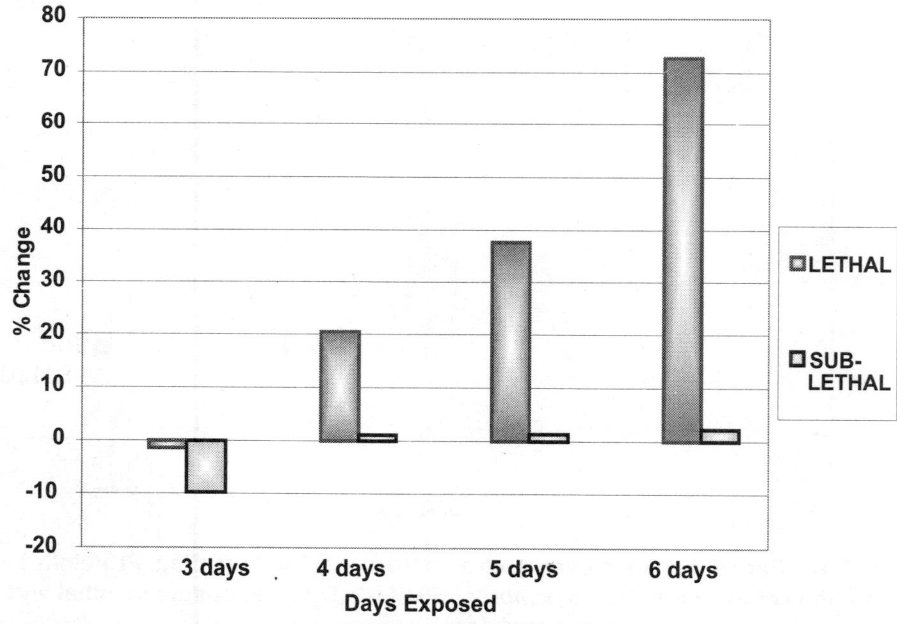

Fig. 5.14 : Per cent change over control in LDH (μ M formozan/mg. Protein/hr) in Haemolymph tubules of Silkworm *Bombyx mori.L.* (PMX NB_4D_2) on exposure to lethal and sub-lethal doses of Selenium.

in silkworm, *Bombyx mori L.* that play a great role in regulating carbohydrate and lipid metabolism. The secretions of corpora cardiaca are released into the tissues which regulate the carbohydrate level, so that it is maintained at an optimal range. According to Samaranayaka (1978), the neurohormonal organ has been identified as a probable site for the action of toxicant in mediating the metabolic reserves. From this study it is clear that selenium

Table 5.15 : Activity of LDH (μ M formozan/mg. Protein/hr) in Fat body of Silkworm *Bombyx mori.L.* (PMX NB_4D_2) on exposure to lethal and sub-lethal doses of Selenium

Dose	3 days	4 days	5 days	6 days
Control	0.147 [b]	0.152 [a]	0.161 [a]	0.169 [a]
Lethal	0.161 [c] (+9.5)	0.178 [b] (+17.1)	0.199 [b] (+23.6)	0.23 [b] (+36.0)
Sub-lethal	0.155 [a] (+5.4)	0.153 [a] (+0.9)	0.163 [a] (+1.5)	0.172 [a] (+1.9)

* Each value is a mean of eight estimates.

** Per cent decrease over control is given in parenthesis.

*** Mean within a column followed by the same letter are not significantly different ($p > 0.05$) from each other according to Duncan's Multiple range test.

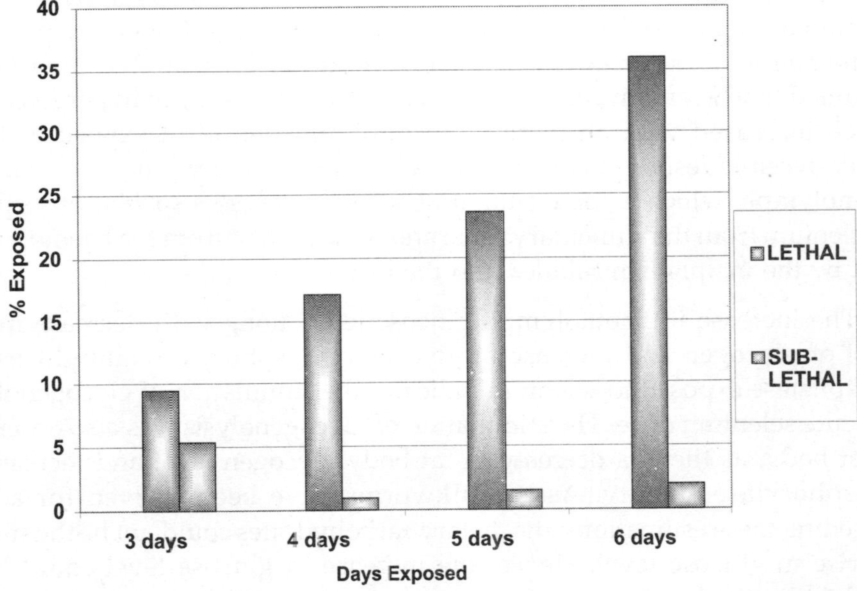

Fig. 5.15 : Per cent change over control in LDH (μM formozan/mg. Protein/hr) in Fat body of Silkworm *Bombyx mori. L.* (PMX NB_4D_2) on exposure to lethal and sub-lethal doses of Selenium.

might have caused an indiscriminate release of neurohormones which ultimately lead to the metabolic imbalance in lethal dose of selenium. Vinson and Dahlman (1989) exhibited decreased gluconeogenesis and simultaneous elevation of regulatory enzymes of glycogenolysis (phosphorylase activity) suggesting hormonal involvement during stress in lepidopteron insects. The literature also described that an increase in glucose and the decline in glycogen content in animals treated with selenium leading to disruption of carbohydrate metabolism and growth inhibition (Opienska and Iwanowski, 1952; Wu *et al.*, 2004; Opienska and Iwanowski, 1952). Bacterial growth and glucose consumption by E.coli were inhibited when selenite was added to culture medium (Holland and Humphrey, 1953). In the present study, increase in glucose level in the haemolymph and fat body with corresponding decrease in the glycogen content clearly indicates a persistent effect of selenium on the carbohydrate metabolism under prolonged periods of exposure to lethal dose. The glycogen stored in the fat body of silkworm will get depleted as and when required for deriving energy for growth and metamorphosis.

Further, glycogen levels of fat body showed a significant decrease in lethal dose of selenium, suggesting breakdown, which is evident from the increased trehalose and glucose levels. In other words, the increase in haemolymph glucose level indicates continuous accumulation. It may therefore presumed that the efficiency of selenium exposed larvae to utilize the available haemolymph glucose level for deriving energy to putforth with the progress of the age in V instar might have been reduced. Present study markedly exhibited that Selenium administration to silkworm results in hyperglycemia, which increased with an increase in dose and period of exposure. Thus hyperglycemic response is related to selenium concentrations in circulating haemolymph, which is the resultant of several processes such as absorption of selenium from the alimentary canal and removal of it from the haemolymph and, by the malpighian tubules into the urine.

The increase in haemolymph glucose level along with decrease in the level of glycogen and increase in glycogen phosphorylase and glucose-6-phosphatase exposed to selenium indicates the stimulation of glycogenolysis by acute selenium dose. The stimulation of glycogenolysis was also observed in fat body, as there is decrease in fat body glycogen level and increase in phosphorylase activity. As the silkworms have been starved for a day preceding these estimations, the dietary carbohydrates could not be the source for rise in glucose level. Hence, the increase in glucose level could have resulted by the breakdown of glycogen reserves by the abnormal elevation in the glycogen phosphorylase and glucose-6-phosphotase activities in silkworms. The abnormal elevation of these enzyme activities might have occurred by the inhibitory effect of the selenium on the release of neuro secretary hormones due to their direct effect on glycolysis or glycogen metabolism. Further the decreased utilization of glucose for energy purposes could also contribute to increase in haemolymph glucose level. In addition to tissue acidosis due to reduced oxygen transport would favour the process of glycogenolysis (Natarajan, 1982; Sharma, 1984; Radhakrishnaiah and Busappa, 1986; Dhavale and Masurekar, 1986). Echner, (1971) showed that anoxic conditions induce rapid glycogenolysis through the activation of phosphorylase. A significant increase in glucose level and depletion in glycogen content in fat body due to glycogenolysis either through the hormonal imbalance and or the other influencing factors resulted primarily in the depletion of carbohydrate energy reserves of silkworm *Bombyx mori L.* on exposure to acute dose of selenium. Further increased depletion of carbohydrate reserves over time of exposure from 4 day to 6 days is a clear indication of high metabolic imbalance and failure of metabolic homeostasis. This is possible that the greater amounts of selenium accumulated within the tissues over time of exposure might have impaired greatly the neuroendocrinal coordinated centers thereby lead to the continuous breakdown of glycogen reserves in fat body of the silkworm by improper stimulation of phosphorylase enzymatic machinery.

The administration of selenium in sub-lethal dose showed that selenium initially exhibited significant glycogenolysis which indicates that selenium even at sub-lethal dose could affect the energy reserves with the influence of factors responsible for it. However the less degree of glycogenolysis compared to the degree observed in the lethal dose suggest that the rate of glycogenolysis is dose dependent at 3 day of exposure. Further, from 4 day onwards insignificantly increased haemolymph glucose level and the enzyme activities did not alter much. The glycogen levels did not show significant changes compared to controls.

The accumulation studies, also, confirms lower levels of selenium in haemolymph, fat body and malpighian tubules compared to lethal dose exposed silkworms. The potential sites of selenium absorption from the environment are the alimentary canal, the respiratory tract and the skin. The apparent physiological function to be affected is oxygen consumption. Any change in the respiratory epithelium of the tracheoles would affect the rate of oxygen consumption. According to Smitha (2002) Selenium at lethal dose found to suppress the rate of oxygen consumption and moderately increased the rate of oxygen consumption at sub-lethal dose.

In the present study the observed hyperglycemic condition may be the result of decreased utilization of glucose, suppression of oxygen consumption in the haemolymph and fat body. Further, the present study corresponding to the decrease in the rate of oxygen consumption, the decrease in the SDH activity in haemolymph and fat body of silkworm exposed to the lethal dose of selenium suggest the suppression of oxidative phosphorylation of the animal (Bonhorst, 1955; Collett *et al.*, 1933; Moxon and Franke, 1935; Woodruff and Gies, 1902; Wolley, 1952; Wright, 1938). Though the carbohydrates were mobilized, the silkworm could not utilize the carbohydrates for the release of energy due to the inhibition of oxidative metabolism. Hence glucose utilization decreased, thereby hyperglycemic condition prevailed in the silkworm under acute selenium stress. The selenium induced decrease in SDH activity can be correlated to the binding of selenium with the enzyme, blockage of -SH groups or impairment of mitochondrial organization (Klug *et al.*, 1953).

It is interesting that the increase in LDH activity in the organs of silkworm exposed to lethal dose of selenium exhibit the silkworm under selenium stress might have relied on anaerobic glycolysis in meeting the energy requirements. Recent studies have shown that oxygen consumption rate was decreased and concomitantly glucose was decomposed to lactic acid in selenium intoxicated silkworm *Bombyx mori L.* (Smitha, 2002). Tsen and Collier (1959) correlated the magnitude of inhibition in LDH activity in mammals. Elevated activities of LDH and pyruvictransaminase were also reported in the serum or plasma of selenium intoxicated mammals. (Buchaman-Smith *et al.*, 1976). Interestingly, in contrary to the lethal dose in silkworm, exposed to sub-lethal dose of selenium exhibited gradual increase in the glucose and trehalose levels in haemolymph and fat body. The levels of glucose and trehalose except the glycogen have revealed significant increase in their concentration. It indicated that in haemolymph and fat body, the glycogenolysis is activated for their immediate requirement of energy in lethal dose. The increased levels of glucose and trehalose in the haemolymph are perhaps due to glucogenolysis during selenium toxicity.

The increased level of glucose in haemolymph and decreased levels in glycogen fat body and variations in other parameters of carbohydrate metabolism increases with the increasing period of the exposure. Hence the toxicity of selenium in sub-lethal dose is dose dependent. The insignificant decrease in haemolymph glucose and significant increased in fat body glycogen at sub-lethal dose of selenium treated silkworm suggest the normalcy as like controls. The decreased levels of glucose-6-phosphotase and glycogen phosphorylase indicate the disruption of carbohydrate metabolism in lethal dose selenium treated silkworms. The lower levels of glucose-6-phosphotase could lead to the decrease in the haemolymph of glucose-6-phosphotase to glucose. In turn phosphorylase is subjected to allosteric inhibition by glucose-6-phosphotase. So that glycogen breakdown was slow, the concentration of which built up in the fat body. In addition to this, glucose-6-phosphotase allosterically activated glycogen synthesis. Further glycogen phosphorylase level also decreased which may be another cause for decreased trend of glycogen to glucose. The overall system is thus regulated both allosterically by substrates and products and by post-translational modification of enzymes in response to selenium.

CHAPTER

6 Protein Metabolism

Introduction

The biological importance of proteins can be judged by the fact that the animals can live for a long time without fat or carbohydrate, but not without protein. Unlike carbohydrates and fats, proteins of living organisms are the structural and functional components rather than a source of energy. Hence the protein compounds are the most important of cell constituents and are described as the "stuff of life" (Swaminathan, 1983). Protein is a kind of basic substance to construct silkworm's body and also is an important material of silk and egg production. Enzymes, hormones and other physiologically active substances are proteins which can adjust an insect's physiological activity (Lehninger, 1984). Proteins can also be decomposed to supply the energy. The ingested protein is decomposed into amino acids and is utilized to regulate physiological processes such as growth and reproduction.

Proteins as they are the source of metabolic currency also can be referred as an important analyte in evaluating the physiological standards of the cell (Young, 1970). During starvation, proteins become the last source of energy, which is used only when there are no carbohydrates and fats available (Sridhara and Bhatt, 1963). Proteins make compensatory metabolic adjustments in tissues through modification or modulation (Bano *et al.*, 1981; Assem and Hanke, 1983). The proteins of every tissue including blood are continuously brokendown to amino acids through hydrolysis, which is common process and involve Proteases in their degradation. Among the proteases, some are lysosomal in origin having acidic pH optimum, some are found in association with peroxisomes, lysosomes and mitochondria possessing neutral pH optimum and other proteases with an alkaline pH optimum are reported in the cytosolic fraction. (Zalkin *et al.*, 1962; Stagni and Debenard, 1968; Ali and Lack, 1965; Davies *et al.*, 1970; Janoff, 1970; Noguchi and Kandtatsu, 1971).

Hydrolysis of proteins into amino acids is the prelude to either further synthesis of new substances or for their oxidation. Very little of energy is liberated and no storage of energy takes place. The amino acids will be mobilized for protein synthesis or utilized for metabolic energy. In the catabolism of amino acids the aminotransferases, the aspartate aminotransferases (AAT) or glutamate-oxaloacetate transferase (GOT) catalyses the interconversion of aspartic acid and α-keto glutaric acid to oxaloacetic acid and glutamic acid. Whereas the alanine aminotranseferase (AlAT) or glutamate pyruvate transferase (GPT) catalyses the interconversion of alanine and keto glutaric acid to pyruvic acid and glutamic acid (Goldstein and Newholme, 1980; Martin *et al.*, 1983). When aminoacids are in excess they are converted to ketoacids which enter carbohydrate metabolic cycle for energy releasing purposes. Wretlind *et al.*, (1959) described the nonspecific nature of enzymes in any organ but their concentration in different tissues varies. Ostradius (1961) reported that plasma aspartate amino transeferases (AAT) or glutamic oxaloacetic acid transaminases were useful indicators of muscular dystrophy and liver necrosis respectively in field case of vitamin E & selenium deficiency in pigs.

The constant breakdown and synthesis of proteins in tissues is always maintained and the concentration of proteins and, size of the tissues is thus kept constant (Schimke, 1974). Hence the dynamic equilibrium of these two ultimately results in homeostasis in an animal (Banks *et al.*, 1976; Grainde and Seglen, 1981; Tavill and Cooksley, 1983). Continuous synthesis of amino acids and its periodical absorption from the intestine constitute amino acid pool of the body from which proteins, enzymes and protein hormones are synthesized by all the tissues including exocrine and endocrine glands. Nagy *et al.*, (1981) reported the alteration of dynamic equilibrium under stress by interfering in the protein synthesis and their breakdown.

Certain enzymes in blood plasma can be sensitive indicators of tissue damage and may provide evidence of tissue affected. Plasma activity of these enzymes is dependent on the equilibrium between rate of release from damaged cells and rate of inactivation or removal from the blood stream. Tollersrud, (1973) studied the activity of AAT, AlAT and Glutamic pyruvic transaminase (GPT) in swine myocardium, liver and skeletal muscle and reflect necropsy in pigs fed diets low in selenium and vitamin E. Therefore the activity of AAT and AlAT indicate the simple selenium deficiency in animals (Tollersrud, 1970; Tollersrud, 1973). Further he found that the activities of AAT, AlAT and LDH were increased in the liver as the level of protein in diet was increased. Thus moderate increases in plasma activities of these enzymes could appear in response to changes in diet composition and protein in need (Hyldgaard and Jensen, 1971). Bengtsson *et al.*, (1978) found that selenium additions to vitamin-E deficient diets decreased the incidence of abnormal elevation of plasma AAT activity.

GDH catalyzes the reversible oxidative deamination of glutamate to keto glutamate and ammonia with pyridine nuclectide NAD or NADP as coenzymes. GDH has been measured in a number of tissues (Clampitt and Hart, 1978) and serum (Caisey and King, 1980) and the authors speculated that its measurement would be a sensitive indicator of hepatic cell injury (Clampitt and Hart, 1978). GDH not only channels the nitrogen from glutamate to ammonia but also catalyzes the amination of α-keto glutamate by using free ammonia (Harper, 1986). Unlike that of transaminases, which are present in both cytosol and mitochondrial fraction, GDH is present only in mitochondria. Bursell, 1963; Knox and Greengard, 1965 studied the shifts in the activities of these enzymes and to varied environmental and physiological conditions (Bonitenko, 1974). Uric acid is the main component of the excretory product *i.e.*, urine in many insect groups, and adopts necessary mechanisms to dispose the uric acid. It is known that uric acid, because it is insoluble, can be stored as a solid and is found in the fat body of many insects at some stage of development (Moloo, 1973; Wigglesworth, 1939) and serve as a site for nitrogen reserve to be utilized further by insects (Ludwig, 1954).

It exhibited that the fat body may degenerate the amino acids into uric acid, which are then transferred into the body fluid and are expelled (Anderson and Patton, 1955). In addition to uric acid, urea and ammonia are also one of the excretory products. It is known that the arginase activity is predominant in the fat metabolism, arginine can be converted into urea and ornithine (Hayashi, 1961). The urea is expelled and ornithine can form those corresponding amino acids through the alteration of the amino group with the α-keto acid and its carbon skeleton can be used to form proline which joins the energy metabolism. The metabolic pathway by which urea is produced in insects is not known, but it is probably, independent of uric acid synthesis (Gilmour, 1961; Chefurka, 1965). Garcia *et al.*, (1956) reported the evidence of ornithine cycle in silkworm based on the presence of arginine, ornithine and urea. Hayashi, 1961 also reported the formation of urea from arginine in silkworms.

Protein concentration in larval blood fluctuates more widely than that of free amino acids and other non protein nitrogen. Palli and Locke, 1988 indicated the fat body as principal site for synthesis of haemolymph proteins. Shigematsu 1958 also reported the fat body as an active site for intermediary metabolism of amino acids. All these enzymes AAT, AlAT and GDH function as a link between protein and carbohydrate metabolism and net outcome is the incorporation of keto acids into TCA cycle. The catabolism of proteins usually results in the production of some of the unwanted nitrogenous end products like ammonia, urea and uric acid. Ammonia toxicity has been posing a problem right from the protozoans to mammals and a variety of adaptations have been observed among animal groups to dispose off the ammonia (Hoar, 1976). Ammonia is produced within the body at the expense of amino acids and their derivatives. Since ammonia is toxic substance, it should be converted into some non toxic forms like urea, uric acid etc., before it is disposed off from the animal subject. The fat body is the primary site of intermediary metabolism as well as a site for storage of metabolic reserves, and was a great influence on the physiological functions of various organs in the body. The fat body also performs detoxification and can store nutrients, nullify the toxin and provide periodical life activity with various biosynthetic metabolism products, it is similar to the liver in the vertebrates in functions like water and electrolyte balance, nutrient conservation, maintenance of blood pH, and removes the end products of nitrogenous metabolism.

The effects of vitamin E and selenium deficiency have been postulated to result from the destruction of cellular membranes of critical cellular components and thus cellular integrity is sustained. Schwartz and Foltz (1957) reported the liver necrosis in rats due to selenium deficiency, which can cause degenerative lesions.

From the literature, it was clear that the biochemistry of selenium is interrelated with other nutritional factors. McCoy and Weswig (1969) described the selenium deficiency results in poor growth and reproductive incapability in rats. Scott (1978) studied the effect of selenium deficiency in diets of chicks to develop muscular dystrophy and pancreatic degeneration etc. Stowe and Brady (1978) suggest the metabolism of several other elements is interrelated with that of selenium.

There are a few studies described alterations in nitrogen metabolism of vertebrates on exposure to selenium. It is known that selenium modulates the functions of a variety of intracellular proteins. Selenium is associated with protein in animal tissues (Burk and Hill, 1993). Spallholz (1994) and very little is currently known about the toxic role of selenium in the biochemical functions of the cell. Abdullaev *et al.*, (1992) studied the effect of selenium on cell viability, cell cycle on protein synthesis and also DNA integrity. It has also been reported that Selenium arrests cell cycle of cancer at low concentration and G1, S, and G2-phases of cell division and change in protein synthesis (Combs and Grey, 1998). The authors suggested that the selenium may interfere with transcription of DNA. It is also evident the growth of E.coli was supported by the synthesis of the enzyme formate dehydrogenases when the medium is supplemented with inorganic selenium compounds (Lester and DeMoss, 1971). Selenium supplementation at 0.25 mg./kg level is sufficient to stimulate aminoacid incorporation into protein in hepatocytes, mitochondria and post mitochondrial supernatant from rat liver, and the increases in incorporation were also consistent with an acceleration of glutathione peroxidase activity and malaondialdehydrogenases (Jia *et al.*, 1982). Katsuma (2004) observed a decrease in cystine protease activity of B.mori on exposure to nucleopolyhedrovirusus.

On the whole, the literature indicates the involvement of selenium in the protein metabolism of mammals. However, the influence of selenium on the protein metabolism of Lepidopteron insects is not clearly known and no such studies were made earlier in the silkworm *Bombyx mori L.* Further, no dose and time dependent studies are also carried earlier on the protein metabolism of the silkworm on exposure to selenium. Hence the present work has designed to study the changes in the levels of soluble, structural and total proteins free amino acids, ammonia and the activities of protease, AlAT, AAT and GDH in fat body and haemolymph of silkworm exposed to selenium.

RESULTS

Total Protein Levels

The data given in the Table 6.1 and Figure 6.1, revealed a significant increase ($p < 0.05$) in total proteins of all organs of silkworm (group 2) at 3 day in lethal concentration of Selenium. But these protein levels are declined significantly ($p < 0.05$) on further exposure to lethal concentration of selenium (groups 5, 8 and 11) at 4, 5 and 6th day of exposure. The per cent decrease of the protein content in haemolymph, fat body and malpighian tubules of silkworm was progressed at 4, 5 and 6th day of exposure periods studied in the order 4 < 5 < 6. In sub-lethal concentrations of Selenium, these protein

Tab le 6.1 : Level of Soluble proteins (mg./gm wet wt.) in Fat body of V instar Silkworm *Bombyx mori.L.* on exposure to lethal and sub-lethal doses of Selenium at 3, 4, 5 and 6 days

Dose	3 days	4 days	5 days	6 days
Control	106.4133 [a]	109.37 [b]	119.57 [b]	130.23 [b]
Lethal	125.54 [c] (+17.9)	97.066 [a] (-11.2)	86.24 [a] (-27.8)	69.78 [a] (-46.41)
Sub-lethal	112.39 [b] (+5.62)	119.63 [c] (+9.39)	134.4 [c] (+12.41)	150.0 [c] (+15.20)

* Each value is a mean of eight estimates.

** Per cent decrease over control is given in parenthesis.

*** Means with in a column followed by the same letter are not significantly different ($p > 0.05$) from each other according to Duncan's Multiple range test.

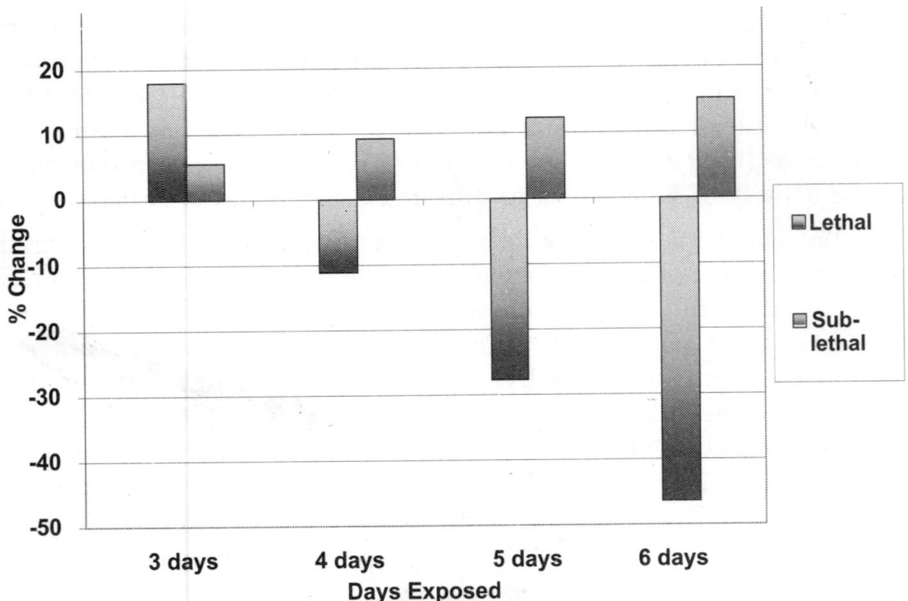

Fig. 6.1 : Per cent change over control in the level of Soluble proteins (mg./gm wet wt.) in Fat body of V instar Silkworm *Bombyx mori.L.* on exposure to lethal and sub-lethal doses of Selenium at 3, 4, 5 and 6 days.

levels recorded a significant increase ($p < 0.05$) in haemolymph, fat body and malpighian tubules of V instar silkworm at 3, 4, 5, and 6 day exposure periods studied in the order 3 < 4 < 5 < 6. Among the exposure periods, the total protein content accumulated was more in haemolymph than in fat body and malpighian tubules in the order haemolymph > fat body > malpighian tubules. The results also revealed that the increase in the protein content of haemolymph, fat body and malpighian tubules of silkworm was more at 3 and 4 day of exposure periods and declined on further exposure to selenium at sub-lethal concentrations.

Soluble, Structural and Total Protein Levels

The data given in Tables 6.2 to 6.7 and Figures 6.2 to 6.7, revealed an elevation in the levels of soluble and structural proteins in fat body and malpighian tubules of silkworm at 3 day in lethal concentration of selenium (group 2). However, these levels are significantly decreased ($p < 0.05$) on further exposure to lethal dose of selenium (groups 5, 8 and 11) at 4, 5 and 6 day of exposure. The per cent decrease was progressed at 4, 5 and 6 day of exposure periods studied , in the order of 4 < 5 < 6. However the levels of soluble and structural proteins in, fat body and malpighian tubules of silkworm could exhibit a significant increase ($p < 0.05$) at all the days of exposure periods studied at sub-lethal dose of selenium (groups 3, 6, 9 and 12). The accumulation

Table 6.2 : Level of Structural proteins (mg./gm wet wt.) in Fat body of V instar Silkworm *Bombyx mori.L.* on exposure to lethal and sub-lethal doses of Selenium at 3,4,5 and 6 days.

Dose	3 days	4 days	5 days	6 days
Control	80.3167[a]	82.8133 [a]	90.533 [b]	98.6767 [b]
Lethal	94.5667 [c] (+17.74)	73.6067 [b] (-11.11)	65.9867 [a] (-27.11)	53.38 [a] (-45.9)
Sub-lethal	81.47 [b] (+1.4)	84.18 [a] (+1.6)	96.13 [c] (+6.18)	125.7 [c] (25.9)

* Each value is a mean of eight estimates.

** Per cent decrease over control is given in parenthesis.

*** Means with in a column followed by the same letter are not significantly different ($p > 0.05$) from each other according to Duncan's Multiple range test.

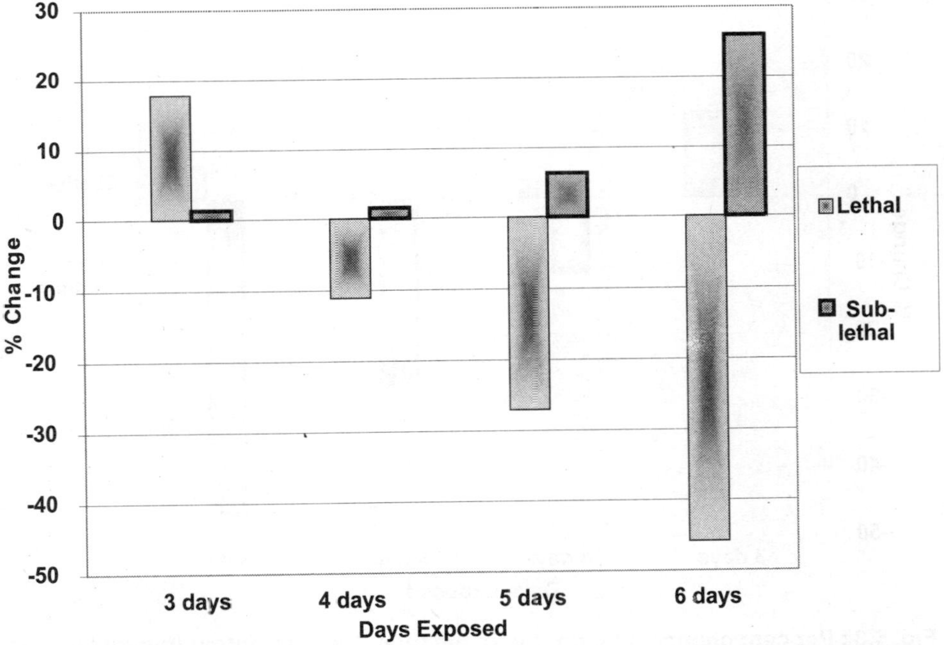

Fig. 6.2 : Per cent change over control in the level of Structural proteins (mg./gm wet wt.) in Fat body of V instar Silkworm *Bombyx mori.L* on exposure to lethal and sub-lethal doses of Selenium at 3, 4, 5 and 6 days.

of structural and soluble proteins in all organs of the silkworm were more at 5 and 6 day and less at 3 and 4 day of exposure periods in the order 3 < 4 < 5 < 6.

Table 6.3 : Total Protein Content (mg./gm wet wt.) in Fat body of V instar Silkworm *Bombyx mori L.* on exposure to lethal and sub lethal doses of Selenium at 3, 4, 5 and 6 days

Dose	3 days	4 days	5 days	6 days
Control	186.35 [a]	192.16[b]	210.57 [b]	229.80 [b]
Lethal	220.37[c] (+18.25)	170.52 [a] (-11.2)	152.38 [a] (-27.6)	123.13 [a] (-46.42)
Sub-lethal	210.32 [b] (+12.8)	221.36 [c] (+18.2)	229.38 [c] (+8.9)	241.69 [c] (+5.1)

* Each value is a mean of eight estimates.

** Per cent decrease over control is given in parenthesis.

*** Means with in a column followed by the same letter are not significantly different ($p > 0.05$) from each other according to Duncan's Multiple range test.

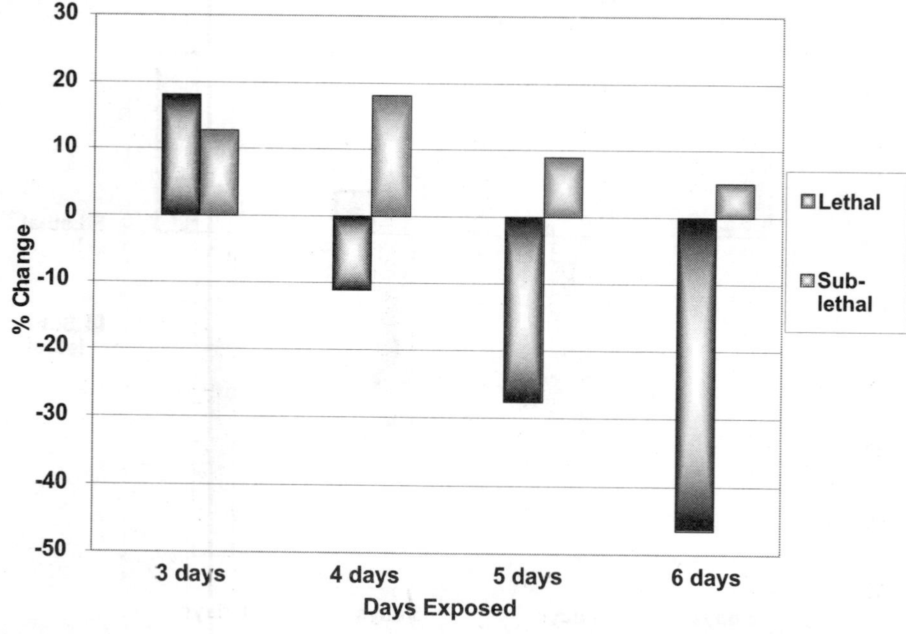

Fig. 6.3 : Per cent change over control in the total Protein Content (mg./gm wet wt.) in Fat body of V instar Silkworm *Bombyx mori L.* on exposure to lethal and sub-lethal doses of Selenium at 3, 4, 5 and 6 days.

Protease Activity

Compared to controls (groups 1, 4, 7 and 10), corresponding to the decrease in protein content, protease activity increased significantly ($p < 0.05$) in fat body and malpighian tubules of silkworm at all the exposure periods studied in the lethal concentrations of Selenium (Tables 6.13-6.15 Figures 6.13-6.15).

Table 6.4 : Level of Soluble proteins (mg./gm wet wt.) in Malpighian Tubules of V instar Silkworm *Bombyx mori.L.* on exposure to lethal and sub-lethal doses of Selenium at 3, 4, 5 and 6 days.

Dose	3 days	4 days	5 days	6 days
Control	59.10 [a]	59.90 [b]	60.70 [b]	62.10 [b]
Lethal	59.826 [a] (+1.22)	56.616 [a] (-5.48)	53.67 [a] (-11.58)	49.38 [a] (-20.48)
Sub-lethal	59.54 [a] (+0.74)	60.33 [b] (+0.71)	61.156 [b] (+0.751)	62.23 [b] (+0.209)

* Each value is a mean of eight estimates.

** Per cent decrease over control is given in parenthesis.

*** Means with in a column followed by the same letter are not significantly different ($p > 0.05$) from each other according to Duncan's Multiple range test.

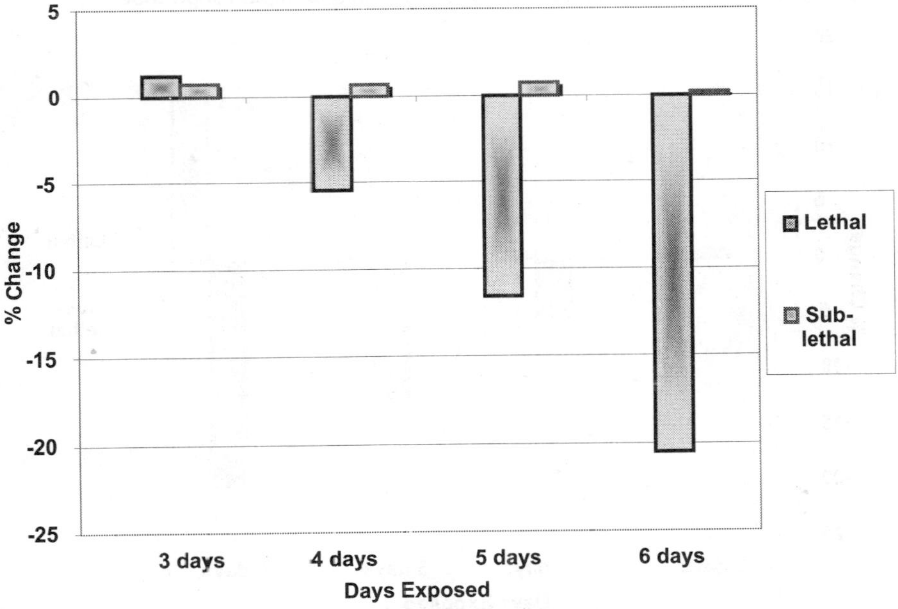

Fig. 6.4 : Per cent change over control in the level of Soluble proteins (mg./gm wet wt.) in Malpighian Tubules of V instar Silkworm *Bombyx mori.L.* on exposure to lethal and sub-lethal doses of Selenium at 3, 4, 5 and 6 days.

This increase was significant ($p < 0.05$) in, fat body and malpighian tubules. Based on the per cent values, it is seen that the increase in protease activity was predominantly more in the organs of silkworm subjected to the lethal concentrations than the sub-lethal ones. Among the periods of exposure, the increase of protease activity in fat body and malpighian tubules of silkworm is less at 3 day (group 2) and greater at 4, 5, and 6 days (groups 5, 8, and 11) of exposure to lethal concentrations. But in the malpighian

Table 6.5 : Level of Structural proteins (mg./gm wet wt.) in Malpighian Tubules of V instar Silkworm *Bombyx mori.L.* on exposure to lethal and sub-lethal doses of Selenium at 3, 4, 5 and 6 days

Dose	3 days	4 days	5 days	6 days
Control	66.74 [a]	67.45 [b]	68.82 [b]	69.97 [b]
Lethal	67.34 [c] (+0.89)	63.8967 [a] (-5.26)	60.2167 [a] (-12.50)	55.76 [a] (-20.30)
Sub-lethal	66.99 [b] (+0.37)	67.9667 [c] (+0.76)	68.933 [b] (+0.16)	80.37 [b] (+14.8)

* Each value is a mean of eight estimates.

** Per cent decrease over control is given in parenthesis.

*** Means with in a column followed by the same letter are not significantly different (p > 0.05) from each other according to Duncan's Multiple range test.

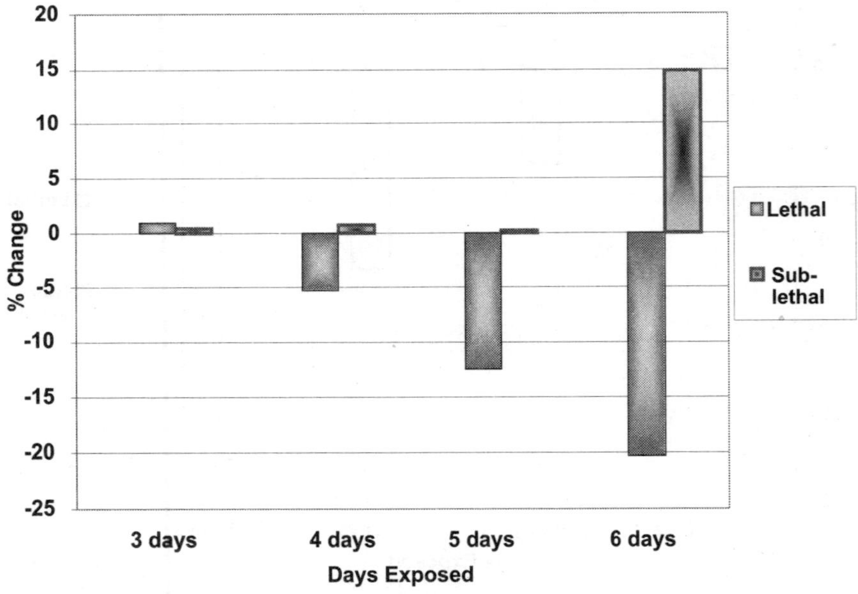

Fig. 6.5a : Per cent change over control in the level of Structural proteins (mg./gm. wet.) in Malpighian tubules of V instar Silkworm *Bombyx mori.L.* on exposure to lethal and sub-lethal doses of Selenium at 3, 4, 5 and 6 days.

tubules of silkworm, though the increase was greater at 5 and 6 days, it was less at 2 days of exposure (3 > 4 < 5 < 6). In sub-lethal concentrations, the increase these parameters in fat body and malpighian tubules of silkworm was more at 3 day (group 3) and declined on further exposure at 4, 5 and 6 days (groups 6, 9 and 12) which was in the order 3 > 4 > 5 > 6 in haemolymph and 3 > 4 > 5 < 6 in malpighian tubules. However, this decrease was insignificant (p > 0.5) in relation to controls (groups 1, 4, 7 and 10).

Table 6.6 : Total Protein Content (mg./gm. wet wt.) in Malpighian Tubules of V instar Silkworm *Bombyx mori.L.* on exposure to lethal and sub-lethal doses of Selenium at 3, 4, 5 and 6 days

Dose	3 days	4 days	5 days	6 days
Control	125.76[a]	127.53[b]	129.71 [b]	132.23 [b]
Lethal	127.43 [a] (+13.2)	120.60 [a] (-5.43)	113.46 [a] (-12.5)	105.20 [a] (-20.4)
Sub-lethal	126.51 [a] (+0.5)	128.25[c] (+0.56)	130.54 [c] (+0.6)	132.30 [b] (+0.05)

* Each value is a mean of eight estimates.

** Per cent decrease over control is given in parenthesis.

*** Means with in a column followed by the same letter are not significantly different ($p > 0.05$) from each other according to Duncan's Multiple range test.

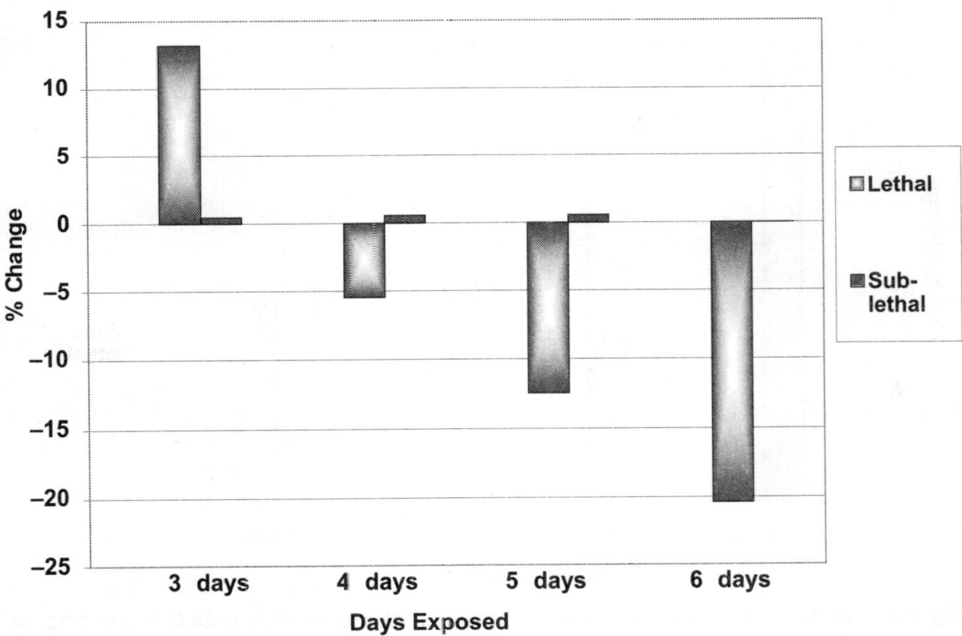

Fig. 6.6 : Per cent change over control in the total Protein Content (mg./gm. wet wt.) in Malpighian Tubules of V instar Silkworm *Bombyx mori.L.* on exposure to lethal and sub-lethal doses of Selenium at 3, 4, 5 and 6 days.

Table 6.7 : Level of Free amino acids Content (mg. of tyrosine equivalents/gm. wet wt.) in Fat body of V instar Silkworm *Bombyx mori.L.* on exposure to lethal and sub-lethal doses of Selenium at 3, 4, 5 and 6 days

Dose	3 days	4 days	5 days	6 days
Control	43.64[a]	46.36[a]	48.33[a]	51.30[a]
Lethal	53.88[b] (+22.31)	55.06[c] (+18.7)	56.58[c] (+17.07)	61.27[b] (+19.43)
Sub-lethal	53.09[b] (+21.6)	52.42[b] (+13.07)	52.36[b] (+8.3)	52.12[a] (+1.5)

* Each value is a mean of eight estimates.

** Per cent decrease over control is given in parenthesis.

*** Means with in a column followed by the same letter are not significantly different ($p > 0.05$) from each other according to Duncan's Multiple range test.

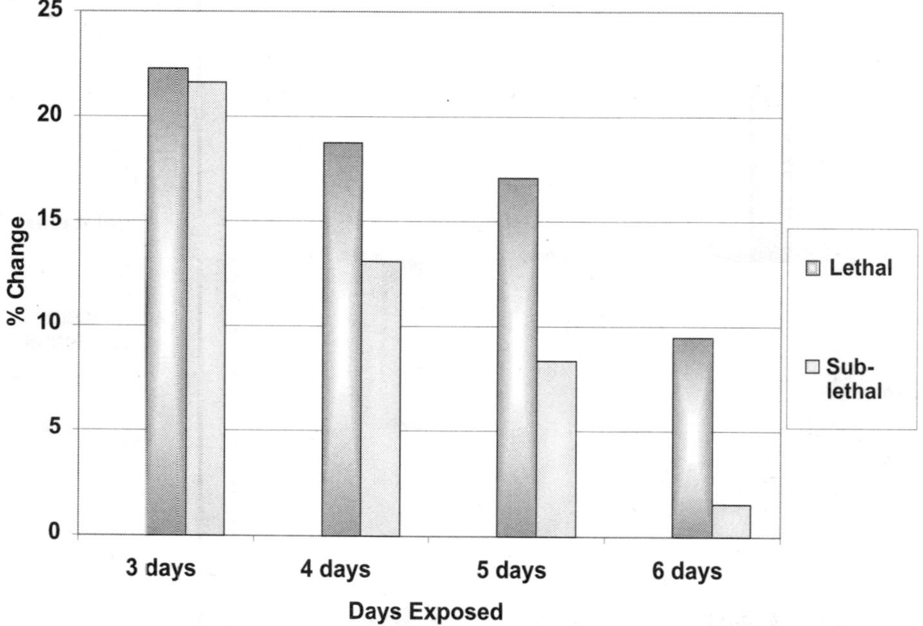

Fig. 6.7 : Per cent change over control in the level of free amino acids Content (mg. of tyrosine equivalents/gm. wet wt.) in Fat body of V instar Silkworm *Bombyx mori.L.* on exposure to lethal and sub-lethal doses of Selenium at 3, 4, 5 and 6 days.

Free Amino Acid Levels

The data given in Tables 6.8-6.10 and Figures 6.8-6.10, revealed that the free amino acid levels increased ($p < 0.05$) in all the organs of silkworm at all exposure periods studied in the lethal concentrations of selenium. In the sub-lethal concentrations also, the levels of amino acids recorded significant

Table 6.8 : Level of Free amino acids Content (mg. of tyrosine equivalents/gm. wet wt.) in Malpighian Tubules of V instar Silkworm *Bombyx mori.L.* on exposure to lethal and sub-lethal doses of Selenium at 3, 4, 5 and 6 days.

Dose	3 days	4 days	5 days	6 days
Control	23.33 [a]	25.56 [a]	26.60 [a]	27.87 [a]
Lethal	26.25 [b] (+12.52)	28.24 [c] (+10.49)	29.8 [b] (+12.09)	32.7 [b] (+17.5)
Sub-lethal	28.50 [c] (+22.16)	28.02 [b] (+9.6)	27.994 [a] (+5.2)	27.962 [a] (+0.3)

* Each value is a mean of eight estimates.

** Per cent decrease over control is given in parenthesis.

*** Means with in a column followed by the same letter are not significantly different ($p > 0.05$) from each other according to Duncan's Multiple range test.

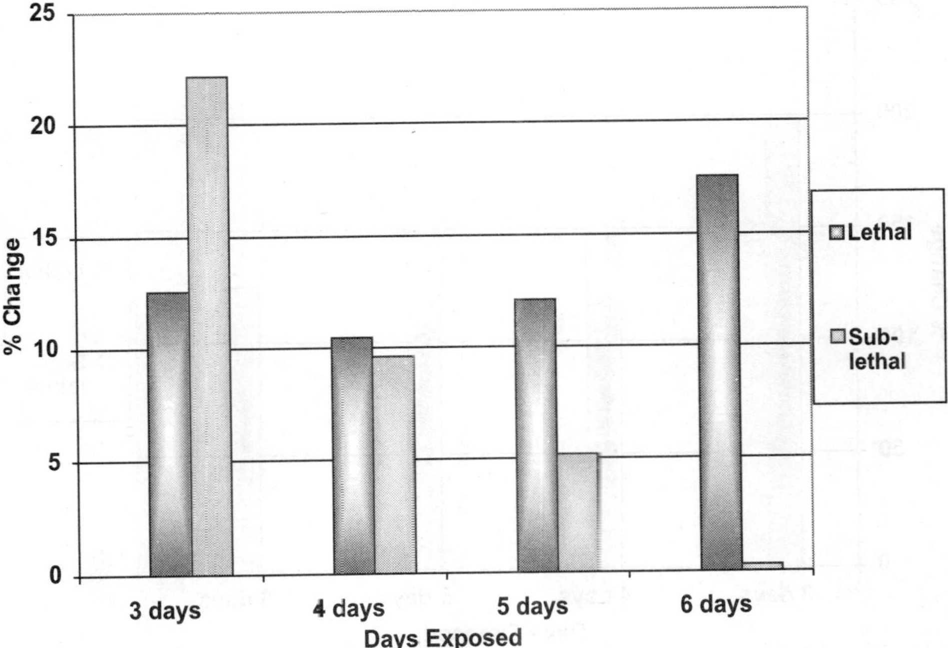

Fig. 6.8 : Per cent change over control in the free amino acids Content (mg. of tyrosine equivalents/gm. wet wt.) in Malpighian Tubules of V instar Silkworm *Bombyx mori.L.* on exposure to lethal and sub-lethal doses of Selenium at 3, 4, 5 and 6 days.

Table 6.9 : Activity of Protease Content (μ moles tyrosine equivalents formed/100 mg. protein/ hr.) in Fat body of V instar Silkworm *Bombyx mori.L.* on exposure to lethal and sub-lethal doses of Selenium at 3, 4, 5 and 6 days

Dose	3 days	4 days	5 days	6 days
Control	0.516 [a]	0.646 [a]	0.701 [a]	0.803 [a]
Lethal	1.54 [b] (+198.4)	1.600 [c] (+147.6)	1.75 [c] (+149.6)	1.806 [a] (+124.9)
Sub-lethal	1.30 [b] (+151.9)	1.030 [b] (+59.44)	0.774 [b] (+10.4)	0.817 [a] (+1.7)

* Each value is a mean of eight estimates.

** Per cent decrease over control is given in parenthesis.

*** Means with in a column followed by the same letter are not significantly different (p > 0.05) from each other according to Duncan's Multiple range test.

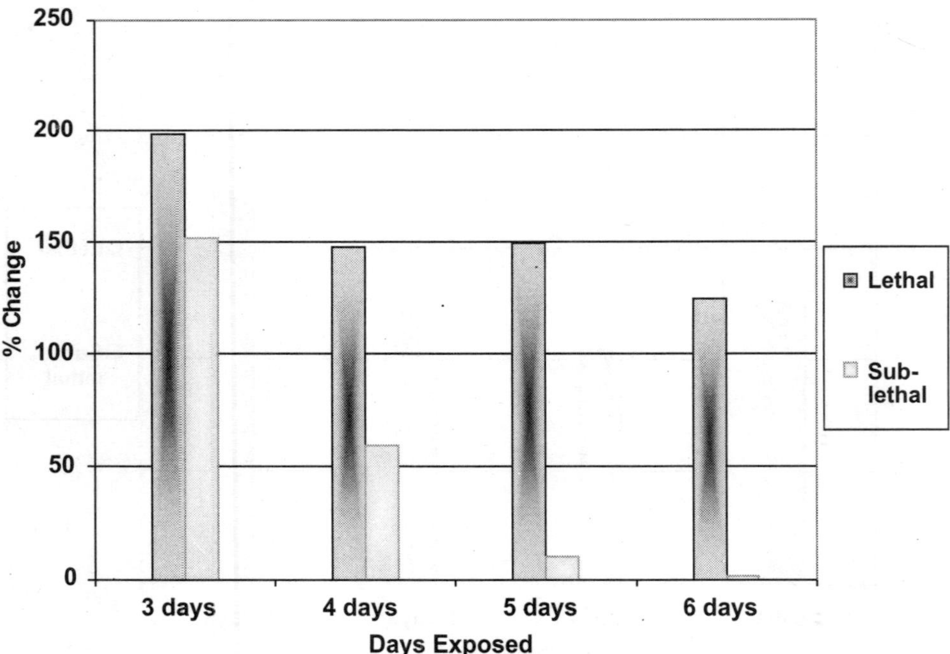

Fig. 6.9 : Per cent change over control in the activity of Protease Content (μ moles tyrosine equivalents formed / 100 mg. protein/hr.) in Fat body of V instar Silkworm *Bombyx mori.L.* on exposure to lethal and sub-lethal doses of Selenium at 3, 4, 5 and 6 days.

Table 6.9a : Activity of Protease Content (μ moles tyrosine equivalents formed/100 mg. protein/hr.) in Malpighian Tubules of V instar Silkworm *Bombyx mori.L.* on exposure to lethal and sub-lethal doses of Selenium at 3, 4, 5 and 6 days

Dose	3 days	4 days	5 days	6 days
Control	0.3553 [a]	0.4540 [a]	0.506 [a]	0.511 [a]
Lethal	0.4157 [c] (+16.90)	0.521 [b] (+14.7)	0 5973 [b] (+17.98)	0.617 [c] (+20.19)
Sub-lethal	0.3947 [b] (+11.18)	0.461 [a] (+1.54)	0.509 [a] +0.59)	0.542 [a] (+6.0)

* Each value is a mean of eight estimates.

** Per cent decrease over control is given in parenthesis.

*** Means with in a column followed by the same letter are not significantly different ($p > 0.05$) from each other according to Duncan's Multiple range test.

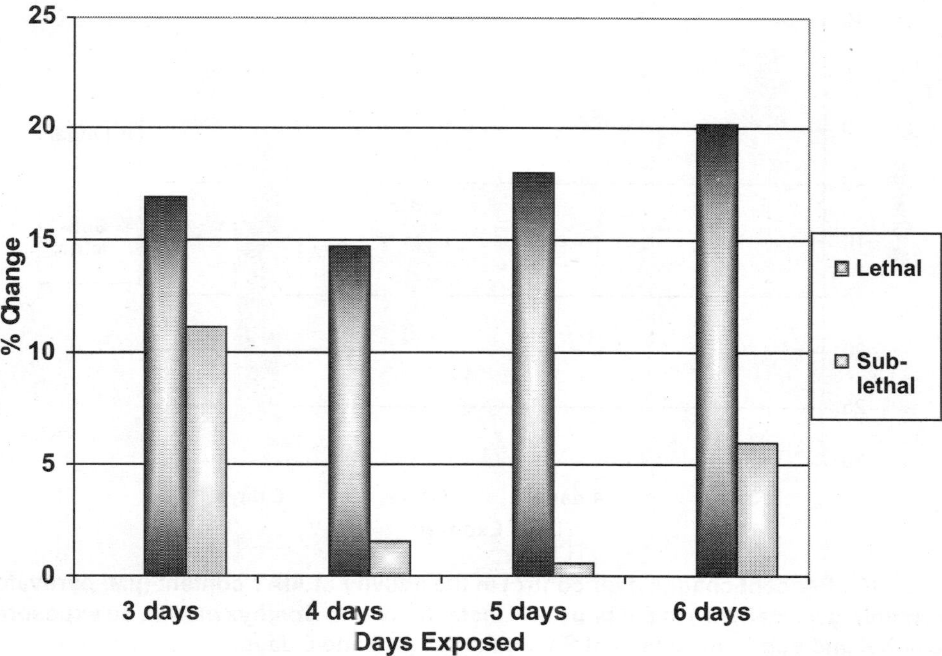

Fig. 6.9a : Per cent change over control in the activity of Protease Content (μ moles tyrosine equivalents formed/100 mg. protein/hr.) in Malpighian Tubules of V instar Silkworm *Bombyx mori.L.* on exposure to lethal and sub-lethal doses of Selenium at 3, 4, 5 and 6 days.

Table 6.10 : Activity of AlAT content (μ M/ pyruvate formed/mg. protein/hr.) in Fat body of V instar Silkworm *Bombyx mori. L.* on exposure to lethal and sub-lethal doses of Selenium at 3, 4, 5 and 6 days

Dose	3 days	4 days	5 days	6 days
Control	0.6490 [a]	0.6827 [a]	0.7230 [b]	0.7483 [b]
Lethal	0.7033 [b] (+8.3)	0.6997 [b] (+2.49)	0.5803 [a] (-19.73)	0.5537 [a] (-26.0)
Sub-lethal	0.6993 [b] (+7.75)	0.7027 [b] (+2.93)	0.7263 [b] (+0.45)	0.8140 [c] (+8.7)

* Each value is a mean of eight estimates.

** Per cent decrease over control is given in parenthesis.

*** Means with in a column followed by the same letter are not significantly different ($p > 0.05$) from each other according to Duncan's Multiple range test.

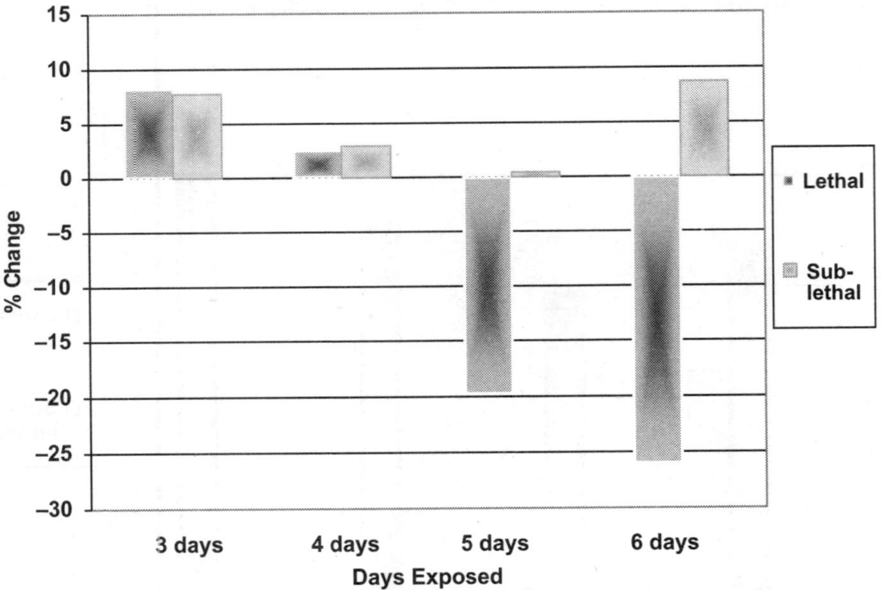

Fig. 6.10 : Per cent change over control in the activity of AlAT content (μM/ pyruvate formed/mg. protein/hr.) in Fat body of V instar Silkworm *Bombyx mori.L.* on exposure to lethal and sub-lethal doses of Selenium at 3, 4, 5 and 6 days.

($p < 0.05$) increase. Based on per cent values, it is seen that the increase in free amino acid levels was more in the fat body and malpighian tubules of silkworm subjected to the lethal concentrations (groups 2, 5, 8 and 11) than the sub-lethal ones (groups 3, 6, 9 and 12). However, the increase in the amino acid levels accumulated is more at sub-lethal concentrations at 3 and 4 day of exposure than the lethal ones.

AAT, AIAT and GDH Activities

The data given in the Tables 6.11-6.21 and Figures 6.11-6.21, show a steep increase in AAT, AIAT and GDH activities in fat bodies and malpighian tubules of silkworm at 3 day (group 2) of exposure to the lethal concentrations of Selenium, relative to controls (groups 1, 4, 7 and 10). However, at 4 day the increase in the activities of these enzymes regressed, which on further exposure led to a significant ($p < 0.05$) decrease in the activities of these enzymes at 4, 5 and 6 days (groups 5, 8, and 11). The activities of AAT, AIAT and GDH also increased in all the organs of the silkworm at 3 day (group 3) of exposure to the sub-lethal concentration of Selenium, but the increase was gradually progressed on further exposure to 4, 5 and 6 days groups (6, 9 and 12). However, the increase observed at 3 day of exposure to the sub-lethal concentration was significantly less than the increase at 3 day in the lethal concentration. The increase of AAT, AIAT and GDH activities in the organs of silkworm exposed to the sub-lethal concentration was in the order 3<4<5<6 mostly. In lethal concentration, the steep increase at 3 day of exposure led to a significant decrease at 4, 5 and 6 days, whereas in the sub-lethal concentrations, the little increase at 3 day gradually progressed with over time of exposure, with a significant difference between 3 and 6 days. Among the organs of silkworm, the increase in activities of AIAT, AAT and GDH at 3 day of exposure to the lethal concentration was more in malpighian tubules than in haemolymph and fat body, in the order malpighian tubules > haemolymph > fat body.

Ammonia and Urea Levels

Related to controls, ammonia levels increased in haemolymph, fat bodies and malpighian tubules at all the exposure periods studied in the lethal concentrations of Selenium (groups 2, 5, 8 and 11). In sub-lethal concentrations showed a significant decrease at all the exposure periods studied in haemolymph of the silkworm and in malpighian tubules a slight increase in the ammonia levels in sub-lethal concentrations but difference in the increase in the ammonia levels in the lethal and sub-lethal concentrations was insignificant ($p > 0.05$) in malpighian tubules. Interestingly, Urea levels significantly ($p < 0.05$) increased in haemolymph, fat bodies and malpighian tubules of V instar silkworm at 3 day (group 2) and 4 days (group 5) of exposure to the lethal concentration of Selenium, however, on further exposure its level decreased at 5 day (group 8) and 6 days (group 11), and this decrease was significant ($p < 0.05$) in the order 5 < 6 in both the organs of silkworm studied. Urea level increased in haemolymph and malpighian tubules of silkworm exposed to the sub-lethal concentrations of the Selenium (groups 3, 6, 9 and 12). This increase was significant in all the days of exposure periods

Table 6.11 : Activity of AlAT content (μM/ pyruvate formed/mg. protein/hr.) in Malpighian tubules of V instar Silkworm *Bombyx mori.L.* on exposure to lethal and sub-lethal doses of Selenium at 3, 4, 5 and 6 days

Dose	3 days	4 days	5 days	6 days
Control	0.2967 [a]	0.3200 [b]	0.3600 [b]	0.4133 [b]
Lethal	0.3533 [c] (+19.07)	0.3000 [a] (-6.25)	0.2467 [a] (-31.4)	0.2133 [a] (-48.4)
Sub-lethal	0.3200 [b] (+7.85)	0.3433 [c] (+6.47)	0.4273 [c] (+18.6)	0.5100 [c] (+23.39)

* Each value is a mean of eight estimates.

** Per cent decrease over control is given in parenthesis.

*** Means with in a column followed by the same letter are not significantly different ($p > 0.05$) from each other according to Duncan's Multiple range test.

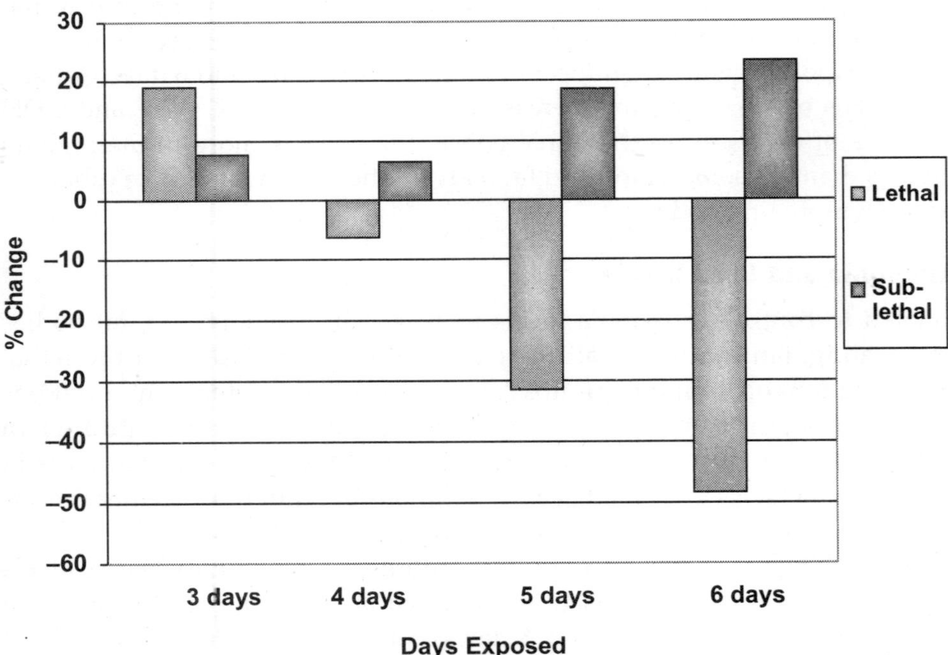

Fig. 6.11 : Per cent change over control in the activity of AlAT content (μM/ pyruvate formed/mg. protein/hr.) in Malpighian tubules of V instar Silkworm *Bombyx mori.L.* on exposure to lethal and sub-lethal doses of Selenium at 3, 4, 5 and 6 days.

Table 6.12 : Activity of AAT content (µM/ pyruvate formed/mg. protein/hr.) in Fat body of V instar Silkworm *Bombyx mori.L.* on exposure to lethal and sub-lethal doses of Selenium at 3, 4, 5 and 6 days

Dose	3 days	4 days	5 days	6 days
Control	0.7333 [a]	0.7643 [a]	0.8157 [b]	0.9340 [b]
Lethal	0.8313 [c] (+13.36)	0.7530 [a] (-1.4)	0.6163 [a] (-24.4)	0.5737 [a] (-38.57)
Sub-lethal	0.7440 [b] (+1.45)	0.8947 [b] (+17.06)	1.1207 [c] (+37.39)	1.3267 [c] (+42.04)

* Each value is a mean of eight estimates.

** Per cent decrease over control is given in parenthesis.

*** Means with in a column followed by the same letter are not significantly different ($p > 0.05$) from each other according to Duncan's Multiple range test.

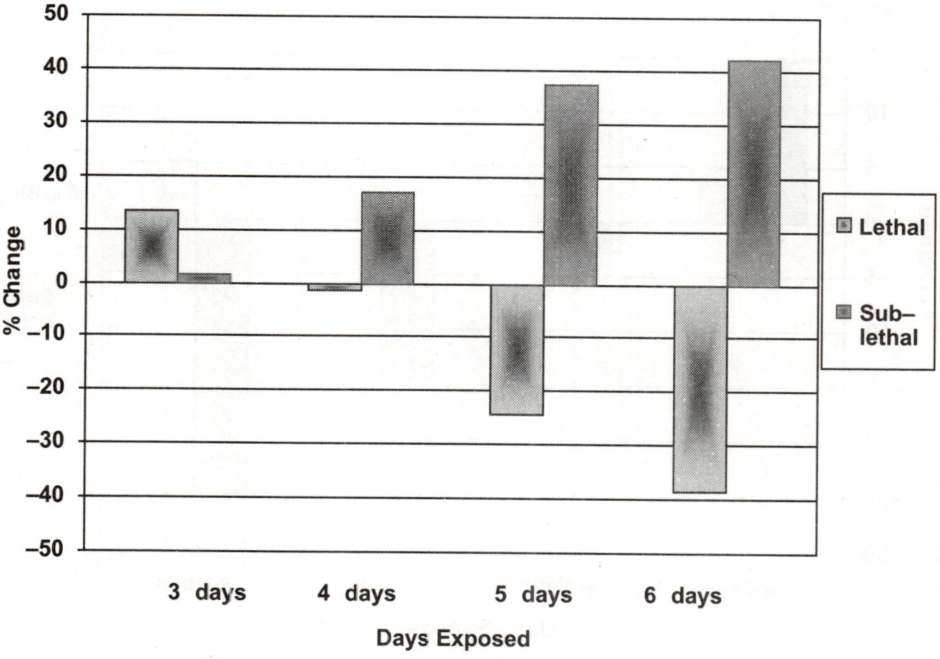

Fig. 6.12 : Per cent change over control in the activity of AAT content (µM/ pyruvate formed/mg. protein/hr.) in Fat body of V instar Silkworm *Bombyx mori.L.* on exposure to lethal and sub-lethal doses of Selenium at 3, 4, 5 and 6 days.

Table 6.13 : Activity of AAT content (µM/ pyruvate formed/mg. protein/hr.) in Malpighian Tubules of V instar Silkworm *Bombyx mori.L.* on exposure to lethal and sub-lethal doses of Selenium at 3, 4, 5 and 6 days

Dose	3 days	4 days	5 days	6 days
Control	0.1830 [a]	0.1947 [b]	0.2013 [b]	0.2267 [b]
Lethal	0.210 [c] (+14.75)	0.1891 [a] (-2.87)	0.1729 [a] (-14.35)	0.1715 [a] (-24.95)
Sub-lethal	0.1893 [a] (+3.44)	0.1997 [c] (+2.5)	0.2127 [c] (+5.6)	0.2383 [c] (+5.12)

* Each value is a mean of eight estimates.

** Per cent decrease over control is given in parenthesis.

*** Means with in a column followed by the same letter are not significantly different ($p > 0.05$) from each other according to Duncan's Multiple range test.

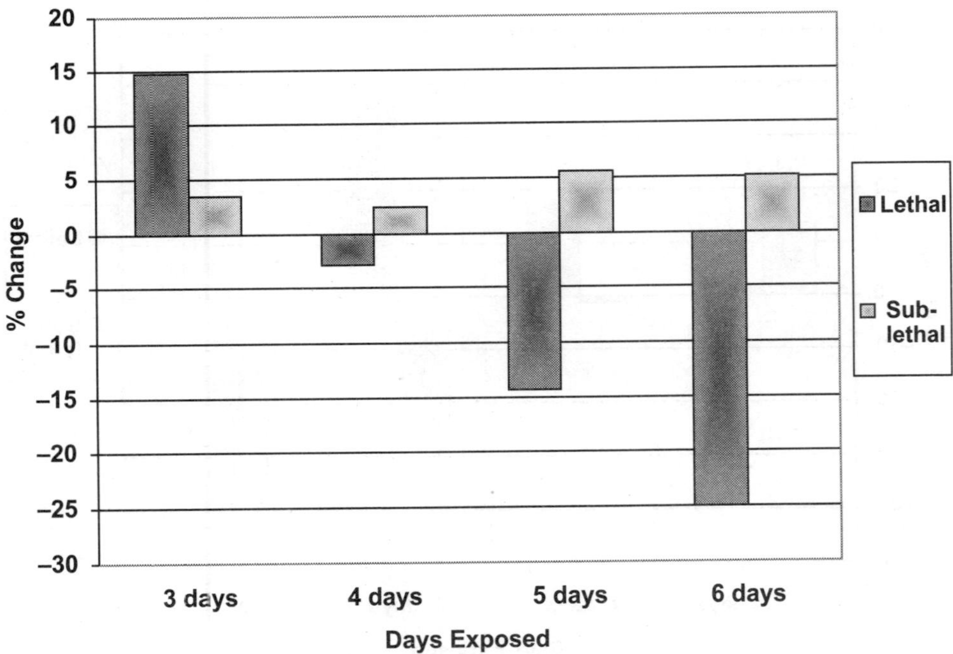

Fig. 6.13 : Per cent change over control in the activity of AAT content (µM/ pyruvate formed/mg. protein/hr.) in Malpighian Tubules of V instar Silkworm *Bombyx mori.L.* on exposure to lethal and sub-lethal doses of Selenium at 3, 4, 5 and 6 days.

Table 6.14 : Level of GDH content (μ M/F ormazon formed/mg. protein/hr.) in Fat body of V instar Silkworm *Bombyx mori.L.* on exposure to lethal and sub-lethal doses of Selenium at 3, 4, 5 and 6 days

Dose	3 days	4 days	5 days	6 days
Control	0.1140 [a]	0.1167 [a]	0.1193 [b]	0.1230 [a]
Lethal	0.1293 [c] (+13.42)	0.1187 [a] (+1.7)	0.1030 [a] (-13.6)	0.1217 [a] (-1.05)
Sub-lethal	0.1264 [b] (+10.8)	0.1350 [b] (+15.68)	0.1487 [c] (+24.64)	0.1643 [b] (+33.57)

* Each value is a mean of eight estimates.

** Per cent decrease over control is given in parenthesis.

*** Means with in a column followed by the same letter are not significantly different ($p > 0.05$) from each other according to Duncan's Multiple range test.

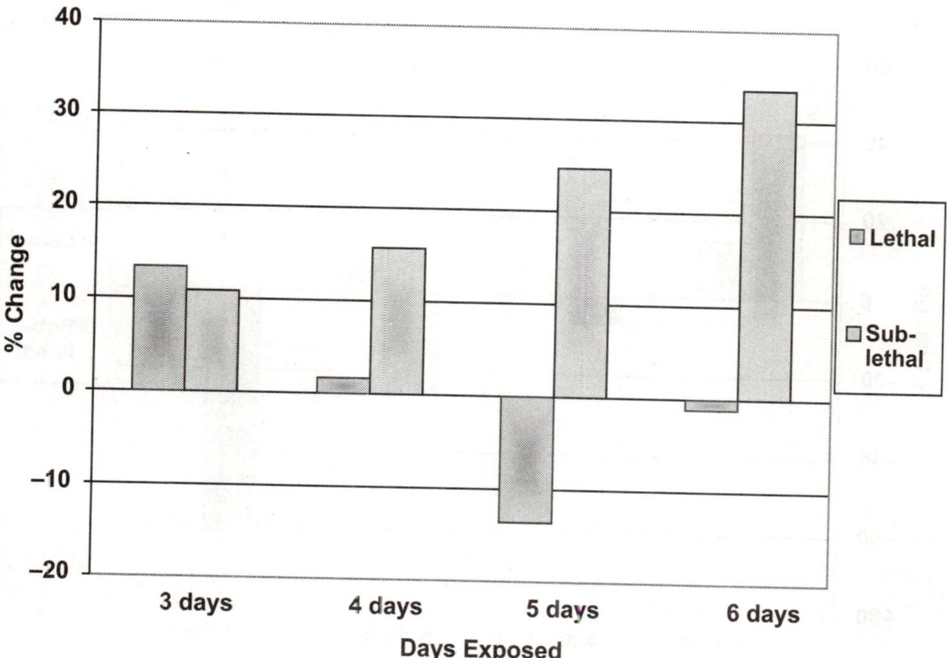

Fig. 6.14 : Per cent change over control in the level of GDH content (μ M/Formazon formed/mg. protein/hr.) in Fat body of V instar Silkworm *Bombyx mori.L.* on exposure to lethal and sub-lethal doses of Selenium at 3, 4, 5 and 6 days.

Table 6.15 : Level of GDH content (µM/Formazon formed/mg. protein/hr.) in Malpighian Tubules of V instar Silkworm *Bombyx mori. L.* on exposure to lethal and sub-lethal doses of Selenium at 3, 4, 5 and 6 days.

Dose	3 days	4 days	5 days	6 days
Control	0.0863 [a]	0.1133 [b]	0.1277 [b]	0.1427 [b]
Lethal	0.1227 [c] (+42.17)	0.1057 [a] (-6.7)	0.0947 [a] (-25.84)	0.0557 [a] (-60.9)
Sub-letha	0.0987 [b] (+14.36)	0.1210 [c] (+6.7)	0.1387 [c] (+8.6)	0.1403 [b] (-1.6)

* Each value is a mean of eight estimates.

** Per cent decrease over control is given in parenthesis.

*** Means with n a column followed by the same letter are not significantly different ($p > 0.05$) from each other according to Duncan's Multiple range test.

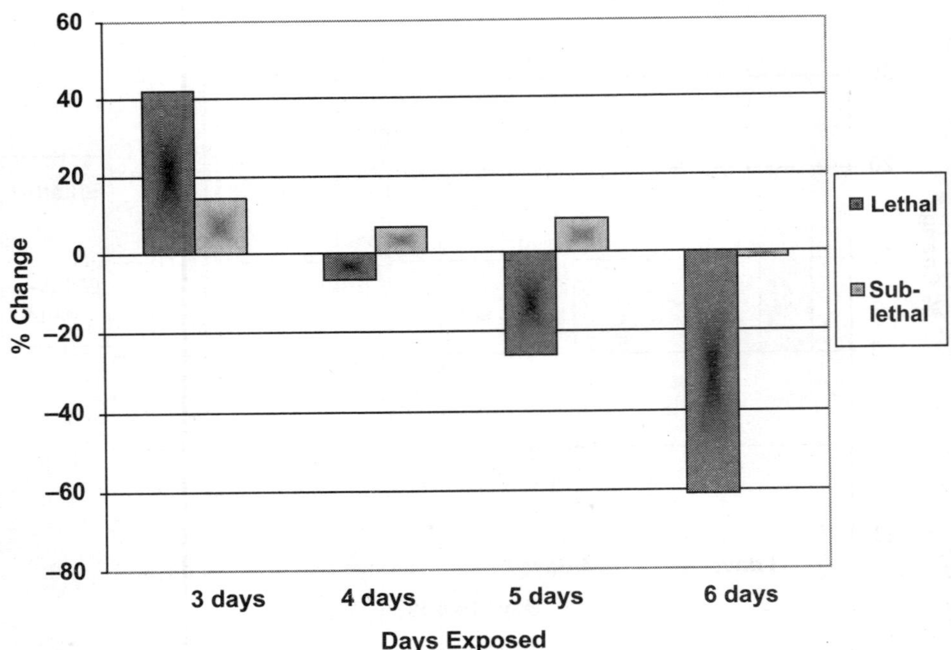

Fig. 6.15 : Per cent change over control in the level of GDH content (µM/Formazon formed/mg. protein/hr.) in Malpighian Tubules of V instar Silkworm *Bombyx mori. L.* on exposure to lethal and sub-lethal doses of Selenium at 3, 4, 5 and 6 days.

Table 6.16 : Level of Ammonia content (μ M/gm. wet wt.) in Fat body of V instar Silkworm *Bombyx mori.L.* on exposure to lethal and sub-lethal doses of Selenium at 3, 4, 5 and 6 days

Dose	3 days	4 days	5 days	6 days
Control	6.193 [a]	6.27 [a]	6.44 [a]	6.68 [a]
Lethal	6.472 [b] (+4.50)	6.842 [b] (+9.12)	7.180 [b] (+11.49)	7.600 [b] (+13.77)
Sub-lethal	6.278 [a] (+1.37)	6.650 [b] (+6.06)	6.357 [a] (+1.28)	6.682 [a] (+0.02)

* Each value is a mean of eight estimates.

** Per cent decrease over control is given in parenthesis.

*** Means with in a column followed by the same letter are not significantly different ($p > 0.05$) from each other according to Duncan's Multiple range test.

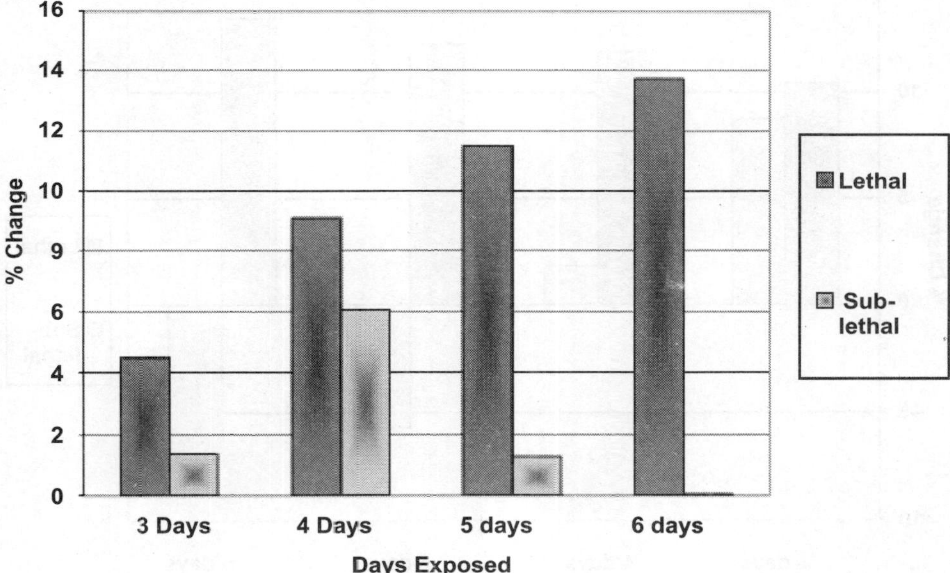

Fig. 6.16 : Per cent change over control in the level of Ammonia content (μ M/gm. wet wt.) in Fat body of V instar Silkworm *Bombyx mori. L.* on exposure to lethal and sub-lethal doses of Selenium at 3, 4, 5 and 6 days.

Table 6.17 : Level of Ammonia content (μ M/gm. wet wt.) in Malpighian Tubules of V instar Silkworm *Bombyx mori.L.* on exposure to lethal and sub lethal doses of Selenium at 3, 4, 5 and 6 days

Dose	3 days	4 days	5 days	6 days
Control	6.44 [a]	6.72 [a]	7.03 [b]	7.01 [b]
Lethal	**7.12 [b]** (+10.4)	7.27 [b] (+11.84)	7.3211 [c] (+12.24)	7.95 [c] (+13.45)
Sub-lethal	7.01 [b] (+8.73)	6.84 [a] (+1.83)	6.63 [a] (-5.68)	6.53 [a] (-6.80)

* Each value is a mean of eight estimates.

** Per cent decrease over control is given in parenthesis.

*** Means with in a column followed by the same letter are not significantly different ($p > 0.05$) from each other according to Duncan's Multiple range test.

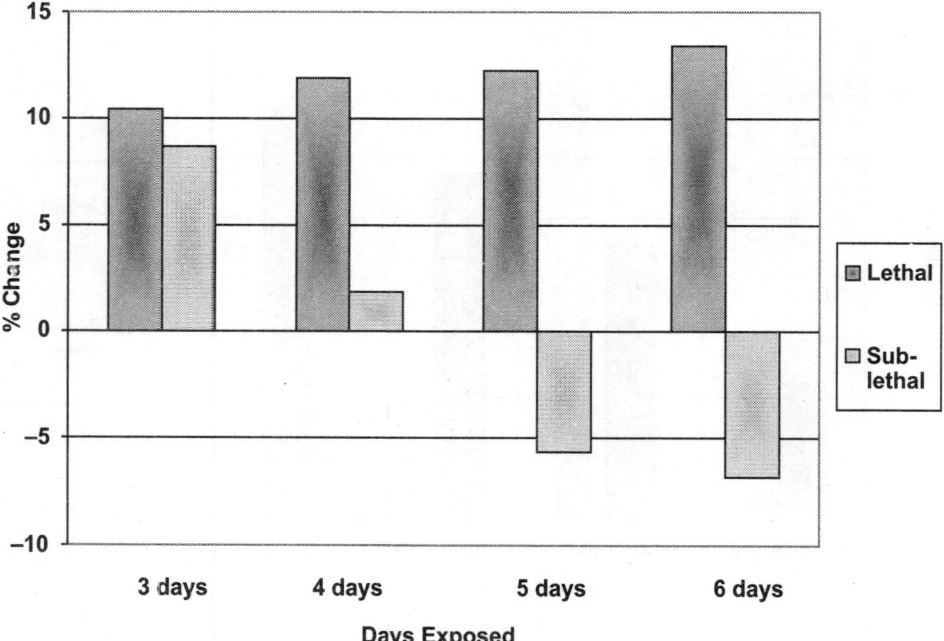

Fig. 6.17 : Per cent change over control in the level of Ammonia content (μ M/gm. wet wt.) in Malpighian Tubules of V instar Silkworm *Bombyx mori. L.* on exposure to lethal and sub-lethal doses of Selenium at 3, 4, 5 and 6 days.

Table 6.18 : Level of Ammonia content (μ M/100 ml.) in Haemolymph of V instar Silkworm *Bombyx mori.L.* on exposure to lethal and sub-lethal doses of Selenium at 3, 4, 5 and 6 days

Dose	3 days	4 days	5 days	6 days
Control	4.5067 [b]	4.7567 [b]	5.09 [b]	5.23 [b]
Lethal	4.69 [a] (+4.06)	5.44 [c] (+14.36)	6.37 [c] (+25.27)	7.25 [c] (+38.68)
Sub-lethal	4.9800 [b] (+10.50)	4.0167 [a] (-15.55)	3.3567 [a] (-34.05)	2.84 [a] (-45.63)

* Each value is a mean of eight estimates.

** Per cent decrease over control is given in parenthesis.

*** Means with in a column followed by the same letter are not significantly different ($p > 0.05$) from each other according to Duncan's Multiple range test.

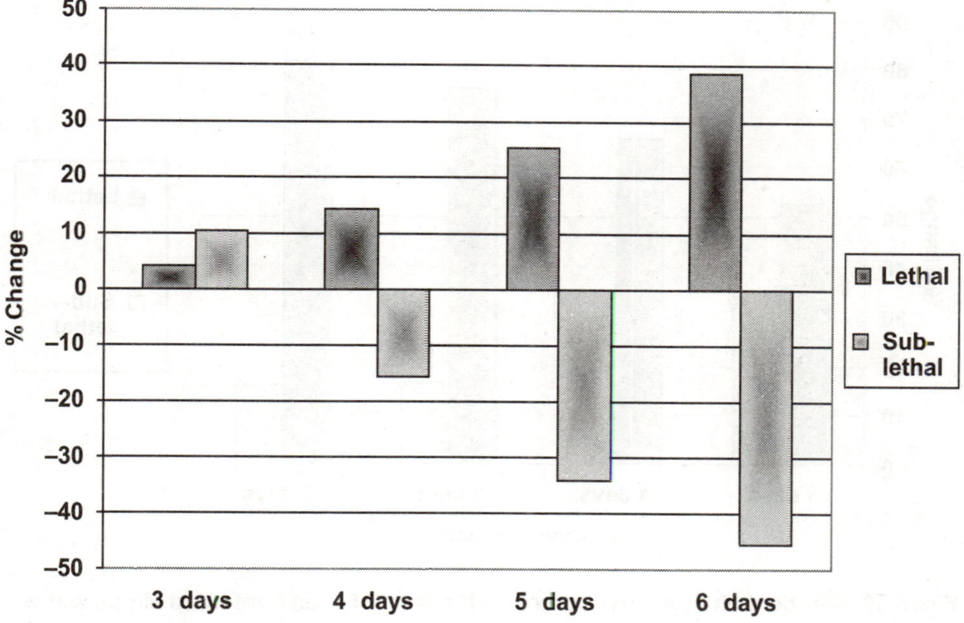

Fig. 6.18 : Per cent change over control in level of Ammonia content (μ M/100 ml.) in Haemolymph of V instar Silkworm *Bombyx mori.L.* on exposure to lethal and sub-lethal doses of Selenium at 3, 4, 5 and 6 days.

Table 6.19 : Level of Urea content (μ M/gm. wet wt.) in Fat body of V instar Silkworm *Bombyx mori. L.* on exposure to lethal and sub lethal doses of Selenium at 3, 4, 5 and 6 days

Dose	3 days	4 days	5 days	6 days
Control	0.7370 [a]	0.8049 [a]	0.8755 [b]	0.9421 [b]
Lethal	0.3476 [c] (+52.83)	0.2736 [c] (+66.00)	0.2094 [a] (+76.08)	0.2950 [a] (+81.26)
Sub-lethal	0.3942 [b] (+46.51)	0.5710 [b]) (+25.05	0.7322 [c] (+16.36)	0.7916 [c] (+15.97)

* Each value is a mean of eight estimates.

** Per cent decrease over control is given in parenthesis.

*** Means with in a column followed by the same letter are not significantly different (p > 0.05) from each other according to Duncan's Multiple range test.

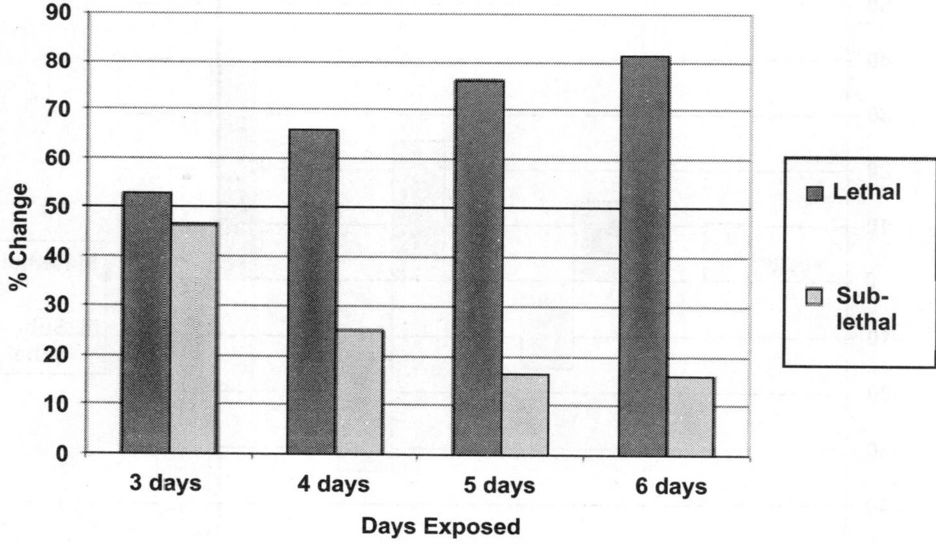

Fig. 6.19 : Per cent change over control in the level of Urea content (μ M/gm. wet wt.) in Fat body of V instar Silkworm *Bombyx mori. L.* on exposure to lethal and sub-lethal doses of Selenium at 3, 4, 5 and 6 days.

Table 6.20 : Level of Urea content (μ M/gm. wet wt.) in Malpighian Tubules of V instar Silkworm *Bombyx mori.L.* on exposure to lethal and sub-lethal doses of Selenium at 3, 4, 5 and 6 days

Dose	3 days	4 days	5 days	6 days
Control	0.3750 [a]	0.3943 [a]	0.4330 [b]	0.5010 [b]
Lethal	0.4967 [c] (+32.45)	0.4550 [c] (+15.39)	0.3273 [a] (-24.41)	0.2950 [a] (-41.0)
Sub-lethal	0.4020 [b] (+7.2)	0.4087 [b] (+3.6)	0.4540 [c] (+4.8)	0.5277 [c] (+5.32)

* Each value is a mean of eight estimates.

** Per cent decrease over control is given in parenthesis.

*** Means with in a column followed by the same letter are not significantly different ($p > 0.05$) from each other according to Duncan's Multiple range test.

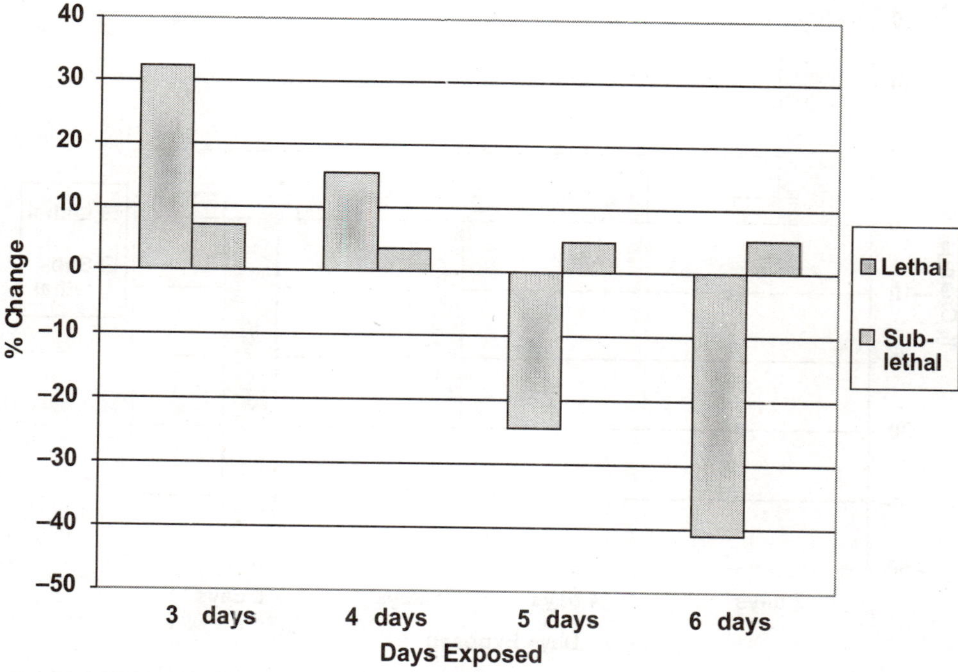

Fig. 6.20 : Percent change over control in the level of Urea content (μ M/gm. wet wt.) in Malpighian Tubules of V instar Silkworm *Bombyx mori. L.* on exposure to lethal and sub-lethal doses of Selenium at 3, 4, 5 and 6 days.

Table 6.21 : Level of Urea content (µ M/100 ml.) in Haemolymph of V instar Silkworm *Bombyx mori. L.* on exposure to lethal and sub-lethal doses of Selenium at 3, 4, 5 and 6 days

Dose	3 days	4 days	5 days	6 days
Control	0.126 [a]	0.1423 [a]	0.1630 [b]	0.1947 [b]
Lethal	0.1570 [c] (+24.6)	0.1527 [b] (+7.3)	0.1160 [a] (-28.8)	0.1127 [a] (-42.11)
Sub-lethal	0.131 [b] (+3.9)	0.155 [c] (+9.13)	0.1847 [c] (+13.3)	0.2017 [b] (+3.6)

* Each value is a mean of eight estimates.

** Per cent decrease over control is given in parenthesis.

*** Means with in a column followed by the same letter are not significantly different ($p > 0.05$) from each other according to Duncan's Multiple range test.

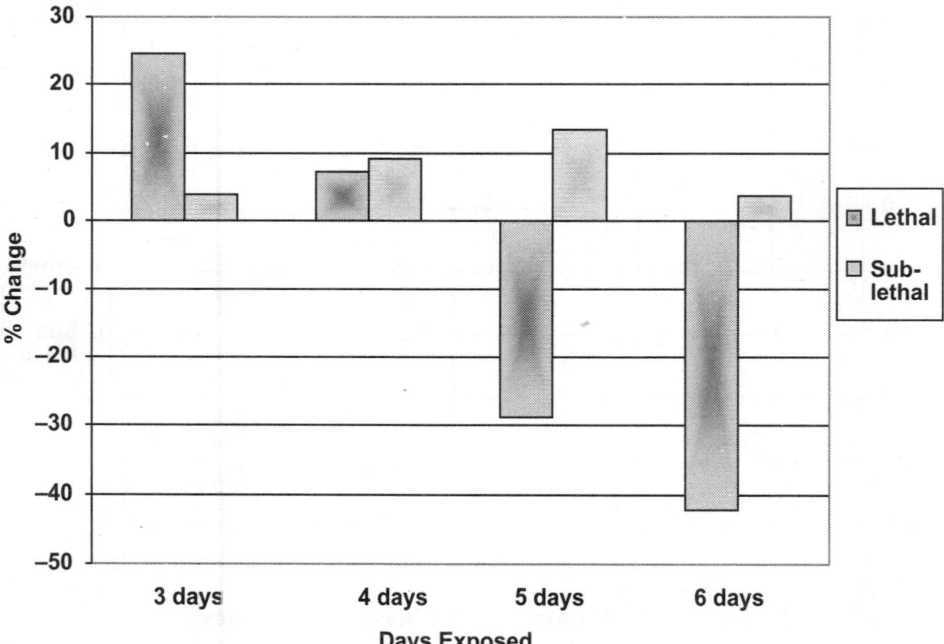

Fig. 6.21 : Per cent change over control in the level of Urea content (µ M/100 ml.) in Haemolymph of V instar Silkworm *Bombyx mori. L.* on exposure to lethal and sub-lethal doses of Selenium at 3, 4, 5 and 6 days.

studied in malpighian tubules and this increase was found insignificant at 6 days of exposure in haemolymph. However, the increase in Urea level observed at 3 day (group 2) exposure to the lethal concentration was significantly ($p < 0.05$) greater than the increase at the respective exposure period in sub-lethal concentration of Selenium (group 3) in haemolymph, fat body and malpighian tubules of V instar silkworm, *Bombyx mori L.* Among the exposure periods studied, the increase in the ammonia levels in haemolymph and malpighian tubules followed the trend 3 < 4 < 5 < 6 days, and the differences in increase between 3 and 4 days were significant. The increase in Urea levels in haemolymph, fat bodies and malpighian tubules at 3 and 4 days was observed in the order 3 > 4. Ammonia level increased in the haemolymph and malpighian tubules at 3 day of exposure to the sub-lethal concentration, whereas decrease of it on further exposure followed the trend 4<5<6 and in haemolymph, and 5<6 in malpighian tubules.

Discussion

According to Young (1970), the protein budget of the cell can be considered as an important analyte in evaluating the physiological standards of the cell. Hydrolysis of protein is quite common and proteases split proteins stepwise into amino acids. The amino acids formed due to protein breakdown will be mobilized for protein synthesis or utilized for metabolic energy production. As the proteins being the most important organic constituents, role of these in the compensatory mechanisms of silkworms can be expected during stressful conditions. The decrease in structural soluble and total protein contents in the haemolymph, fat body and malpighian tubules of selenium treated silkworms suggest the suppression of protein synthesis and/or utilization of protein for energy purposes. Suppression of protein synthesis is observed in the silkworm exposed to the lethal dose of selenium indicates the breakdown of these proteins due to active selenium toxic stress. Generally the breakdown of proteins dominates over synthesis and enhanced proteolytic activity (Harper *et al.*, 1979).

From the present study, it is evident that the breakdown of proteins is associated with steep elevation in protease activity and free amino acids level in the silkworm exposed to the lethal doses. The maintenance of proteins in a highly organized state requires an active continuous supply of energy. If protein metabolism is impaired, the organ structures breakdown and proteins partially denatures in their configuration. Dudley *et al.*, (1984) exhibited that heavy metal intoxication leads to ultra structural changes in the organ systems, which are generally associated with decreased protein synthetic activities.

Proteases hydrolyze proteins and peptide bonds result in the production of amino acids as end products. Increase in protease activity, lysosomal enzymes in the organs of silkworm exposed to the lethal dose of selenium could be due to the damage resulted in high dose of selenium to lysosomes resulting in the leakage of these enzymes into the cytosol (Singaraju *et al.*,

1991). In addition, an increase in a proteolytic activity can be due to the destruction of organ systems and there by the biochemical functions of cellular activities (Karel and Saxena, 1975 and also due to impairment of protein synthetic potentials (Garg *et al.*, 1989). As the silkworms are exposed to selenium for longer period, the intensity of the proteolytic activity increased with the increase in exposure period from 3 day to 6 days. The steep increase in the rate of accumulation of selenium over the time of exposure could be the primary reason for the progressive tissue degradation and destabilization.

However the sub-lethal dose could not cause a significant increase in 5 and 6 days of exposure except at 3 and 4 days. From this it is clear that selenium in lethal dose induce protease activity which leads to the formation of more free amino acids content causing toxicity. The effect of selenium on amino acids and protease activity is dose and time dependent. The aspartate aminotranseferases (AAT), alanine amino transeferases (AlAT) serve as a strategic link between carbohydrate and protein metabolism under physiological and pathological conditions and under environmental stress (Knox and Greengard, 1965).

In the present study the trend in the activities of both AAT and AlAT exhibits that there is a great conversion of amino acids into the keto acids to be utilized for energy purposes. It is likely that the pyruvate formed through AlAT activity may be converted to acetyl co-A to be metabolized further through the TCA cycle. Localization of AlAT and AAT (Katanuma *et al.*, 1962) in both mitochondria and cytosolic fractions of the cells have been confirmed.

A close correlation appears to exist between the mitochondria integrity and transaminase levels. (Carofoli *et al.*, 1964; Bonitenko, 1974) and any alteration in the organization of mitochondria is bound to alter the levels of enzymes associated with it. The increase in the activities of transaminase observed in the present study is in agreement with reports in literature showing their consistent increase with the enhanced gluconeogenesis (Knox and Greengard, 1965). GDH catalyses, the reversible oxidative deamination of glutamate to a keto glutarate to ammonia with pyridine nucleotide as a co-enzyme. This reaction serves as a link between protein and carbohydrate metabolism through the TCA cycle. The increase in GDH activity indicates either the increased mitochondrial permeability or the lysosomal damage or the induced synthesis of the enzyme (Johanson and Barrington, 1970). Hence it is known that GDH plays a crucial role in oxidative deamination (Harper *et al.*, 2005). The increase in the level of GDH activity coincides with the increase in the ammonia found in malpighian tubules, fat body and haemolymph of silkworm exposed to selenium at lethal dose shows the production of it through nucleotide deamination and oxidative deamination and this suggests that the fat body is the site for ammonia production, detoxification and its mobilization. It is evident that excess of uric acid liberated from tissues is not converted which means that the fat body tissue is not able to detoxify all the excess ammonia either produced by the fat bodies per se or being transported from other tissues. Hence it is accumulated in the haemolymph probably malpighian tubules could not filter out all the ammonia from the haemolymph; hence accumulation of ammonia in large amounts is seen even in malpighian tubules. Sub-lethal dose did not show significant increase in ammonia level either in tissues or in haemolymph indicates that sub-lethal dose of selenium could not exert toxic effect on silkworm protein metabolisam.

Chapter

7

Histology

Introduction

Digestion and absorption of nutrients to various tissues has acquired great significance in the physiology of an animal. Metabolic activities of different physiological systems affect when sufficient quantities of vitamins, minerals, amino acids, proteins and carbohydrates are not reached the tissue. Certain trace elements like–Se, Ni, Zn and cobalt play a good role in the nutrition. The activities of the cell are carried out most efficiently within a narrow range of conditions. It is therefore important that the environment within the cell and in the animal in general should be kept as near optimal as possible, a process known as 'Homeostasis'. When this balance is not maintained, ultimately pathological changes and structural modification of a cell will occur. There is a persistent relationship between the histopathological changes and progression of external symptoms.

In the present chapter, an attempt has been made to study the histological aspects of some tissues such as fat body and malpighian tubules of *Bombyx mori L.* and changes under exposure to selenium.

Normal Histology of Malpighian Tubules

Excretion is the removal, from the body, of harmful products of internal metabolism. The faces are not normally included in this category. Since during its passage through the alimentary canal the food is morphologically external to the body and the process of defaecation is otherwise known as egestion. There are two main aspects of excretion namely carbonaceous and nitrogenous. Carbonaceous excretion is the removal of the carbon dioxide resulting from cellular respiration and it is carried out by the respiratory surface. Nitrogenous excretion is the removal of the wastes of nitrogenous metabolism especially that of amino acids.

The excretory system is primarily responsible for homeostasis, which maintains a constant level of salts and water and osmotic pressure in the haemolymph. Toxic compounds absorbed from the environment are also eliminated. Some molecules entering the body from the environment may be too large or too toxic to be dealt with by the excretory system. Hence various tissues are involved in metabolizing them to detoxify or more readily extractable substances. Generally, toxic materials are eliminated from the body in the form of fluid urine, which is composed of unselective substances of the haemolymph. Useful compounds in the urine are reabsorbed and others in excess may be added to the urine. The excretory organs of arthropods, are very varied and only in the primitive Peripatus is there a series of segmental paired organs comparable to annelids. In crustaceans there is a single pair of excretory organs in one segment, which may be either the antennary or maxillary segment. This suggests that with increasing efficiency it has been possible to reduce the number of excretory organs from a segmental series to one pair, but the remaining pair is not the same in all species. The opposite extreme is seen in insects which, in the adult form, are usually land animals requiring to conserve water. Excretion is performed by numerous fine out growths of the front of the hindgut called malpighian tubules. The length of the tubules ranges from 2–100 mm in different insects and each tubule is one cello thick with one or a few cells encircling the lumen. Each malpighian tubules is functionally divisible into two parts; the distal part absorbs from the haemocoel and secretes into the lumen a solution of sodium and potassium urates; in the proximal part the secretion of carbon dioxide causes the precipitation of the uric acid, and sodium and potassium bicarbonates are reabsorbed. The uric acid passes on to the hindgut and is voided with the faeces, thus achieving nitrogenous excretion with the minimum of water loss. Under transverse section microvilli and plasma membrane with more number of mitochondria were observed (O' Donnel *et al.*, 1985). Misra (1981) exhibited, gradual degeneration of cells alongwith its nuclei in malpighian tubules of *Hieroglyphus nigroreletus* under stress conditions.

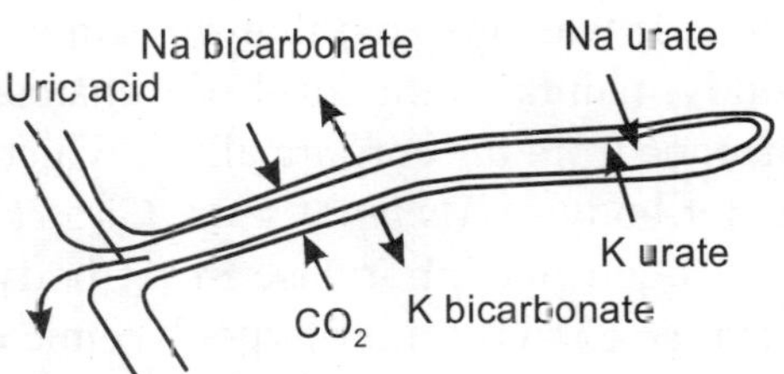

Fig. 7.1 : Malpighian tubules summarizing the chemical processes involved.
Source : An introduction to functional systems in animals by Springthorpe (1973).

Normal Histology of Fat Body

The insect fat body is the principal organ of intermediary metabolism site for the requirement of the physiological activity and is similar to the liver of mammals in function.

The fat body is derived from mesoderm of the coelomic sac and composed of fat contained cells and its surface is covered by thin membrane. They are almost circular in shape during young ages and become multiangular in the older larval stage. It has one circular nucleus and some times more than two nuclei. Fat body principally has the trophocytes and in addition, it may have urate cells, hemoglobin, tracheal cells, mycetocytes and some other oenocytes. The structure of a trophocyte may vary according to its developmental stage and nutritional status. Urate cells characteristically contain large crystalloid spherules of uric acid. Haunerland *et al.*, (1990); and Schin et al., (1977) reported that the fat body is regionally differentiated to perform different functions such as storage in perivisceral body and synthesis in perivisceral body as observed in many insects of Lepidoptera. In accordance with metabolism, the fat body serves as the aimed tissues affected by various hormones such as juvenile hormone, moulting hormone. Fat body also serves to store fifty per cent of glucose ingested to meet the requirement of energy consumption.

The fat body also takes part in the metabolism of proteins and amino acids. Synthetic ability of protein in the fat body is related to the brain and carpus cardiacum and is regulated by the neuro hormones. According to Palli and Locke (1988), 90 per cent of total haemolymph proteins are synthesized by the fat body in larval insects. Tojo *et al.*, (1980), studied the regulatory mechanism of protein synthesis in *Bombyx mori L.* which is under hormonal control. Juvenile hormone is the factor, which suppresses the protein synthesis, which again restarts at the end of V instar when juvenile hormone disappears from the haemolymph. Fat body accumulates carbohydrates in the form of glycogen during its active feeding periods for utilization at the time of moulting period. It was reported that the conversion of glycogen to trehalose in the fat body maintains the level of trehalose under the control of hyperglycemic hormone from the corpora allata, which activates glycogen phosphorylase in the fat body of *Manduca sexta*. Gies *et al.*, (1988) reported that the activity of glycogen phosphorylase in fat body was regulated by adepokinetic like hormone (AKH) under hypoglycemic condition.

The fat body also can synthesize the vitamin-C and contain a lot of xanthin oxidase and degenerate the amino acids into uric acid into body fluid to be expelled out. The arginine activity is quite high, it can be transformed into urea and ornithine by arginase. It was described that ultra structural changes in skeletal muscle and myocardium of selenium deficient pigs (Van Vleet *et al.*, 1976 and Van Vleet *et al.*, 1977). Muth (1963) reported the muscular degeneration or weakness in sheep due to selenium deficiency.

Results

1. *Histopathological changes in malpighian tubules:* Severe pathological changes were observed in the malpighian tubules of group 2 (Plate-V b) like cloudy swellings and degenerations of tubular cells. The swollen tubular cells projected into the lumen of the tubules, which reduced the size of the lumen. Some of the tubular cells exhibited granular cytoplasm. Some of the tubules were dilated and necrosis was seen in the proximal tubules.

In group 5 (Plate-VI b) also malpighian tubules showed noticeable changes, the nuclei of the tubular cells were not visible and those which could be seen appear to be pyknotic (A degenerative state of the cell nucleus). The cytoplasm of many tubular cells was granular. Necrosis in proximal tubules was evident, but the extent of damage was relatively less than in group 2 (Plate-V b) silkworms. Silkworms in group 8 (Plate-VII b) exhibited tubular cell oedema, round cell infiltration, tubular cell necrosis. But the extent of damage was more than that of group 4 (Plate-VI b) silkworms. Silkworms in group 11 (Plate-VIII b) exhibited severe degenerative changes as seen by wide spread disintegration of malpighian tubules. Necrosis of tubular cells was most pronounced. Presence of casts in tubular lumen, aggregation of chronic inflammatory cell in the interstitium was observed. In group 3 (Plate-V c) silkworms showed necrosis in the tubular cells. The nuclei of the most of the oedematus tubules were not visible and appeared pyknotic and were in the process of nuclear degeneration. In group 6 (Plate-VI c) silkworms, there were no appreciable changes and moderate tubular necrosis was observed.

In group 9 (Plate-VII c) silkworms exhibited hyperplasia of tubular tufts together with necrosis in tubular epithelium and cellular infiltration in interstitium. In group 12 (Plate-VIII c) silkworms did not exhibit any pathological changes except limited signs of necrosis.

2. *Histopathological changes in Fat bodies:* Changes were observed in fat bodies of group 2 (Plate-I b), group 5 (Plate-II b), group 8 (Plate-III b) and group 11 (Plate-IV b) of silkworms compared to the controls. Silkworms in group 2 (Plate-I b) exhibited with hypertrophoid condition. Vacuoles appeared in the cytoplasm were some what less and the membranous sheath surrounding the fat cells were slightly destructed. Similarly, in group 5 (Plate II b) silkworms also showed extensive cell necrosis. Hyperplasia and fatty degeneration were conspicuous. However the degenerative lesions were severe than those in group 2 (Plate-I b). In group 8 (Plate-III b), the fat body section showed severe structural alterations like cell necrosis of reticulo-endothelial cells and hyperplasia. Scattered area of fatty degeneration of fat body was also evident. In group 11 (Plate-IV b) also appeared massive cell necrosis, cell outline disappearance, degeneration of nuclei were the most characteristic features. Hypoplasia of reticulo- endothelial cells was observed. Appreciable changes were noticed in group 3 (Plate-I c) pushing of the nucleus to the peripheral regions of the fat body cells, degeneration of the nucleus, pyknotic clubbing of nuclei due to cytoplasmic disappearance. In the group 6 (Plate-II c) silkworms exhibited only mild structural changes, insignificant necrosis was observed. Significant changes like degeneration of nuclei, dissolution of cytoplasm were markedly noticed in group 9 (Plate-III c). Whereas, in group 12 (Plate-IV c) no conspicuous changes were observed except a mild necrosis.

Discussion

In a majority of insects toxic chemicals that enter the tissues are excreted often after being metabolized. The changes frequently resulted in the compound become less toxic, but the converse is sometimes true and toxicity is enhanced. Some compounds notably those that are water soluble are metabolized to components that are subsequently incorporated into the insect's primary metabolic pathways. Most of the lipophylic substances are first converted into water soluble components and are excreted. Many different enzyme systems are known to be involved in these reactions and some systems are almost certainly ubiquitous. This process may occur in a variety of tissues as there is no organ comparable with the liver *i.e.*, the focus for comparable reactions in vertebrates. Activity of the appropriate enzymes often occurs in the midgut, fat body and malpighian tubules. Different species differ widely in their ability to metabolize toxic substances. Amongst plant feeding insects this variation contributes to host pant specificity. The caterpillar of *Manduca sexta,* for example habitually feeds on alkaloid containing plants, including tobacco and it is able to do his because it detoxifies the alkaloids (Snyder *et al.*, 1994). Although the end products of this metabolic process are commonly excreted, there sometimes sequestered. Sequestration may also occur without any prior metabolism. In some species and the compound has been stored in the cuticle, perhaps minimizing the risk to the insect. But the other species store the defensive substances in glands or in the haemolymph. Similarly silkworm fat bodies accumulate most of the toxic substances for the detoxification. Greater accumulation of selenium in groups 2, 5, 8 and 11 might have resulted in extensive degeneration of structure of fat body may be due to the failure of detoxification mechanisms. The most significant changes observed are cell necrosis, fatty degeneration and hyperplasia. Most histological alterations described in fat body of silkworms are available on exposure to pollutants like BHC, malathion and phosphamidon and silkworm exposure to pathogens like Bm NPV and CPV and the changes observed are vacuolization, fatty generation, nuclear degeneration, hyperplasia and cell necrosis (Brown, 1963; Chattoraj and Sharma, 1964; Gawrilescu and Peters, 1931; Hoskins, 1940; Ingram, 1955; Lockau and Ludicke, 1952; McMullen, 1965; Misra, 1981). The changes exhibited initially the appearance of destructed membranous of sheath surrounding the fat cells and hypertrophied could be correlated with excessive selenium concentration in haemolymph. Consequently, extravasations of selenium ions diffusing out into surrounding areas might be responsible for excessive damage. Misra 1981, reported that the fat cells are either destroyed or dissolute and scattered nuclei and hypertrophied on exposure to insecticides. Xeros, (1956) reported that the fat body nuclei contained the typical virogenic structure. Jagadish Naik, (2005) reported that 50 per cent tukra fed larvae exhibited mild destructivity and normal vacuolization appeared in the cell of cytoplasm of fat body. The present study has shown that selenium ions exert toxic effect on fat body tissue since soft tissues retain only a small fraction of dietary toxicant (Shupe *et al.*, 1962). It is likely that the structural alterations observed in the present study are consequent of the selenium tissue retention. Further the alterations observed in the fat body of silkworm are dose dependent and also time dependent. The findings have been further substantiated by biochemical disobsorbents observed in the fat bodies of silkworm treated with different doses of selenium.

The disarranged fat tissue vaculations in fat body cells followed by the shrinkage of fat cells and dissolution of tubular structure suggest that the depletion in its glycogen reserves. Corresponding to the cellular damage to the fat body tissue the decrease in proteins, increase in ammonia, impaired oxidative metabolism reflects the potent toxicity of selenium to fat body.

Eventhough in the presence of sub-lethal dose of selenium is decreased the selenium treated silkworm exhibited some histopathological changes were more at higher selenium dose and at 6 days of exposure. This could be attributed to sodium selenite, which is toxic due to its great solubility and stability. The lower amounts of sodium selenite resulted in very mild histopathological changes in the sub-lethal treated silkworm fat body groups 3, 6, 9 and 12. Accumulation and excretion studies have also confirmed the marked decrease in the absorption of selenium in silkworm and less accumulation in the fat body, as wells as marked increase of faecal selenium excretion.

In insects both the malpighian tubules and hind gut function together as excretory organs. The malpighian tubules collect the filtrate from the haemolymph and pass this primary urine to the hind gut. Insect excretion has been reviewed extensively (Springe, 1990, Nicholson, 1993 and Pannabecker, 1995). Since malpighian tubules are mainly concerned with the elimination of undetoxified and unwanted substances from the haemolymph of the silkworm, it is more prone to the toxicity of various toxic pollutants. Selenium treated silkworms in all the groups exhibited significant alterations in the architecture of malpighian tubules. The histopathological changes were in the direct proportion to the dosage and period of selenium administration.

Areas of cloudy swellings, degeneration and necrosis of malpighian tubules could be resulted due to increased selenium ions. Similar to the histopathological changes observed in the selenium exposed silkworms in the present investigation are also reported by the earlier workers in different experimental toxicants and insecticides. Misra (1981) reported that those pesticides are excreted through the malpighian tubules. He also pointed out that malpighian tubules are severely damaged in BHC, Malathion and phasmomidon experimental silkworms. He presumed that in the presence of toxic levels of pesticides in the haemolymph the tubular structure of malpighian tubules is selectively damaged by its passage. According to Misra (1981), pesticide exposed malpighian tubules appear degeneration of the cells along with their nuclei, narrowing of the lumen of the tubules and hypertrophied condition. Histopathological alterations like necrosis of Microvilli, cloudy degeneration of tubular cells in malpighian tubules of poisoned insects have been nóticed (Hoskins, 1940; Lockau and Ludicke, 1952; McMullen, 1965). The findings of pioneer investigations showing extensive destruction to the malpighian tubules of selenium intoxicated silkworm, substantiate the observations of the above studies. Higher levels of selenium in the haemolymph and malpighian tubules also support the cytotoxicity to the tubular cells the malpighian tubules.

On the other hand sub-lethal dose of selenium also produced certain histopathological changes in 3, 6, 9 and 12 groups of silkworms. The physiological and biochemical alterations are very less and more or less similar to controls in the 9 & 12 groups of silkworms. Correspondingly the structural damage to malpighian tubules in these groups is very less particularly at 6 days of exposure.

Plate–I

a, b & c : Transverse sections of the fat body of V instar Silkworm *Bombyx mori L.* (PM X NB_4D_2) exposed to lethal and sub-lethal doses of Selenium at 3 day. X 450(H&E)

a : Group 1 (Control)

b : Group 2 (Lethal)

c : Group 3 (Sub-lethal)

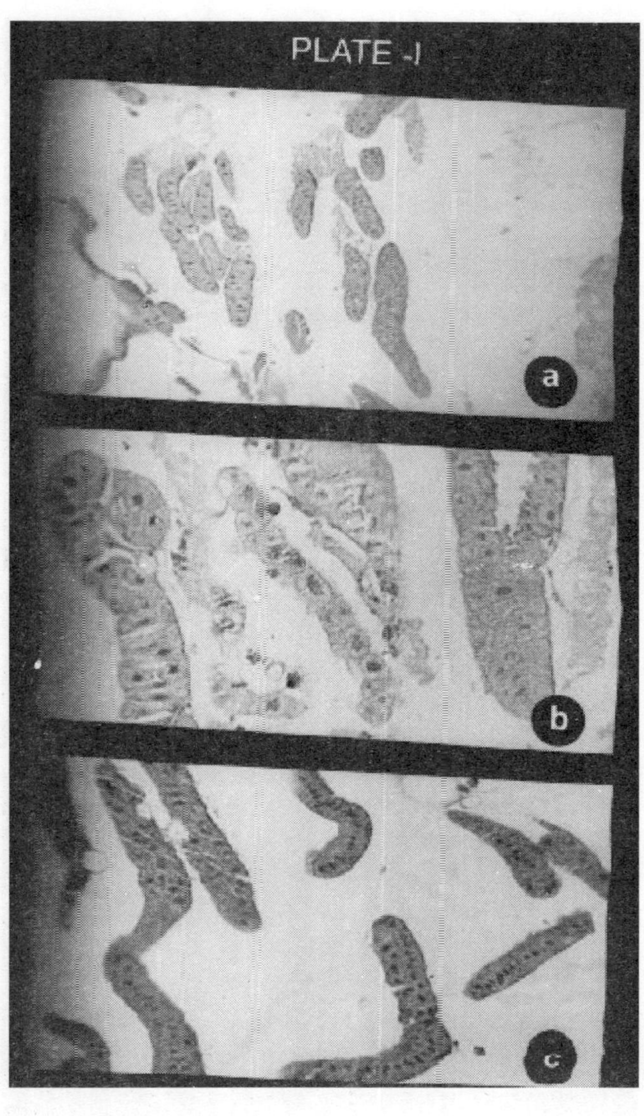

Plate-II

a, b & c : Transverse sections of the fat body of V instar Silkworm *Bombyx mori L.* (PM X NB_4D_2) exposed to lethal and sub-lethal doses of Selenium at 4 day. X 450(H&E)

a : Group 4 (Control)

b : Group 5 (Lethal)

c : Group 6(Sub-lethal)

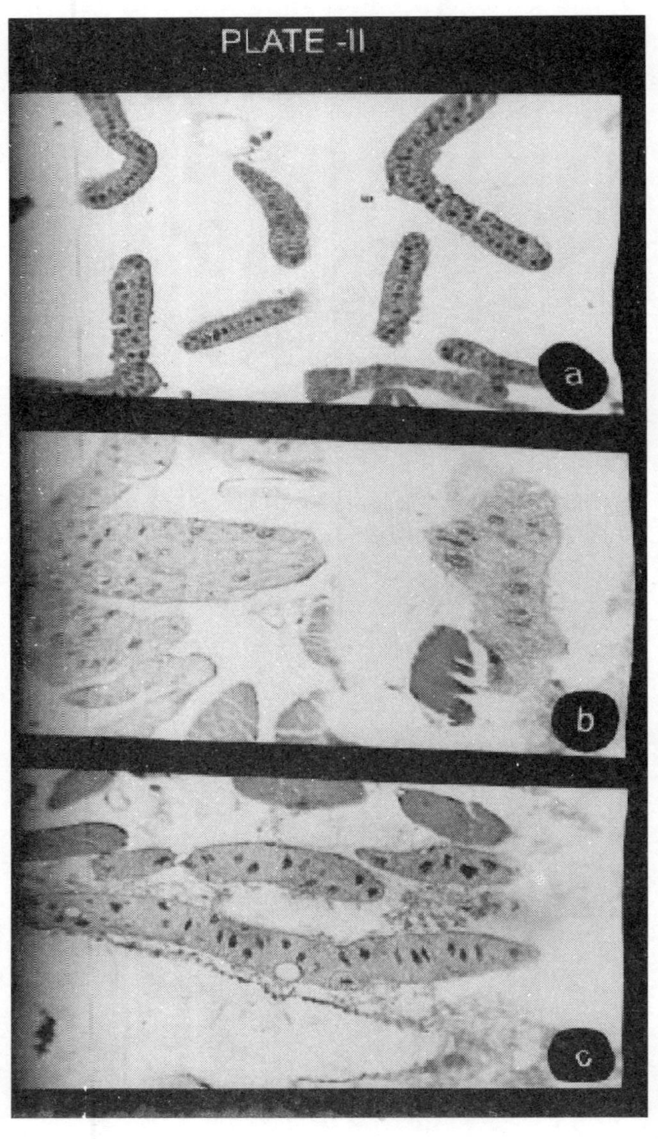

Plate-III

a, b & c : Transverse sections of the fat body of V instar Silkworm *Bombyx mori L.* (PM X NB_4D_2) exposed to lethal and sub-lethal doses of Selenium at 5 day. X 450(H&E)

a : Group 7 (Control)

b : Group 8 (Lethal)

c : Group 9 (Sub-lethal)

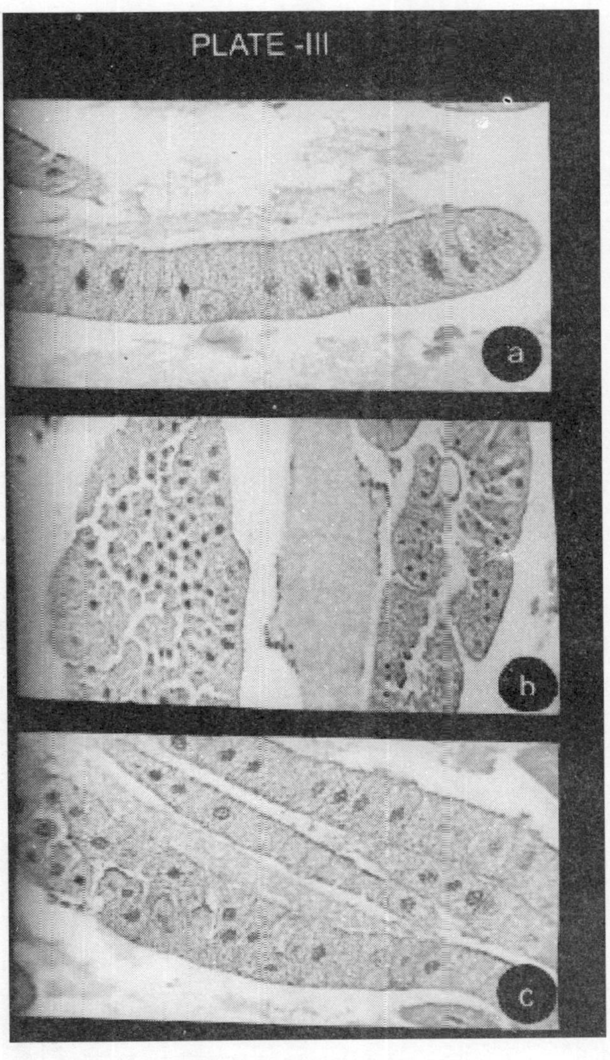

Plate-IV

a, b & c : Transverse sections of the fat body of V instar Silkworm *Bombyx mori L.* (PM X NB_4D_2) exposed to lethal and sub-lethal doses of Selenium at 3 day. X 450(H&E)

a : Group 10 (Control)

b : Group 11 (Lethal)

c : Group 12 (Sub-lethal)

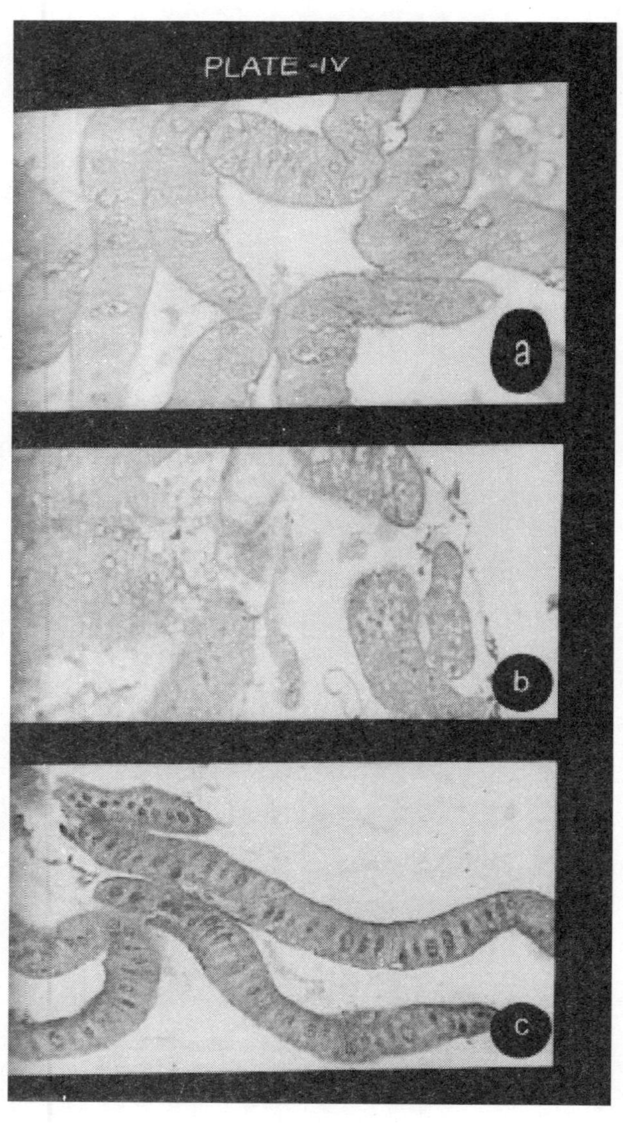

Plate-V

a, b & c : Transverse sections of the malpighian tubules of V instar Silkworm *Bombyx mori L.* (PM X NB_4D_2) exposed to lethal and sub-lethal doses of Selenium at 3 day. X 450(H&E)

a : Group 1 (Control)

b : Group 2 (Lethal)

c : Group 3 (Sub-lethal)

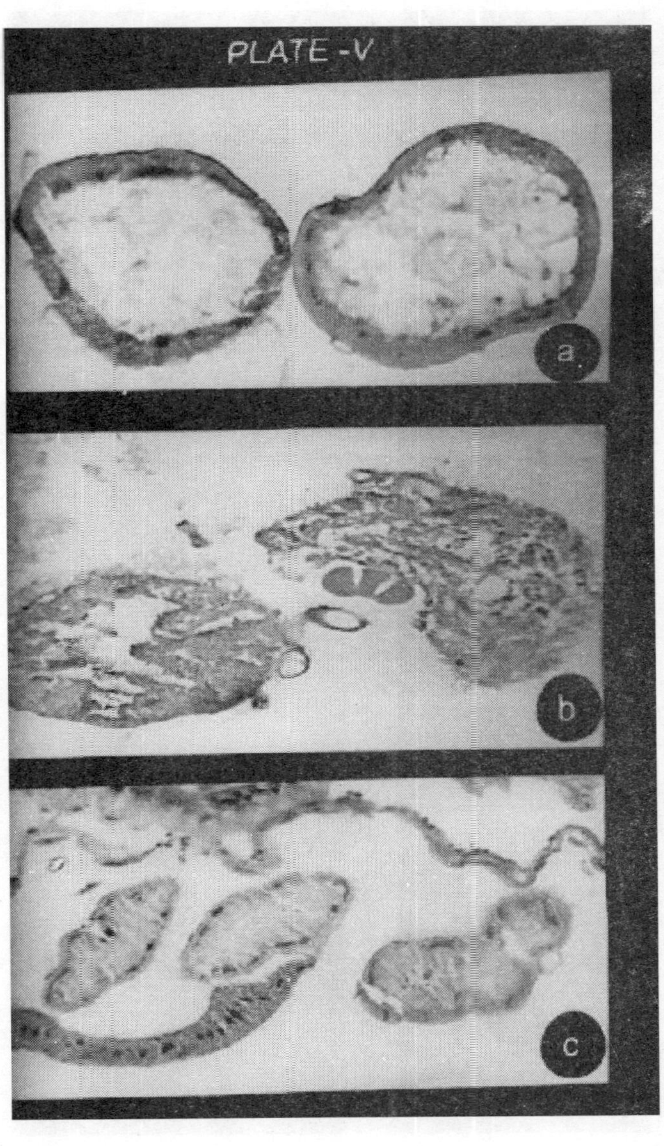

Plate-VI

a, b & c : Transverse sections of the malpighian tubules of V instar Silkworm *Bombyx mori L.* (PM X NB_4D_2) exposed to lethal and sub-lethal doses of Selenium at 4 day. X 450(H&E)

a : Group 4 (Control)

b : Group 5 (Lethal)

c : Group 6 (Sub-lethal)

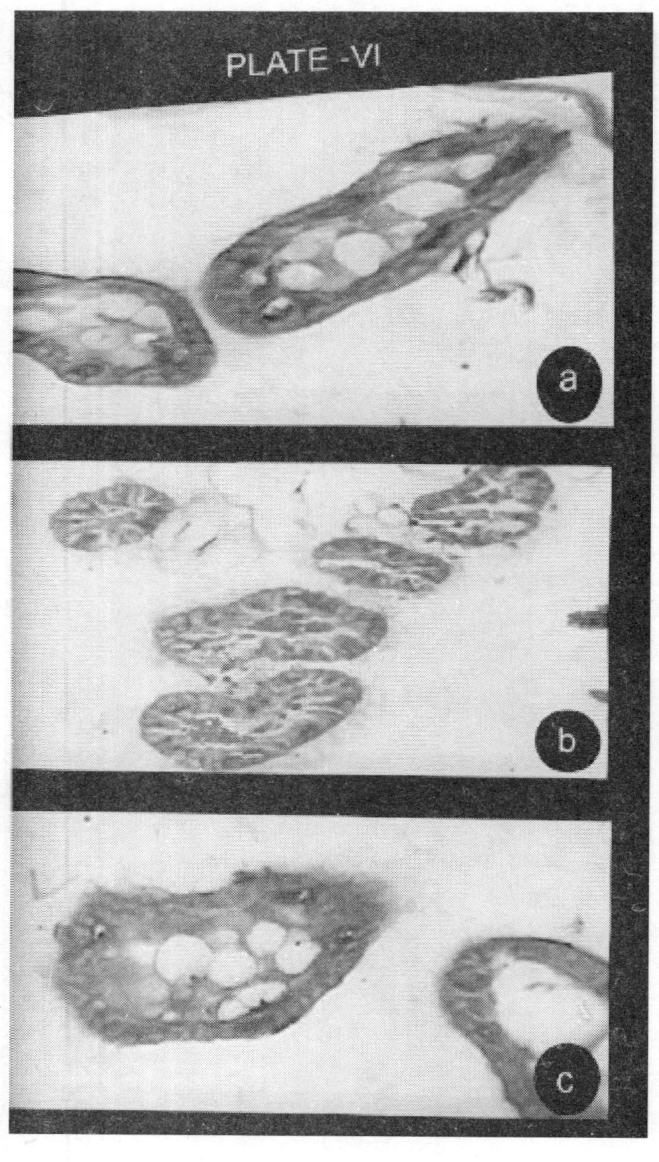

Plate-VII

a, b & c : Transverse sections of the malpighian tubules of V instar Silkworm *Bombyx mori L.* (PM X NB_4D_2) exposed to lethal and sub-lethal doses of Selenium at 5 day. X 450(H&E)

a : Group 7 (Control)

b : Group 8 (Lethal)

c : Group 9 (Sub-lethal)

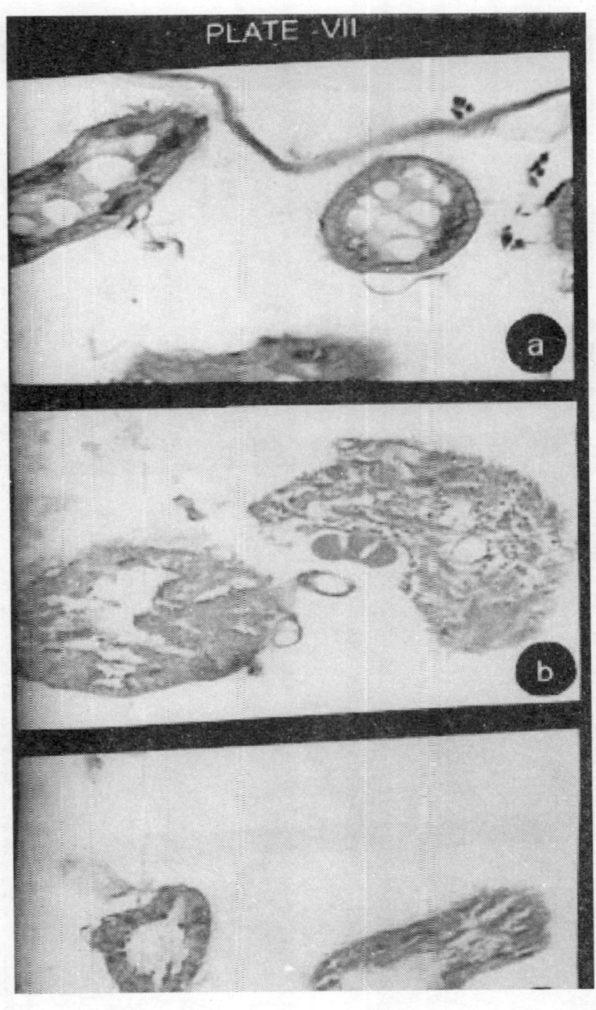

Plate–VIII

a, b & c : Transverse sections of the malpighian tubules of V instar Silkworm *Bombyx mori L.* (PM X NB_4D_2) exposed to lethal and sub-lethal doses of Selenium at 6 day. X 450(H&E)

a : Group 10 (Control)

b : Group 11 (Lethal)

c : Group 12 (Sub-lethal)

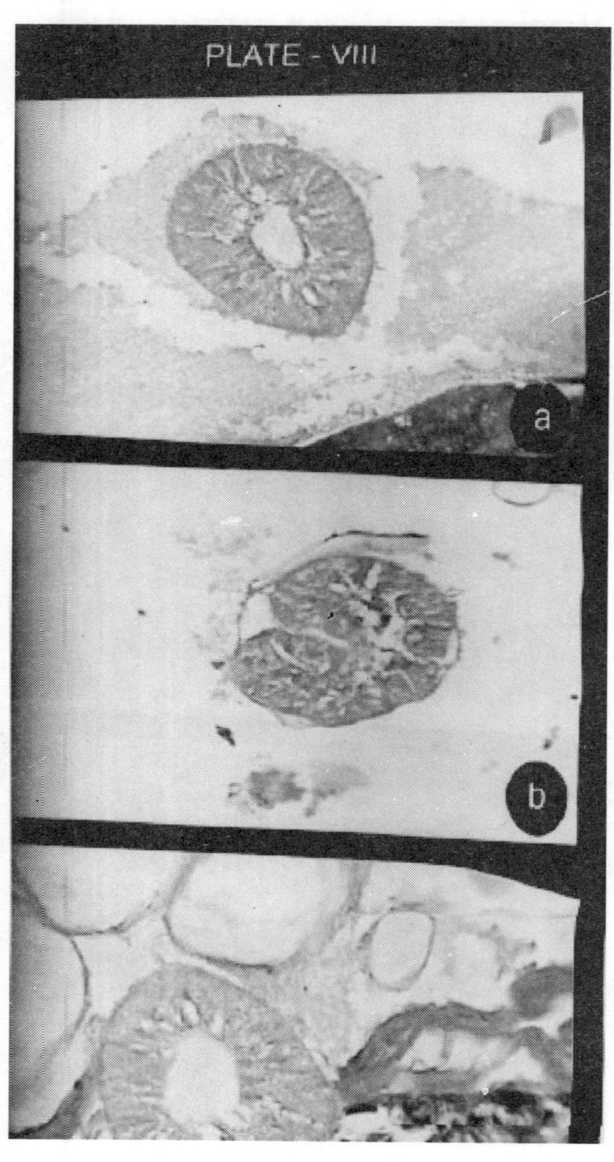

CHAPTER

8

Cocoon Commercial Characters

Introduction

The cocoon is the raw material used for reeling raw silk. It is in fact, a protective shell made up of a continuous and long proteinaceous silk filament made up of sericin and fibroin secreted from the silk glands of the mature silkworm prior to pupation for self-protection from adverse climatic factors and natural enemies. Economics of silk reeling industry and the quality of reeled product depend largely on the quality of cocoons used for reeling.

Size of the cocoon generally indicates the quantity of silk filament and percentage of silk in the cocoon and also the nature of the bave. Size of the cocoon, is generally indicated by the number of cocoons per litre and the number may vary from 110 to 150 with UV/BV cocoon and more with the multivoltine cocoons. The extent of tightness or firmness indicates the shell texture and compactness of the cocoon. The air and water permeability of cocoons in boiling is largely dependent on the hardness of the cocoon shell. The deflossed cocoon has a granular surface wrinkled with convolutions. The sparseness/closeness of the convolutions indicates the degree of granulation. The outer layers of the cocoon have the coarser granules than in the inner layers. The important commercial character of cocoons is "weight". It indicates the approximate quantity of raw silk that can be reeled from it. The quantity of cocoons used to produce one unit of raw silk is called "Renditta", probably derived from rendition. The weight depends on the race, which may range from 1 gram to 3 grams. Shell weight is an another important as it is the shell that yields silk for reeling, largest shell weight may range from 300 mg as in pure races to 350 to 500 mg as in hybrids. Indian multivoltine hybrids weighs hardly 150 mg, and it is still less in multivoltine pure races. The ratio between the weight of silk shell and the whole weight or the cocoon calculated as a percentage gives us the shell ratio. The Indian multivoltine hybrids contain shell ratio from 12 to 15 per cent while newly evolved hybrids 16-19.1 per cent and the multivoltine pure varieties contain from 10-12 per cent and the Japanese reeling cocoons contain as high as 19-25 per cent. The filament length of a cocoon varies according to the breed. The multivoltines can yield above 500 mts. of silk filament and 700-1000 mts. or filament can be unwound from the cocoons of bivoltine races.

Cocoon crop quality and quantity is generally depended on the vigour of silkworm breeds and also is influenced by the mulberry leaf quality (Venugopala Pillai *et al.*, 1987). According to Bajpeyi *et al.*, (1991), the raw silk production per hectare of land is approximately 52 kgs in China and 40 kgs. in Japan. Whereas in India, it is only 31 kgs. It can be said that the low productivity in India, is due to poor quality of leaf. There were many studies to improve quality and quantity of cocoons by supplementing with nutrients such as sugars, proteins, lipids, vitamins etc. (Nagarajan and Radha, 1990; Masilamani *et al.*, 1991; Bajpeyi *et al.*, 1991). However, a few studies were reported (Nagarajan and Radha, 1990; Masilamani *et al.*, 1991; Radhakrishnaiah and Chamundeswari, 1994; Sailaja *et al.*, 1997). Narasimha Murthy and Govindappa, (1988), demonstrated that supplementation of cobalt improved the larval weights shell weight and ERR. Bajpeyi *et al.*, 1991, added calcium, magnesium and iron to mulberry leaves and observed significant enhancement of rearing rate and silk content in the cocoon. Radhakrishnaiah and Chamundeswari, (1994) found that zinc and nickel are acting as supplements to stimulate the protein synthesis. There are reports available on the dietary administration of several vertebrate hormones and prostaglandins enhancing both developmental and metabolic processes of silkworm *Bombyx mori L.* (Bharathi, 1993; Bharathi, 1995; Chaudhury and Medda, 1986 and 1992; Bharathi, 1993 and 1995; Megadum and Hooli, 1988 and Magadum and Magadum, 1993.)

Many reviews on the dietary effect of selenium in animals revealed that the selenium supplementation stimulated the growth in animals. Selenium, although required in only of small amounts in animals, has an essential metabolic role as part of the enzyme glutathione peroxidase that protects cell membranes against oxidative damage (Hoekstra, 1975). Severe deficiency of selenium in the diets of sheep was reported which was characterized by clinical symptoms of white muscle disease and mortality in lambs. Supplementation with selenium increase wool production, body weight gain and reproductive rate was reported in sheep (Wilkins *et al.*, 1982, Langlands *et al.*, 1991, Langlands *et al.*, 1994; Whelan *et al.*, 1994). Deka *et al.* (1999) described the role played by selenium in the improvement of silk protein function, which resulted in increased cocoon commercial parameters of Eri silkworm, *Philosamia Cynthia L.*

In the present study an attempt was made to study the impact of selenium on exposure to lethal (32.39 μg/kg body wt.) and sub-lethal doses (6.47 μg/kg body wt.) of selenium on cocoon commercial characters of silkworm *Bombyx mori L.*

Results

From the data presented in the Table 8.1 and Figure 8.1, it is seen that the cocoon commercial characters such as single cocoon length, cocoon width, cocoon weight, shell weight, shell percentage, filament weight and filament length registered a significant decrease ($P < 0.05$) when compared to controls (groups 1, 4, 7 and 10) in all silkworms (groups 2, 5, 8 and 11) on exposure to lethal dose of selenium. The per cent decrease at lethal dose was progressed towards 6 day and was in the order $3 < 4 < 5 < 6$ days.

In sub-lethal dose all the cocoon characters registered an elevation in all groups of V instar silkworms (groups 3, 6, 9 and 12)) exposed at 3, 4, 5, and 6 days. Based on per cent values, this increase was high at 6 day exposure period and followed the trend $3 < 4 < 5 < 6$.

Discussion

Cocoon characteristic features determine the quality, quantity and cocoon commercial value of the silk. The quality of the cocoon, mainly depend on the healthy larval growth which in turn reflects on the quality and quantity of mulberry leaves, fed during silkworm rearing besides adopting advanced rearing technology. In the present investigation the cocoon commercial characters such cocoon length, cocoon width, cocoon weight, shell ratio, filament weight, and filament length of silkworm cocoon are significantly decreased when exposed to lethal dose of selenium when compared to controls. Venkat Reddy *et al.* (1991) reported that the lethal and sub-lethal doses of fenvelrate might have exerted its effect on the silk gland of the silkworm. As a result the protein synthesis might have hindered and reduced the spinning activity and ultimately resulted in poor silk emission. Metabolism of selenium on silkworm is still not fully understood and also not clear whether selenium acts as protein inhibitor/inducer. However in vertebrates many reports (Wilkins *et al.*, 1982; Langlands *et al.*, 1991 and 1994; Whelan *et al.*,1994) suggest that supplementation with selenium can increase wool production, body weight gain and reproductive rate. (Langlands *et al.*, 1991) reported that concentration of selenium in plasma 0.06 and 0.024 were associated with deficiencies in reproducing ewes and supplementation resulted in increased wool growth and fibre diameter.

Compared to controls, all the cocoon characters, such as cocoon length, cocoon weight, filament length, filament weight, shell ratio, etc. have

Table 8.1 : Cocoon commercial characters of V instar Silkworm *Bombyx mori L.* exposed to lethal & sub-lethal doses of Selenium

Days exposure	Dosage	Cocoon length (mm)	Cocoon width (mm)	Cocoon weight (gm.)	Shell weight (gm.)	Shell Percentage %	Filament length (mt.)	Filament weight (mg.)
3 days	Control	31.82 **b**	17.56 **b**	1.44 **b**	0.25 **b**	15.2 **b**	541.04 **b**	218.19 **b**
	Lethal	30.4 **a** (- 4.46)	15.81 **a** (- 9.96)	1.16 **a** (- 19.4)	0.178 **a** (- 28.0)	11.56 **a** (- 23.9)	367.91 **a** (-31.9)	199.19 **a** (- 8.7)
	Sub-lethal	37.22 **c** (+16.9)	21.34 **c** (+21.5)	1.85 **c** (+20.47)	0.35 **c** (+40.0)	18.5 **c** (+21.7)	765.54 **c** (+41.0)	250.89 **c** (+14.9)
4 days	Control	32.99 **b**	18.23 **b**	1.48 **b**	0.268 **b**	15.72 **b**	580.2 **b**	230.2 **b**
	Lethal	21.12 **a** (-35.9)	12.26 **a** (-33.1)	0.96 **a** (-35.1)	0.14 **a** (-47.0)	10.20 **a** (-35.0)	240.86 **a** (-58.0)	160.00 **a** (-30.4)
	Sub-lethal	38.77 **c** (+17.5)	22.46 **c** (+23.2)	1.88 **c** (+27.02)	0.4. **c** (+49.2)	19.19 **c** (+22.07)	823.06 **c** (+42.0)	270.62 **c** (+17.5)
5 days	Control	33.86 **b**	19.01 **b**	1.52 **b**	0.301 **b**	16.3 **b**	628.29 **b**	232.45 **b**
	Lethal	15.42 **a** (-54.4)	10.89 **a** (-47.37)	0.85 **a** (-44.07)	0.11 **a** (-63.4)	8.40 **a** (-48.4)	220.15 **a** (-64.0)	150.29 **a** (-35.0)
	Sub-lethal	39.96 **c** (+18.0)	23.51 **c** (+23.7)	1.95 **c** (+28.2)	0.451 **c** (+49.9)	20.0 **c** (+22.7)	898.20 **c** (+43.9)	274.8 **c** (+18.2)
6 days	Control	34.40 **b**	19.8 **b**	1.56 **b**	0.34 **b**	17.8 **b**	775.4 **b**	245.09 **b**
	Lethal	12.80 **a** (-67.9)	9.4 **a** (-52.5)	0.61 **a** (-60.8)	0.101 **a** (-70.0)	6.25 **a** (-64.0)	214.78 **a** (-72.0)	100.47 **a** (-59.0)
	Sub-lethal	40.84 **c** (+18.7)	24.75 **c** (+25.0)	2.01 **c** (+28.9)	0.53 **c** (+55.8)	22.00 **c** (+23.5)	1110.2 **c** (+43.0)	292.3 **c** (+19.3)

* Each value is a mean of eight estimates.

** Per cent decrease over control is given in parenthesis.

*** Means with in a column followed by the same letter are not significantly different ($p > 0.05$) from each other according to Duncan's Multiple range tests.

registered a significant increase on exposure to sub-lethal dose of selenium. It can be attributed that selenium in lower dose might be responsible for promotion of silk synthesis. The results indicate that selenium in minute quantities trigger the protein synthesis in the silkworm. The results were also inconformity with the significant growth of silkworm on exposure to sub-lethal dose of selenium. It is known that selenium deficiency produce marked decrease in growth and greatly interfere with efficiency of food utilization by animals. In the present study, supplementation of selenium in sub-lethal dose to silkworm might have shown impact on the efficiency of feed utilization and growth. Thereby the increased energy status could be utilized for protein synthesis. From the above discussion, it can be concluded that the toxicity of selenium on silkworm cocoon commercial characters is having adverse impact on administration of lethal dose.

However, in the silkworm exposed to sub-lethal dose of selenium the cocoon commercial characters were improved. Thus selenium influenced the bio-chemical, physiological pathways to improve the cocoon commercial characters. It can be assumed that the harmful microbial flora of silkworm might have been eliminated in the sub-lethal doses of selenium without affecting the silkworms, which ultimately improved the general health of the silkworm leading to betterment of cocoon commercial characters.

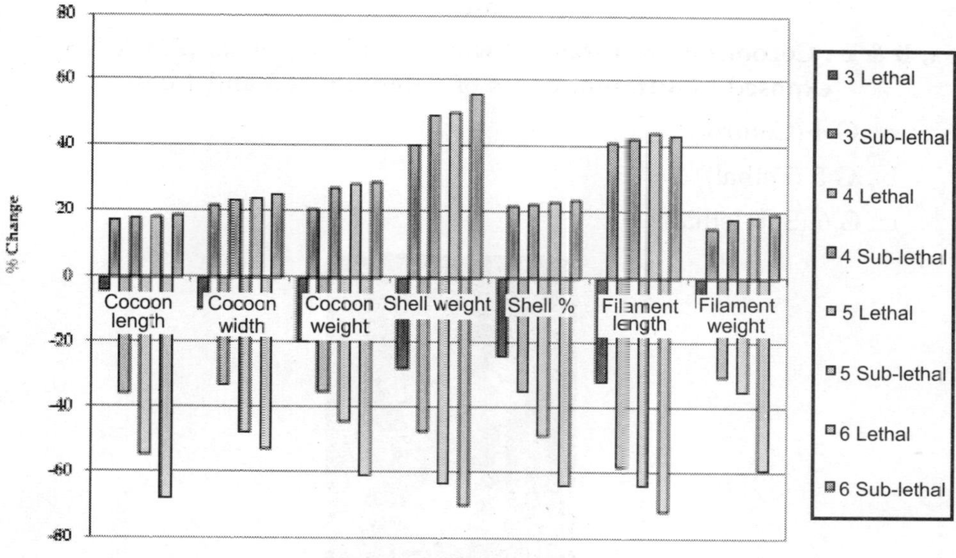

Fig. 8.1 : Per cent change over control in Cocoon Commercial Characters of V instar *Bombyx mori L.* exposed to lethal and sub-lethal dose of Selenium.

Plate-IX

a, b & c : Cocoons of V instar Silkworm *Bombyx mori L.* (PM X NB_4D_2) exposed to different doses of Selenium at 3 day.

a : G 1 (Control)

b : G 2 (Lethal)

c : G 3 (Sub-lethal)

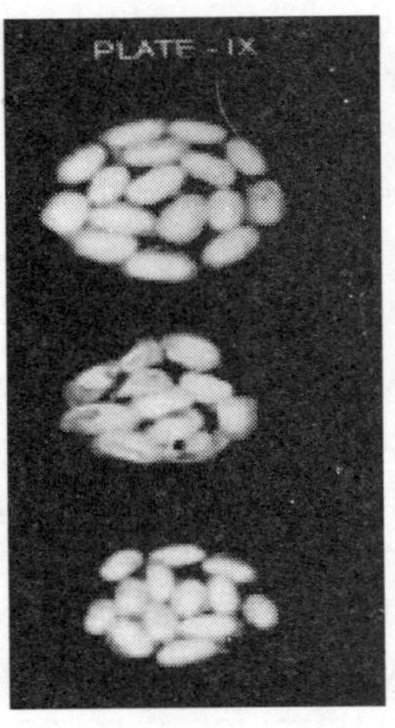

Plate-X

a, b & c : Cocoons of V instar Silkworm *Bombyx mori L.* (PM X NB_4D_2) exposed to different doses of Selenium at 3 and 4 day.

a : G 4 (Control)

b : G 5 (Lethal)

c : G 6 (Sub-lethal)

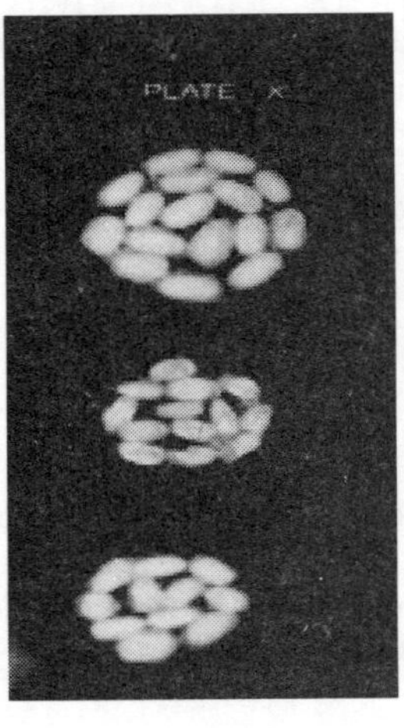

Plate-XI

a, b & c : Cocoons of V instar Silkworm *Bombyx mori L.* (PM X NB_4D_2) exposed to different doses Selenium at 3, 4 and 5 day.

a : G 7 (Control)

b : G 8 (Lethal)

c : G 9 (Sub-lethal)

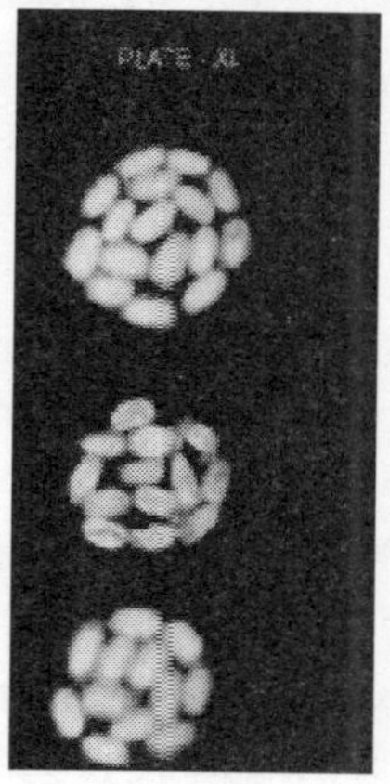

Plate-XII

a, b & c : Cocoons of V instar Silkworm *Bombyx mori L.* (PM X NB_4D_2) exposed to different doses of Selenium at 3, 4, 5 and 6 day.

a : G 10 (Control)

b : G 11 (Lethal)

c : G 12 (Sub-lethal)

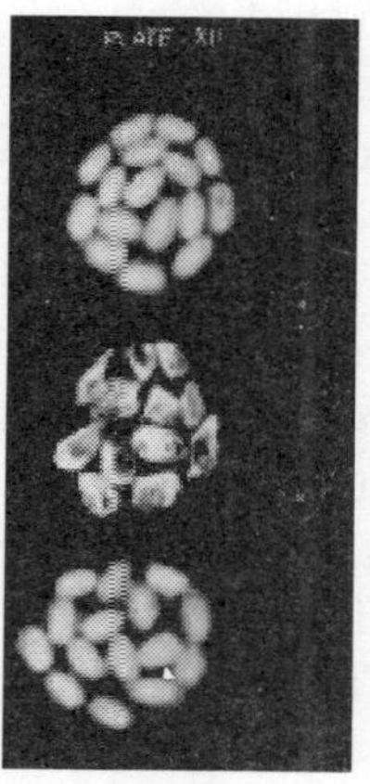

CHAPTER

9

Summary and Conclusion

Some nutritional, bioaccumulation, excretion, carbohydrate metabolism, protein metabolism and cocoon commercial characters have been studied in the silkworm *Bombyx mori L.* with reference to lethal and sub-lethal doses of selenium and changes have been correlated with histological changes in fat body and malpighian tubules of V instar silkworm.

1. To begin with the toxicity of selenium, nutritional parameters has been evaluated using lethal dose (32.38 µgm/kg. body wt.) and sub-lethal (6.47 µgm/kg) doses of selenium. Selenium ingestion caused a significant loss of body weight and decrease in faecal output, which apparently, were due to decreased consumption of food. The changes in the nutritional parameters appeared as a dose and time dependent in the lethal dose of selenium treated silkworms. The treatment with sub-lethal dose of selenium showed significant changes in all nutritional parameters. The changes in the nutritional parameters appeared as dose and time dependent sub-lethal treated silkworms.
2. The bioaccumulation studies revealed that selenium bioaccumulation increased with increase in Selenium dose and period of exposure. The rate of bioaccumulation increased with period of exposure in silkworms, which received the sub-lethal dose of selenium, were significantly less compared to the silkworm treated with lethal dose of selenium. The rate of bioaccumulation of selenium was also very less. The amount of excretion through faeces increased in both lethal and sub-lethal selenium treated silkworms with the period of exposure and dose. Further, the effect of sub-lethal dose on the excretion of selenium was significantly less than the silkworm exposed to lethal dose of selenium. The excretion of selenium through faecal matter increased with dose and period. However, the rate of excretion

increases with the period of exposure when compared to the lethal dose.

3. As the carbohydrates are primary source for energy, shifts in them were observed in silkworm. Exposure to lethal dose of selenium resulted in the increase in haemolymph glucose and trehalose levels with corresponding decrease in the fat body glycogen and increase in glycogen phosphorylase and glucose-6-phosphotase activities. It indicated that an acceleration of glycogenolysis in fat body and decrease in peripheral utilization of glucose was observed. The abnormal elevation of these enzyme activities might have occurred by the inhibitory effect of the selenium and the release of neurosecretory hormones due to their direct effect on glycolysis or glycogen metabolism. Further the decreased utilization of glucose for energy purposes could also contributed to increase in haemolymph glucose level.

   These hyperglycemic changes were more in higher doses whereas in sub-lethal doses the changes were less and decreased with the period of exposure. Silkworm treated with the sub-lethal dose of selenium showed again hyperglycemia, which was less in degree compared with hyperglycemia appeared in lethal dose.

4. Since the building up and breaking down of protoplasm is concerned with protein metabolism, effects of lethal dose and sub-lethal dose of selenium on silkworm *Bombyx mori L.* were assessed. All protein fractions (soluble, structural and total) showed a gradual decrease in haemolymph, fat body and malpighian tubules of silkworm exposed to lethal dose of selenium. Further the decrease was accompanied with increased levels of free amino acids and the activities of proteases, AAT, AlAT and GDH. The results indicated proteolysis and enhancement of transdeamination reactions. The elevation of ammonia and decrease in urea was also observed in all the tissues studied. The selenium effect on protein metabolism is dose and time dependent, thus the proteolysis increased with increase in dose and time of exposure. The silkworm treated with the sub-lethal dose of selenium showed similar effects of lethal dose by selenium on 3 day whereas 4 day onwards sub-lethal dose showed insignificant changes especially at 5, 6 days of exposure.

5. Microscopic study of tissues such as fat body and malpighian tubules revealed interesting pathological changes in all the lethal dose of selenium treated silkworms. The changes in tissues are dose and time dependent. In sub-lethal dose of selenium treated silkworms, mild to severe changes were observed on the 3 day of exposure. Whereas

very mild and insignificant changes were observed in the sub-lethal selenium treated silkworm on further exposures at 4, 5 and 6 days.

6. Cocoon characteristic features such as cocoon length, width, cocoon weight, shell weight, shell ratio, filament length and filament weight on exposure to lethal and sub-lethal doses of selenium were evaluated. Significant decrease over control was observed in silkworms on exposure to selenium. These inhibitory changes may be attributed to the impairment of protein synthetic activity due to toxic stress as induced by the selenium. Whereas significant increase of these characters over control was observed in the sub-lethal dose of selenium exposed silkworms. These findings indicate the role played by selenium in the enhancement of silk production in the silkworms exposed at sub-lethal dose.

   On the whole the results of this investigation throw light on the commercial aspects of sericulture in determining the lethal and sub-lethal doses for V instar silkworms, with reference to selenium. This also helps in determining the safe periods/safe sub-lethal dose of the selenium which directs to provide suitable quantity of selenium as a nutritional stimulant in the silkworm rearing. This knowledge will be helpful in understanding for the nutritional studies of other trace elements. Further the results of this project are expected to understand indirectly the economic values for the maintenance of cocoon production under normal and micronutrient supplementation conditions.

Bibliography

Abe, T. & R., Nakaya., 1951.The Mechanism of the effectiveness of the Selenite Medium (for salmonella). *Japan J. Bacteriol.* **6** : 463-465.

Abel T, Bhatt R, Maniatis T., (1992). A Drosophila CREB/ATF transcriptional activator binds to both fat body–and liver-specific regulatory elements. *Genes Dev.*, **6:** 466–480.

Abdullaev, F.I. C. Mac Vicar & G.D. Frankel., 1992. Inhibition of Selenium of DNA and RNA Synthesis in normal and Malignant Human cells in vitro. *Cancer Letters,* **65:** 43-49.

Ahmad, T.A. & Chaplin, A.E., 1984. The Effect of Experimental Conditions on the Activity of Pyruvate Kinase from the Aductor Muscle of the Mussel. *Mytilus edulis (L). J. Anim. Morphol. Physiol.,* **31:** 107-118.

*Aizawa, K. & Murai, S., 1957. *Seibutsu Butsurikagaku.,* **4:** 23-26.

Albert, R., 1973. Accumulation of Toxic Metals with Special Reference to their Absorption, Excretion and Biological Half-times. *Environ. Physiol. Biochem.,* **3:** 65–107.

Alfthan, G., 1984. A Micromethod for the Determination of Selenium in Tissues and Biological Fluids by Single test tube Fluorimetry,. *Anal. Chem. Acta.* **165:** 187-194.

Ali, S.Y. & Lack, C.H., 1965. Studies on the Tissue Activator of Plasminegen. Distribution of Activator and Proteolytic Activity in the Sub-cellular Fractions of Rabbit Kidney. *Biochem. J.,* **96:** 63.

Allaway W.H., Moore D.P., Oldfield J.E. & Muth O.H., 1966. In: Selenium Assimilation in Animals. *J. Nutr.* **88:** 411.

Anderson, A.D. & Patton, R.L., 1955. Uric and Synthesis in Insects. *J. exp. zool.,* **128:** 443-451.

Arthur, J.R., 1991. The Role of Selenium in Thyroid Hormone Metabolism. Can. *J. Physiol. Pharmacol.,* **69:** 1648-52.

Ashida, M. & Wyatt G.R., 1979. Properties and Activation of Phosphorylase Kinase from Silkmoth Fat Body. *Insect. Biochem.* **25:** 102-108.

Assem, H. & Hanke, 1983. The Significance of the Aminoacids during Osmotic adjustments in Telecast fish-1 changes in the Euryhaline. *Sarotherodon mossambicus. Comp. Biochem. Physiol.,* **74(A):** 531-536.

*Audas-A., Hugan-G-R., & Razniak-H,. 1995. *Journal of Toxicology and Env. Health,* **44(1):** 115-122.

Banuelos, G.S., Ajwa, H.A., Mackey, B., Wu, L. & Cook, C., 1997. Evaluation of Different Plant species used for Phytoremediation of high Selenium. *Journal of Environment Quarterly,* **26:** 639-646.

Bonhorst, C.W., 1955. Selenium poisoning. Anion Antagonisms in Yeast as Indicators of the Mechanism of Selenium Toxicity. *J. Agr. and Food Chem.* **3:** 700-703.

Baines SB, Fisher NS, Stewart R., 2002. Assimilation and Retention of Selenium and other Trace elements from Crustacean foodby Juvenile Striped bass (*Morone saxitalis*). *Limnol Oceanogr* **47:** 645–655.

Bajpeyi, C.M., Singh, R.N. & Thangavelu, K., 1991. Supplementary Nutrients to increase Silk Production. *Indian Silk,* **30(7):** 41-42.

Band, I.L., 1977. Comparative Study of the Quantitative Evolution of Glycogen and Trehalose during Starvation of *Bombyx mori L. Anm. Aliment,* **31(3):** 323-329.

Banks, P., Bartley, W. & Birt, L.M., 1976. In: *The Biochemistry of the Tissues. John Wiley and Sons, New York.* **2:** 23-28.

Bano, Y., S.A & Tariq, H., 1981. Effects of Sub-lethal Concentration of DDT on Muscle Constituents on an air Breathing cat fish, *Ani. Sci.,* **90:** 33-37.

*Barker, S.B. & Summerson, W. H., 1941. *J. Biol. Chem.,* **138:** 535.

Bed ford, J., (1977). The Carbohydrate levels of Insect Haemolymph. *Comp. Biochem. Physiol.* **57:** 83-86.

Benchamin, K.V & Nagaraj, C.S., (1987). *Appropriate Sericulture Techniques, Silkworm Rearing Techniques,* 63-106.

Bengtsson G., Hakkarainen J., Jonsson L., Lannek N. & Lindberg, P., 1978. Requirement for Selenium (as selenite) and Vitamin E (as tocopherol) in weaned pigs. The Effect of valuing alfa Tocopherol levels in a Selenium Deficient diet on the Development of the VESD Syndrome. *J. Anim. Sci.,* **46:** 143.

Benjamin, N. Berg and Henry Simms, (1960). Nutrition and Longevity in the Rat II Longevity and onset of Disease with Different levels of Food Intake. *J. Nutr.* **71:** 255-262.

Benjamin, N Berg, (1960). Nutrition and Longevity in the Rat I. Food intake in Relation to size, Health and Fertility. *J. Nutr.* **71:** 242-254.

*Bergmeyer, H. O., 1965. In: *Methods in Enzymatic Analysis (ed.) Academic Press, New York,* pp. 40.

Bharathi, D., 1993b. Effect of PGF2¦Áon the Organic Constituents of Haemolymph of Silkworm Larvae, *Bombyx mori L.J.Seric.* **1:** 225-228.

Bharathi, D., 1995. Effect of Vertebrate Pituitary Extract on the Nitrogen Turnover in the Faecal Matter of *Bombyx mori L. J. Seric.* **3:** 71-74.

Bharathi, D. and Miao Yun-gen(çŇÔÆ,ù). 2002. Effect of Vertebrate Hormones and Prostaglandins on Growth, Silk quality and Metabolic Activities of *Bombyx mori L.* Journal of Zhejiang University SCIENCE , **3(3):** 344-347.

Bhosale, S.H., Yadwad, V.B & Kallapur, U.L., 1988. Residual toxic effect of Ekalux EC-25 on the Biochemical Constituents of the Fat Body V instar B.mori. *Ind. J. Seric.,* **XXVII(2):** 73-77.

Bonitenko, Y.U., 1974. Isoenzymes of Aspartate Amino Transferse (AAT) in Acute Aichloro Ethane Poisoning. *Gig. Tr. Prof. Zabol.,* **7:** 46-47.

Bopp B.A., R.C. Sonders & J.W.Kesterson, 1982. Metabolic Fate of Selected Compounds in Laboratory Animals and Man. *Drug. Metab. Rev.,* **13:** 271–318.

Brain Research, 2004. *Brain Research Reviews,* **45(3):** 164-178.

Broome, C.S., 2004. *The American Journal of Clinical Nutrition,* **80(1):** 154-162.

Brown, H., 1945. The Determination of Uric acid in Human Blood. *J. Biol. Chem.*, **158:** 601-608.

Brown, A.W.A., 1963. Insecticide Resistance in Arthropods. *World Health Organisation, Geneva*, pp.23-28.

Buchaman - Smith, J.G., E.C. Nelson, & A.P. Tillman, 1969. Effect of Vitamin. E and Selenium Deficiencies on Lysosomal and Cytoplasmic Enzymes in Sheep Tissues., *J. Nutr.* **99:** 387-394.

Burk R.F., D.G. Brown, R.J. Seeley & C.C. Scaief III, 1972. Influence of Dietary and Injected Selenium on whole body Retention, route of Excretion and Tissue Retention of Selenium in the Rat. *J. Nutr.*. **102:** 1049-1055.

Burk R.F., and Hill KE. Regulation of Selenoproteins. *Annu Rev Nutrition. 1993.* **13:** 65-81.

Bursell, E., 1963. Aspects of the Metabolism of Aminoacids in the Tsetsefly, Glossina (Diptera). *J. Insect. Physiol.*, **9:** 317-335.

Caisey, J.D & King, D.J., 1980. Clinical Chemical Values for some Common laboratory Animals. *Clin. Chem.*, **26**: 1877-1879.

Cameron, C.A., 1880. *Science, Proc. Roy. Dublin Soc.*, **2:** 231.

Campbell, T.W., H.G. Walker and G.M. Coppinger. 1952. Some Aspects of the Organic Chemistry of Selenium. *Chem.Rev.* **50:** 279-349.

Candy, D.J & Kilby, B.A., (1959). Site and Mode of Trehalose Biosynthesis in Locust, *Nature London*, **183:** 1594-1595.

Candy, D.J & Kilby, B.A., (1961). The Biosynthesis of Trehalose in the Locust Fat Body, *J. Biochem.*, **78:** 531-536.

Carla R., Raltson J. & Lloyd Blackwell, Nicolas V.C. Raltson, 2006. Effects of Dietary Selenium and Mercury on House Crickets (Acheta domesticus L.). Implications of Environmental Coexposures. *Environmental Bioindicators.* **Vol (1):** 98-109.

Caroll, N.V. Longley, R.W. & Roe, J.H., 1956. Glycogen Determination in Liver and Muscle by use of Anthrome Reagent. *J. Bio. Chem.*, **220:** 583-593.

Carr, A., Sawicki, E and Ray, F.E., 1958. 8-Selenopurines. *J. Org. Chem.* **23:** 1940-42.

Challenger, F., 1951. Biological Methilation. *Advan. Enzymology.* **12:** 429-491.

Chandrasekhar, P.M. & Geetha Bali., 1987. Glycogen Level and Glycogen Phosphorylase Activity in the eggs of Silkworm *Bombyx more* (L.). Proc. *Ind. Acad. Sci.*, **96(1):** 49-54.

Chapman, R.F. In: *The Insects Structure and Function 4th edition, Cambridge University Press.*

Chefurka, W. 1965. Intermediary Metabolism of Carbohydrates in Insects. In: *The Physiology of Insecta. (ed.) M. Rockstein Academic Press, New York*, **2:** pp. 670.

Chen, P.S., 1966. Aminoacid and Proteca Metabolism in Insect Development. In: Advances in Insect Physiology (eds) J.W.L. Beamert, J.E., Treherne & V.B. Wiggleswroth, *Academic Press, London and New York*, **3:** 53-132.

Chitra, C., & Sridhara, S. 1973. Transport of Sugars by the Fat Body of the Silkworm, Bombyx mori (L.). *J. Insect. Physiol.*, **19:** 2053-2061.

Chaudhuri, A., Medda, A.K.,1986. Changes in Protein and Nucleic acid Content of Gonads of Silkworm, Bombyx mori at different Developmental Stages after Thyroxine Treatment. *Proc.Natl.Acad.Sci.*,**56:** 301-306.

Chaudhuri, A., Medda, A.K., 1992. Thyroxine Induced Alterations in Glycogen Content of fat Body of female Silkworm, Bombyx mori (Race-Nistari) during larval, pupal and adult stages Development. *Annals of Entomol.* **10:** 17-21.

Chattoraj, A.N. and Sharma, V.P., 1964. Water loss in *Periplaneta Americana (L.)* with the application of certain insecticides. *Beitr. Ent.*, **14:** 525-532.

Clampitt, R.B. & Hart, R.J., 1978. The Tissue Activities of some Diagnostic Enzymes ten Mammalian Species. *J. Comp. Pathol.*, **88:** 607-621.

Clegg, J.S & Evans, D.R., (1961). Blood Trehalose and Flight Metabolism in the Blow Fly, *Science*, **134:** 54-55.

Clyburn, B.S., Richardson, C.R., Montgomery J.L., Pollard G.V., Herring A.D., & Miller, M.F., 2001. Effect of Selenium Source and Vitamin E level on Performance and Meat Quality of Feed lot Steers. In "Science and Technology" in the Feed industry. (T.P. Lyons and K.A. Jacques, eds) P.P. 377-392. *Noltingham Univ. Press. Nottingham, U.K.*

Collett, M.E., M. Rheinberger & E.G. Little., 1933. On the Question of the Specificity of the Intracellular Dehydrogenases. V. Toxicity of Arsenic, Selenium and Tellurium Compounds to the Dehydrogenase Systems of Frog and Fish Muscle. *J. Bio. Chem.* **100:** 271-275.

Combs, G.F. Jr., Clark, L.C., Turnbull, B.W., 1997. Reduction of Cancer Risk with an Oral Supplement of Selenium. *Biomed. Environ. Sci.* **10:** 227-34.

Combs, G.F. Jr. & Grey, W.P. 1998. Chemophreventive Agents Selenium, *Pharmace Ther.*, **79:** 179-92.

Cori, G.T. & Cori, C.F., 1945. The Enzymatic Conversion of Phosphorylse 'a' to 'b'. *J. Biol. Chem.*, **158:** 321-332.

Cori G.T. & Illingworth, B. & Keller, D.J., 1955. Muscle Phosphorylase In: Methods in Enzymology. *Vol. 1 (eds.) S.P. Colowick and No. Kaplan, Academic Press, New York,* pp. 200- 205.

Corvillain, B., Contempre, B., Longombe, A.U., Goyens, P., Gervy-Decoster, L., Lamy, F.J., Vander Pas, J.B., (1993). Selenium & Thyroid, how the Relationship was Established. *Am. J. Clin. Nutr.*, **57 (2 Suppl.):** 244-248.

Crompton, M. & Birt. I.M., (1967). Changes in the amounts of Carbohydrates Phosphagen and related Comps during the Metamorphosis of the Blow Fly. Lucilia Cuprina. *J. Insect. Physiol.*, **13:** 1575-1592..

*Daniels, R.A., 1996. *Biological Trace Element Research*, **54:** 155-199.

Davies, D.T.P., Kradaver, K. & Weissmann, G., 1970. Neutral Protease of Gramtocyte Lysosomes : Inhibition and Activation. *Fed. Proc.*, **29(1):** 784.

Davis, R.A. and Fraenkel, G., (1940). The Oxygen Consumption of Flies during Flight. *J. exptl. Biol.* **17:** 402-407.

Davis, N.C. & Smith, E.L., 1955. Assay of Proteolytic Enzymes. *Meth. Biochem. Anal.*, **2:** 215-257.

Dean RL, Locke M, and Collins JV, 1985. Structure of Fat Body. In: *Comprehensive Insect Physiology, Biochemistry, and Pharmacology*, Vol 3, ed Kerkut GA, Gilbert LI. Pergamon Press, Oxford, 155–210.

Deka, J., M.R.H. Azad, S. Saharia, D. K. Sharma and A. Borkotoki, (1999). Effect of Sodium Selenite on Nutritional Indices, Cocoon Characters, Silk gland, Protein and Productivity of Silk yarn of ERI Silkworm, (*Samia cynthia ricini*). *Proceedings of NSTS, 3, Department of Sericulture, University of Agric. Sciences, GKVK, Bangalore.*

Delvi, M.R., 1972. Eco-physiological Studies on in the Gross Hopper, *Poicoelocerus pictus. Ph.D Thesis, Bangalore University, Bangalore India;* pp. 166.

Delvi, M.R. & Pandian, T.J., 1972. Rates of Feeding and Assimilation in Grass Hopper, *Poicoelocerus pictus*. *J. Insect. Physiol.* **18:** 1829- 43.

*Denuce, J.M., 1958. *Z. Naturforsch.* **13(b):** 215-218.

Dezwaan, A. 1977. Anaerobic Energy Metabolism in Bivalve Molluscs. *A. Rev. Oceanogr. Mar. Biol.,* **15:** 103-187.

Dhavale, M.D & Masurekar, U.B. 1986. Valuations in the Glucose and Glycogen Content in the Tissues Sylla Serrata under the Influence of Cadmium Toxicity. *Geobios,* **13:** 139-142.

Dhavale, M.D., Masureker, V.B. & Giridhar, B.A., 1988. Cadmium Induced Inhibition of Na+ / K+ ATPase Activity in Tissues of Crab, Scylla serrata (Forskal). *Bull. Environ. Contam. Toxicol.,* **40:** 759-763.

Dingwall, D. 1962. Rev. Article. Selenium Analogues of Biologically Active Sulphur Compounds. *J. Pharm. and Pharmacol.* **14:** 765-775.

Dow, J.A.T. and Davies, S.A., (2003). Integrative Physiology and Functional Genomics of Epithelial Function in a Genetic Model Organism. *Physiol. Rev.* **83:** 687-729.

Downer, R.G.H., (1985). Lipid Metabolism In: *Comprehensive Insect Physiology, Biochemistry and Pharmacology.* **Vol.10:** ed. G.A. Kerkut and L.I. Gilbert, pp. 77-113. *Oxford; Pergmon Press.*

Duchateau, G. & Florkin, M., 1959. Surla trehalosemie des insects etsa signification. *Arch. Intern. Physiol.,* **67:** 306.

*Dudley, H.C., 1936. *Amer. J. Hyg.,* **123:** 169.

Dudley, E.R., Svododa, D.J. and Klassen, C.D., 1984. Time Course of Cadmium Induced Ultrastructural Changes in Rat Liver. *Toxicol. Appll. Pharmacol.,* **76:** 150-160.

Duncan, D.M., 1955. Multirange and Multiple Tests. *Biometrics.* **42:** 7-42.

Echner, I.A., 1971. Demonstration of Phosphorylase and Uridine Diphosphate Glucose-glycosyl Transferase Activities. *J. Histochem. Cy to Chem.,* **19 (2):** 133 (Eng.).

Ehrhardt, P., (1962). Untersuchungen zur Stotwech selphysiologie von Megoura viciac Buckt. *Einer phloemsaugender Aptade Z. Vergl. Physiol.* **46:** 169-211.

F.I. Ferguson, J.C., 1982. A Comparative Study of the Net Metabolic Benefits derived from the Uptake and Release of Free Aminoacids by Marine Invertebrates. *Biol. Bill.,* **162:** 1-17.

Fiske, C.H. and Subba Row, Y., 1925. The Colorimetric Determination of Phosphorus. *J. Biol. Chem.,* **66:** 375-400.

Finney, D.T., 1971. *Probit Analysis, 3rd edition, Cambridge University Press, London and New York,* pp. 333.

Fleet, J.C., 1997. Dietary Selenium Repletion may Reduce cancer Incidence in People at high risk who Live in Areas with low Soil Selenium. *Nutr. Rev.* **55:** 227-29.

*Florkin, M., 1935. *Arch. Insect Physiol.,* **40:** 283-290.

*Frankel, G., 1940. *J. Exp. Biol.,* **17:** 18.

Franken berger, W.T., Benson, S., 1994. *Selenium in the Environment.* Marcel Dekker, New York.

Friedman, T.E. & Hangen, G.E., 1942. Collection of Blood for the Determination of Pyruvic and Lactic acids. *J. Biol. Chem.,* **144:** 67-77.

*Frost, D.V. & Hish, P.M., 1975. *Annev. Rev. Pharmacol.*, **15:** 259-284.

Fukuda, T., 1957. Biochemical Studies on the Formation of the Silk Protein IV. The Conversion of Pyruvic acid to alanine in the Silkworm Larva. *J. Biochem. (Tapar)*, **44:** 505 (1957); Conversion of Pyruvic acid to alanine in the Silkworm Larva. *Nature*, **180:** 245-247.

*Garcia, I., Tixier, M. & Roche, J., 1956. *C.R. Soc. Biol.*, **150:** 66.632.

Garg, V. K., Garg, S.K. & Tyagi, S. K., 1989. Manganese Induced Hematological and Biochemical Anamolies. *J. Environ. Biol.*, **10 (4):** 349-353.

Gawrilescu, N. and Peters, R.A., 1931. Biochemical Lesions in Vitamin B Deficiency. *Biochem. J.*, **25:** 1397-1409.

Geigy. R. Huber. M. Weinman, D. & Wyatt. G.R., 1959. Demonstration of Trehalose in the Vector of African Sleeping Sickness the tsetse Fly. *Acta Trop.* **16:** 255-262.

Ge H.H, Cai. XJ, Tyson J.F, Udon PC, Deniyer ER, Block E., 1996. Identification of Selenium species in Selenium enriched garlic, onion and broccoli using HPLC with inductively coupled plasma mask spectrometry detection. *Anal. Commun.* **33:** 279-281.

Gies A., Fromm T. & Zicgler R., 1988. Energy Metabolism in Starving Larvae of *Manduka sexta. Comparative Biochemistry and Physiology*, **91A:** 549-55.

Gilmour, D., 1961. The Biochemistry of Insects. *Academic Press, New York*, pp. 58-73.

Glenn M.W., Martin J.L. & Cummins L.M., 1964 "A Study of Sodium Selenite Toxicosis in Sheep. *Ames.J.Vet.Res*, **25:** 1495.

Goldstein, L. & Newholme, E.A., 1980. The Formation of Alanine from Aminoacids in Diaphragm Muscle of the Rab. *Bio. Chem. J.*, **154 (2):** 555-558.

Govindappa, S. & Swami, K.S., 1965. Electrophoretic Characteristics of Subcellular Components and their relation to Enzyme activities in Amphibian Muscle Fibres. Indian. *J. Exp. Biol.*, **3(4):** 209-212.

Grainde, B. & Seglen, P.O., 1981. Effects of Aminoacids Analogues on Protein Degradation in rat Hepatocytes. *Biochemica. Acta. Biophysica. Acta.*, **676:** 43-50.

Groff J.L., Gropper S.S. & Hunt S.M., 1995. Microminerals. In: Advanced Nutrition and Human Metabolism. *Minneapolis: West Publishing Company, Mineapolis*, pp 381-384.

Gullan, P.J. and Cranston, P.S., (2000). *The Insects: Outline Entomology. Blackwell Publishing, UK ISBN. 1405111135.*

Gussin, A. E.S. & Wyatt G.R., (1965). Membrane-bound trehalase from Cecropia silkmoth muscle. *Archs. Biochem. Biophys.* **112:** 626-634.

Hammond P.B. & Beliles R.P., 1980. Metals. In: Casarett and Doulls Toxicology, *The Basic Science of Poisons. 2nd ed;* J. Doull, C.D. Klaassen, and M.O. Amdur, *eds. Macmillan Pub., New York*, pp. 409-467.

Hanamura, Y. Hayashiya, K. Natio, K. Matsura, K & Nishida, J., 1962. Food select by Silkworm Larvae. *Nature*, **194:** 754- 755.

Harper, H.A. 1986. In Harper's review of biochemistry (Eds) D.W. Martin, P.A. Mayes and V.M. Rodwell, *20th edition, Lange Medical Publications, Maruzer Company Ltd., California.*

Harper, H.A., 1986. In: Harper's review of Biochemistry. (Eds) D.W. Martin, P.A. Mayes, and V.W. Rodwell, *20th edition, Lange Medical Publications, Marizen Asia, Singapore*, 29-45.

Harper, H.A., Rodwell, V.M. & Mayer, P.A., 1979. In: *Review of Physiological Chemistry, 17th edition, Longe Medical Publications, Maruzer Company Ltd., Caligornia.*

Harrison, J.H., Conrad, H.R., 1984. Effect of Selenium intake on Selenium utilization by the non- lactating cow. 1: *J. Dairy. Sci.*, **67(1):** 219- 23.

Harshfield, R.D & H.L. Klug., 1950. The Effect of Selenium on Anacrobic Glycolysis of rat Liver Homogenate. *Proc. South Dakota Acad. Sci.*, **29:** 94-98.

Haunerland N.H. Nair K.N. & Bowers W.S., 1990. Fatbody Heterogenesity during Development of Heliothis zea. *Insect Biochemistry*, **20:** 829- 37.

Hawkes W.C., Allen F.Z., Oehler L., 2003. Absorption, Distribution and Excretion of Selenium from Beef and Rice in Healthy North American men. 1: *J.Nutr.* **133 (11):** 3434- 42.

*Hayashi, Y., 1961. *J, Seric. Jap.*, **30:**13.

Heinz, G.H., Pendleton, G.W., Krynitsky, A.J. & Gold, L.G. 1990. Selenium Accumulation and Elimination in Mallards. *Arhives of Environ. Contam. and Toxicol.*, **19:** 374-379.

Heliovera, K. and Vaisemen, R., 1993. Incests and Pollution. *CRC Press, Boca Raton, Florida.*

Heller. J., Szarkowska, L.L. & Michalek, H., 1960. Ubigu none (Co-enzyme) in Insects. *Nature*, **188:** 491.

*Hemmingsen, A.M., 1924. Skand. *Arch. Physiol.*, **45:** 204-210.

Hoar, W.S., 1976. General and Comparative Physiology. (Eds. W.D. MC Elroy, C.P. Swenson, *2nd Edition, Prentice Hall, India Pvt. Ltd., New Delhi*, pp. 1056-1196.

Hogan, G.R. & Raziak, H.G. 1991. Selenium Induced Mortality and Tissue Distribution Studies in Tenebrio Molitor Coleoptera: Tenebrionidae, *C. Environ. Entamor*, **20:** 790-798.

Hoekstra, W.G., 1975. Biochemical Function of Selenium and its Relation to Vitamin-E. *Federation Proceedings*, **34:** 2083- 2089.

Holland, J. & G.F. Humphrey., 1953. The Metabolism of Paramecium Candatun. II. The Effect of Respiratory Inhibitors. *Australia J. exptl. Biol. Med. Sci.*, **31:** 299-310.

*Hopkins L.L., Hope A.L. & Baumann C.A., 1966, *J. Nutri.*, **88:** 61.

Horie, Y. (1959) Blood Trehalose and Fat Body Glycogen in the Silkworm *Bombyx. mori.*, *Nature*, **188:** 583-586.

Horie, Y., (1961). Physiological Studies on the Alimentary Canal of the Silkworm, *Bombyx mori L.* 111. Abscrption and Utilization of Carbohydrates, *Bull. Seric. Exp. Jpn.*, **16:** 287-309.

*Horie, Y., (1967), *J. Insect. Physiol.*, **13:** 1163.

*Horie, Y., 1959. *Bull. Seric. Exp. Sta.*, **15:** 365.

*Horie, Y., 1963, *Arch. Biochem. Biophysics*, **14:** 417.

Hoskins, W.M., 1940. Recent Contributions of Insect Physiology to Insect, Toxicity and Control. *Hilgradia*, **13:** 307-386.

Howden, G.F. & Kilby, B.A., (1956). Trehalose and Trehalase in the Locust. *Chem. & Ind.* 1453-1454.

Huckabee, W.E., 1961. Relationship of Pyruvate and Lactate during Anaerobic Metabolism. V. Coronary adequacy. *Am. J. Physiol.*, **200 (6):** 1169-1179.

Hutterer, F., Klion, F.M., Wengraf, A., Schaffner, F & Poper, H., 1969. Hepatocellular Adaptation and Injury Structural and Biochemical Changes following Dieldrin and Methyl Butter Yellow. *Lab. Invest.*, **20:** 455-464.

Hyldgaard- Jensen J.F., 1971. Lactate Dehydrogenase in Pigs *Thesis, Munksgaard, Copenhagen.*

Ingram, R.L., 1995. Water loss from Insects treated with Pyrethrum. *Ann. Soc. Amer.*, **48:** 481-485.

*Institute of Medicine., 1996. *Food and Nutrition Board, Washington.*

*Ito, T. & Horie, Y., 1959. *Arch. Biochem. Biophysics,* **80:** 174.

*Ito, T. & Horie, Y., 1959. *Bull. Seric. Exp. Stp.,* **15:**1959.

*Ito, T. & Tanaka, M., 1959. *Biol. Bull,* **116:** 195.

*Ito, T., Horie, Y. & Ishikawa, S., 1958. *J. Insect. Physiol.,* **2:** 313.

J.E. Spallholz., 1994. On the Nature of Selenium Toxicity and Carcinostatic Activity. *Free Radical Biology and Medicine,* **17:** 45-64.

*Jaffe W.G. and Mondragon M.C., 1969. *J.Nutr.,* **97:** 431.

James, S., Clegg, R. & Evans, David, (1961). Blood Trehalose and Flight Metabolism in the Blow Fly Phormia Regina, *science,* **134:** 54-55.

Janoff, A., 1970. Neutral Proteases of Human PMN Lysosomes: Possible Role in Joint Disease, *Feb.,* **29:** 7813.

Javier Martin F. - Romero, (2001). Selenium Metabilosm in Drosophila. Selenoproteins, Selenoprotein in RNA Expression, Fertility and Mortality. *J. Biol. Chem,* **Vol-276, issue 32:** 29798-29804.

Jia, XA. Zhou L.H., Wu, Y.N., Xia Wou, Xieng, R.H., Yog, J.G., Ji Zs, Wag P, Zhong Y.L., (1982). Relationship between Selenium and Protein Synthesis in Cells and Sub-Cellular Fractions in Liver. *J.Trace Elem. Electrolytes Health Dais.* **3(1):** 27-34.

*Johanson, B.E. and Barrington, D. 1970. *J. Invert. Dermatol.,* 3-85.

Karel, A.K. & Saxena, S.C., 1975. Acute Toxic Effect of Chlordane on Serum Proteins of *Merionvs hurrianae. Arch. Inter. Physiol., Biochem.,* **83:** 283 – 288.

Katanuma, N., Mikumo, K., Matsuda, M. & Okada, M., 1962. *J. Vitaminol.,* **8:** 68.

Katsuma, S., Tanake, G., Shimada, T and Kabayashi, M., (2004). Reduced Cystine Protease activity of the Haemolymph of *B. mori* larvae influenced with FP.25-inactivated *Bombyx mori* Nucleopolyhedrosis, Results in the Postmortem Host Degeneration. *Arch. Virol.* **149:** 1773-82.

Keeley LL, (1985). Physiology and Biochemistry of Fat Body. In: *Comprehensive Insect Phy. and Pharmacology,* Vol 3, ed Kerkut GA, Gilbert LI. Penguin Press, Oxford, 211-248.

Kilby, B.A., 1963. The Biochemistry of the Insect Fat Body. In: *Advances in Insect Physiology,* **1:** 111-174.

Kimurak. Dept. of Biochemistry, Faculty of Medicine, Tottori University from Article in Japanese "Role of Essential Track Elements in the Disturbance of Carbohydrate Metabolism."

*Klug H.L., Lampson G.P., Moxon A.L., 1950. *Proc. S.Dakota Acad.Sci.,* **29:** pp 57.

Klug, H. L., A.L. Moxon, D.F. Peterson & E.P. Painter., 1953. Inhibition of Rat Liver Succinic Dehydrogenase by Selenium Compounds. *J. Pharmacol. and Expt. Therap.,* **108:** 437-441.

Knekt, P., Marniemi, J., Teppo, L., Heliovera M. and Aromaa, A., 1998. Is Low Selenium Status a Risk Factor for Lung Cancer. *Am. J. Epidermiol.,* **148:** 975-982.

Knop, W. 1884-85. *Ber. Verhandl, K. Sa Chs. Ges. Wiss. Math-Phys. Classe,* 39.

Knox, W.E. & Greengard, O. 1965. In: Introduction to Enzyme Physiology, Advan. Enzyme. *Regnl (Ed.) G. Weber, Vol.3, Pergoman Press, New York,* pp. 247-248.

Kondo, Y & Watanabe, T., 1957. Studies on the free Amino Acids and related Compounds in the Silkworm, *Bombyx mori L.* (II) On the free Aminoacids and related Compounds Fin Silkworm Larval, *J. Seric. Sci. Jpn.*, **26:** 289-305.

*Krebs, H.A., 1954. In: *The Enzymes, Academic Press, New York,* **2:** 247-250.

Krishnamohan Reddy, B., 1986. Metabolic Modulation of Fatigue with Special Reference to Lactate and Ammonia Metabolism in different Skeletal Muscle Fibre types of Albino rat. *Ph.D. Thesis, S.V. Univ, Tirupati, India,* pp. 44-52.

Krishnswamy, S., Narasimhanna, M.N., Suryanarayana, S.K & Kumararaj, S., (1973). Sericulture manual 11-Silkworm hearing. *Food and Agriculture Organisation of the United Nations, Rome,* 131.

Krishnaswamy, S., 1978. New Technology of Silkworm Rearing. *Buli. No.3. C.S.R&T.I., Mysore,* p.23.

Krishnaswamy, S., 1986. New Technology of Silkworm Rearing. *Bulletin No.7, C.S.R. & T.I., Central Silk Board. Mysore,* pp. 16-20.

Kurz, 2002. *Osteoartritis and Cartilage,* **10(2):** 119-126.

*Kuwana, 1937. *Japan J. Zool.,* **7:** 273-303.

Langlands, J.P., Donald, G.E., Bowles, J.E. and Smith, A.J., 1991a. Subclinical Selenium Insufficiency 1. Selenium Status and the Response in Liveweight with Selenium. *Australian Journal of Experimental Agriculture,* **31:** 25-31.

Langlands, J.P., Donald, G.E., Bowles, J.E. and Smith, A.J., 1994. Selenium Concentration in the blood of Ruminants Grazing in New South Wales. 4. Relationship with Tissue Concentrations and Wool Production of Marino Sheep. *Australian Journal of Agricultural Research,* **45:** 1701-1714.

Lee Y.L & Lardy H.A., 1965. Influence of Thyroid Hormone on L-glycero Hosphate Dehydrogenase and other Dehydrogenases in various Organs of Rats. *J. Biol. Chem.,* **240:** 1427.

Lehninger, A.L., 1979, 1984. In: *Biochemistry, Kalyani Publications, Ludhiana, New Delhi.*

Lehninger, A.L., 1984. In Bio-Chemistry., 2nd edition, *Kalyani Publishers, Ludhiana, New Delhi,* 54-66.

Lemly, A.D., 1997. A Teratogenic Deformity Index for Evaluating Impacts of Selenium on Fish Populations. *Ecotoxicol. Environ. Saf.* **37:** 259-266.

Lemly, A.D., 1998. Assessing the Toxic Threat of Selenium to Fish and Aquatic Birds. *Environmental Monitoring and Assessment,* **43:** 19-35.

Lester RL, DeMoss J.A., 1971. Effects of Molybdate and Selenite on Formate and Nitrate Metabolism in E. coli. *J. Bacteriol.* **105:** 1006-1014.

Levander, O.A., 1991. Scientific Rationale for the. 1989 Recommended Dietary Allowances for Selenium. *J. Am. Diet. Associ.* **91:** 1572-1576.

Levander, O.A., 1997. Nutrition and Newly Emerging Viral Diseases: An over view. *J. Nutr.,* **127:** 9485-9505.

Levander O.A. & Argrett L.C., 1969. *Toxicol. Appl. Pharmacol.* **14:** 308.

Levander, O.A. & Beck, M.A. 1997. Interacting Nutritional and Infectious Etiologies of Keshan disease. Insights from Coxsackle virus B-induced Myocanitis in Mice deficient of Selenium or Vit. E. *Biol. Trace Elem. Res.,* **56:** 5-21.

Lockau and Ludicke., 1952. Die Darstellung von radioaktiuem O, 0-Diathyl 0-p-nitrophenylmonothiophosphat, seine Aufnahme und Weiterleitung in Insektenkerper. Z. *NATURFORSCH.*, **76:** 389-397.

Longtin, R., 2003. INCl, *J.of The National Cancer Institute,* **95(2):** 98-100.

Lowry. O.H. Rosen brough, N.J. Farr, A.L. Randall, R.J., 1951. Protrein Measurement with the Folin-phencl Reagent. *J. Biol. Chem.,* **193:** 265-275.

Ludwig I.D., 1954. Changes in the Distribution of Nitrogen in the Blood of the Japanese Bettle. *Physiol. Zool.,* **27:** 325-334.

Ludwig, T.G. & Bibby, 1969. Geographic Variations in the Prevalence of Dental Caries in the United States of America caries. *Res.* **3:** 32 – 43.

Lucky, T.D., 1968. Insecticide Homolygosis. *J. Econ. Entomol.,* **61:** 7-12.

Maag, D.D., Orsborn J.S. & Clompton J.R. 1960, *Amer. J. Vet. Res.,* **21:** pp 1049.

Magadum, S.B., Hooli, M.A., 1988. Effect of Thyroxine on the Polyvoltine Silkworm, the Pure Mysore breed of *Bombyx mori L., Envt.Ecol.***6:** 863-868.

Magadum, V. B., Magadum, S.B.,1993. Effect of Testosterone Proprionate on the Economic Traits of Silkworm, *Bombyx mori L. Korean J. Sci.* **35:** 69-72.

Martin, D.W., Mayers, P.A. & Rodwell, V.W., 1983. In: Harper's Review of Bio Chemistry. *Lange Medical Publications, Maruzen, Asia,* pp. 26-42.

Martin, J.L., Gerlackh, 1969. *Anal. Biochem.* **29:** 257.

Masilamani, S., Subramaniyam, R.K., Chikkanna & Noamani, M.K.R., 1991. The Role of Secondary Metabolites of mulberry leaf in Silkworm Feeding. *Indian Silk,* **30(1):** 44-46.

Mathuan, S., Sudha, P.M., & Pethimuthu, S.M., 1989. Effect of Bacillus Thurigiensis on the Midgut of B. mori larvae: A Histochemical and Histopathological Study. *J. Pathol.* **53:** 217-227.

Matsushma., Osamu., Katayama., Heizavuro., Yamala & Koji., 1987. The Capacity for Intracellular Osmoregulation Mediated by FAA in three Bivolve molluscs., *J. Exp. Mar. Biol. Ecol.* **19 (1):** 93-99.

Mautner, H.G., 1956. The Synthesis and Properties of some Selenopurines and Selenopyramidines. *J. Am. Chem. Soc.* **78:** 5292-94.

Mautner, H.G. and Kumbler, W.D., 1956. 2-Phenyl Selenosemicarbazide and related compounds. Dipole movement and Spectroscopic measurement on Analogus Ureides, Thioureides and Selenoureides. *J. Am. Chem. Soc.* **78:** 97-101.

Mayland, H.F., 1994. Selenium in Plant and Animal Nutrition. In: *Frankenberger, W.T. Jr. Benson, S. Editors. Selenium in the Environment, New York, Marcel Dekker,* p. 29-45.

McCoy, K.E.M. & WesWig, P.H., 1969. Some Selenium responses in the rat not related to Vitamin E. *J. Nutr.* **98:** 383-389.

McMullen, 1965. The Symptoms and Histopathology of Poisoning by Maneb in *Oncepltvs Fascitus. J. Canad. Ent.,* **97:** 1200-1208.

* Miller W.P. & Williams K.T., 1940. Jourl. Arg. Res; **60:** pp.163.

Miller, P.A., 1985. Structure and Physiology of the Circulatory System In: *Comprhensive Insect Physiology, Biochemistry and Pharmacology.* G.A. Kerkut and LI Gilbert, Eds. **3:** 289-354. Pergamon Press, Oxford.

Misra, D.S., 1981. Toxicological and Histopathological Studies of some Insecticides on certain Insects. *Ph.D. Thesis, Department of Entomology and Agric. Zoology, Faculty of Agriculture, Banaras Hindu University, Varanasi.*

Moloo S.K., 1973., Accumulation and Storage sites of Uric acid in the Developing eggs of Schistocerca Gregaria, *J. of Entemology, A,* **48:** 85-8.

Moore & Sutherland., 1981. *From "Selenium" published by Authors, New York.*

Moore, S. & Stein, W.H., 1954. A Modified Ninhydrin Reagent for the Photometric Determination of Aminoacids and related Compounds. *J. Biol. Chem.,* **211:** 907-913.

Morris, O.N., 1962. Progressive Histochemical Changes in Virus Infected Fat Body of the Western eak looper. *J. Insect. Pathol,* **4:** 454-464.

Moxon, A.L. & K.W. Franke., 1935. Effect of certain Salts on Enzyme Activity. *Ind. Eng. Chem.* **27:** 77-81.

MP Bansal & Parminder Kaur, 2005. Selenium, a Versatile Trace Element: Current Research Implications. *Ind. J. of Experimental Biology.* **Vol. 43:** 1119-1129.

Mullins, D.E., (1985). Chemistry and Physiology of the Haemolymph, In: *Comprehensive Insect Physiology and Pharmacology, Vol. 3. Kerkut, G.A., and Gilbert, L.F: (Editors). Pergmon Press:* 355-400.

Murphy, T.A. & Wyatt, G.R., 1965. The Enzymes of Glycogen and Trehalose Synthesis in Silkmoth fat body *J. Biol. Chem.,* **240:** 1500-1508.

Muth, O.H. 1963. White Muscle Disease, a Selenium Responsive Miopathy, *J. An. Med. Assoc.,* **142:** 272- 277.

Nachlas, M.M., Margulies, S.I. & Seligman, A.M., 1960. A Colorimetric Method for the Estimation of Succinate Dehydrogenase Activity. *J. Biol. Chem.,* **235:** 499.

Nagarajan, P. & Radha, N.V., 1990. Supplementation of Amino acids through Mulberry leaf for increased Silk Production. *Indian Silk,* **29(4)**: 21-22.

Nagy, I. Sohar, I. Bekessey, Kavaes, G. & Guba, F., 1981. Pros. Ann. Meet, *Bio. Chem.* **21:** p. 59.

Naik, P.R., 1985. Effect of Perimethrin on Consumption and Utilization of Food and Water in *Bombyx mori L.* and *Philosamia ricini* Hutt. *Thesis, Bangalore University, Bangalore.* PP. 119.

Nammalwar, P., 1983. Heavy Metal Pollution in the Marine. *Environment Sci. Rep,* **13:** 158-160.

Narasimha Murthy, C.V., Govindappa, S., 1988. Effect of Cobalt on Silkworm Growth and Cocoon Crop Performance. *Indian J Seric.,* **XXVII(1)**: 45-47.

Natarajan, G.M., 1982. Effect of Zinc Sulphate on the Tissue Glycogen content of Air breathing Climbing Perch, Anabas Scandens (cuvier). *Comp. Physiol. Ecol.,* **7:** 37-39.

Natelson, S., 1971. In: Practical Clinical Biochemistry (ed.) Varlely, H. 4th edition. *ELBV. London,* 161-162.

National Research Council Food and Nutrition Board. Recommended Dietary Allowances. 10th ed. Washington, DC, National Academy Press, 1989.

Nelson, N. & Somogyi, M., 1952. A Photometric Adaptation of Somogyi Method for the Determination of Glucoses. *J. Biol. Chem.,* **35(7):** 1092-1100.

Nicholson, S.W., 1993. The Ionic basis of Fluid Secretion in Insect Malpighian Tubules. Advances in the last ten years. *J. Insect. Physiol.,* **39:** 451-458.

Noguchi, T. & Kandatsu, M., 1971. Purification and Properties of a new Alkaline Protease of rat Skeletal Muscle. *Agric., Biol. Chem.,* **35 (7):** 1092-1100.

Nyberg, S., 1991. Multiple use of Plants - Studies on Selenium Incorporation in some Agricultural Species for the Production of Organic Selenium Compounds. *Plant Foods for Human Nutrition;* **41:** 69-88.

O' Donnel, M.J. Maddrell, shp., Skaer, H.Le B & Harrison, J.B., 1985. Elaborations of the Basal Surface of Cells of Malpighian Tubules of an Insect. *Tissue & Cell,* **17:** 865-81.

Olson, O.E., 1969. Selenium as a Toxic Factor in Animal Nutrition. In: *Proc. Gorgia. Nutr. Conf., Atlanta.* P. 68.

Opienska - Blanth, J., & Iwanowski., 1952. The Effect of Selenium on the Growth and Glucose Metabolism in Liquid.

Oser, B.L, 1965. Blood analysis, Hawks Physiological Chemistry, *Tata Mc Graw Hill Publishing Co. Ltd., Bombay, New Delhi,* pp. 1047.

Ostradius K., 1961., Nutritional Muscular Dystrophy in Pigs. Studies on the etiology, diagnosis and therapy, *Thesis, Uppsala.*

Palli S.R. & Locke M., 1988. The Synthesis of Haemolymph Proteins by the Larval Fat Body of an Insect. *Calpode ethlius* (Lepidoptera, Hesperiidae), *Insect Bio-chemistry,***18:** 405-3.

Pannabecker, T., 1995. Physiology of Malpighian Tubules. *Annu. Rev. Entmol.* **40:** 493-510.

Pant, R. Katiar, S.K. & Jaiswal, G., 1982., Effect of Feeding Hexachlorobenzeen and Acetyl Choline to *Philosamia ricini* larvae during development. *Curr. Sci.,* **51:** 732- 737.

Pant, R. & Katiar, S.K., 1983. Effects of Malathion and Acetyl Choline on Developing Larvae of *Philosamia ricini* (Lepidoptera : Saturnidae). *J. Bio. Sci.,* **5:** 89-95.

Passow, H. Rophestein, A and Clarkson, T.W., 1961. The General Pharmacology of Heavy Metals. *Pharmacol. Rev:,* **13:** 183-224.

Parker, D.R., Paise, A.L., 1994. Vegetation Management Strategies for Remediation of Selenium-Hontaminated Soils. In: Frankenberger Jr. W. T. and Benson, S.(Eds). *Selenium in the Environment. Marcel Decker, New York,* pp. 327-342.

Patterson, B.H. & Levander, O. A., 1997. Naturally Occurring Selenium Compounds in Chemoprevention Trials: *A work shop summary. Cancer epidemiol Biomakers Prev;* **6:** 63-9.

Pawar, V.M & Rama Krishnan, N., (1977). Biochemical Changes in Larval Haemilymph of Spodoptera Litura Fibricus due to Nuclear Polyhedrogis Virus Infection, *Indian J. expt. Biol.* **15:** 755-758.

Pehrson, B., 1993. Selenium in nutrition with Special reference to the Biopotency of Organic and Inorganic Selenium Compounds. *Biotechnology in the Feed Industry.* **1993:** 71-90.

Petrusewiez, K & Mac. Fayden, A., 1970. Productivity of Terrestrial Animals. *IBP Handbook No. 13, Blackwell Scientific Publications, Oxford and Eden Berg. Pp.* 190.

Pilat, M., 1935. Histological Researches into the action of Insecticides on the Intestinal tube of Insects. *Bull. Ent. Res.,* **26:** 165-180.

Ponz, F., 1952. Efecto del arsenitoy del selenito sobre la absorcion intestinal de glucose. *Rev. Espan. Fisiol.* **8:** 261-267.

Prasad, N.R., 1990. Contributions to Pathobiology og Silkworm *Bombyx mori L.* infected with endoparasite Exorista (Wild). *Ph.D., Thesis University of Mysore, Mysore, India.* Pp. 10-90.

Prsser, T.S., Sylvestar, M.A. & Low, W.M., 1994. Bioaccumulation of Selenium from Natural Geologic Sources in Western States and its Potential Consequences. *Environ. Management,* **18:** 423-436.

Processer, C.L. & Brown, P.A. Jr., 1979. In: Comparative Animal Physiology (eds). *III Edition, W.B. Sanders Co., Philadelphia. Raaltd., H.G.S. Van Pesticide,* **2(3):** 39.

Radhakrishnaiah, K. & Busappa, B., 1986. Effect of Cadmium on the Carbohydrate Metabolism of the fresh water field crab Oziotelpnusa senex (Fabricius). *J. Environ. Biol.,* **7(1):** 17-21.

Radhakrishna, P.G., 1989. Effect of Organophosphorous Insecticides on food Utilization in the Silkworm *Bombyx mori L. Ph.D Thesis. Bangalore University, Bangalore, India.*

Radhakrishnaiah, K. & Chamundeswari, P., 1994. Effect of zinc and nickel on the Larval and Cocoon characters of the Silkworm, *Bombyx mori* (L.). *Sericologia,* **34**(2): 327-332.

Rani and Lalitha., 1996. *Biological Trace Element Research,* **51(3):** 225-234.

*Rao, C.G.P., 1990. How is Silk Produced? *Indian Silk,* **35:** 6-8. 18.

Reinfelder, J.R., Fisher, N.S., 1994. The Retention of Elements Absorbed by Juvenile Fish (*Menidia menidia, M. beryllina*) from Zooplanktonic Prey. *Limnol. Oceangr.* **39:** 1783-1789.

Reitman, S. & Frankel, S., 1957. A Colorimetric Method for the Determination of Serum Glutamic Oxaloacetate and Glutamic Pyruvic Transaminases. *Am. J. Clin. Path.* **27:** 56.

Roe, F.J.C., Lancaster, M.C., 1964. Natural Metallic and other Substances as Carcinogens. *Br. Med. Bull.* **20:** 127-133.

Roeder, K.P., 1953. Reflex Activity and Ganglion Function. In: *Insect Physiology, John Wiley and Sons, Publishers, New York and London,* pp 463-487.

Rosenfield, I. & Beath, A., 1964. *Selenium, Geo-Botany, Bio-chemistry, Toxicity and Nutrition, Academic Press, New York.*

Rotruck JT, Pope AL., Ganther HE, Swanson AD, Hafeman DG, Hoekstra WG., 1973. Selenium: Biochemical Role as a Component of Glutathione Peroxidase. *Science,* **179:** 588-590.

Rowan, A.N. & Newsholme, E.A., (1979). Changes in the contents of Adenine Nucleotides and Intermediates of Glycolysis and the Citric and Cycle in Flight muscle of the Locust upon Flight and their Relationship to the Control of the Cycle. *Biochem. J.* **178:** 209-216.

Russow, M.W., Murray, S.C., Wurzelwan, J.I., Woosley, J.T. & Sandler, R.S., 1997. Plasma Selenium levels and the risk of Colorectal Adenomos. *Nutr. Cancer,* **28:** 125-9.

Sailaja, K., Rani, P.P., Mohan, P.M. & Bharathi, D., 1997. Effect of Cobalt on the Growth pattern of Silkworm *Bombyx mori* L. *Environ. and Eco.,* **15** 1, 130-132.

Sakamoto, E. & Horie, Y., 1979. Quantitative change of Phosphorus Compounds in Haemolymph during Development of the Silkworm *Bombyx mori L. J. Seric. Sci.,* Japan; **48:** 319-326.

Sakamoto, E. & Horie, Y., 1979. Quantitative changes of Phosphorous Compounds in Haemoloymph during Development of the Silkworm *Bombyx mori L. J. Insect Physiol.,* **9:** 509-519.

Saito, S., 1963. Trehalose in the Body Fluid of the Silkworm *Bombyx mori L. J. Insect. Physiol.,* **9:** 509-519.

Samaranayaka, M., 1978. Insecticide induced Release of Neuro Secretory Hormones. In. Pesticide and venom neurotoxicity (eds.) D.L. Shankland, R.M. Holling Worth and T. Smyth. *Plenum. New York.*

*Saito, S., 1963. *J. Insect. Physiol,* **9:** 509.

Sawicki, E. and Carr, A., 1957. Structure of 2,1,3-Benzoselenadiazole and its derivatives. 1. Ultraviolet visible absorption spectra. *J. Org. Chem.* **22:** 503-506.

Schimke, R.T., 1974. In: *New Sciences (Eds) F.O. Schmitt and F.G. Worder, Cambridge, Massachusetts,* **111:** pp. 813-825.

Schin K., Lanfer H. & Carr E., 1977. Cytochemical and Electrophoretic Studies of Hemoglobin Synthesis in the Fat Body of a Midge, Chironomous thummi. *J. of Insect Physiology,* **23:** 1233- 42.

Schmidt, A.P. & Platzer, E.G., 1980. Changes in Body Tissue and Haemolmph Composition of *Culex Pipens* in response to infection Romanomermis culicivorax. *J. Invert. Pathol.,* **36:** 240- 254.

Schmid-Hempel, P., 2005. Evolutionary Ecology of Insect Immune Defenses. *Annu. Rev. Entomol.* **50:** 529-551.

Schwartz, K. and Foltz, C.M., 1957. Selenium as an Integral part of Factor 3 against dietary necrotic Liver Degeneration. *J. Am. Chem. Soc.* **79:** 3292.

Scott, M.L., 1978. Vitamin E. pp. 133-210 In: Handbook of Lipid Research. 2. The Fat Soluble Vitamins, H.F. DeLuca, ed. *New York, Pienum Press.*

Scriber, J.M. and Slansky, F. J.R., 1981. *The Nutritional Ecology of Immature Insects. Ann. Rev. Entomol.* **26:** 183-211.

*Shamberger, R., 1985. The Genotoxicity of Selenium. *Mutat. Res.,* **154:** 29-48.

Sharma, K.C., 1984. Effects of Mercury Pollution the general Biology and Carbohydrate metabolism of a fresh water Murrel, *Channa puactatus (Bloch). Geobios,* **11:** 122-127.

Shigematsu, H., 1958. Synthesis of Blood Protein by the Fat Body in the Silkworm *Bombyx mori L. Nature,* **182:** 880-882.

*Shigematsu, H., 1956. *Nippon Sanshigaku Easshi,* **25:** 1232-127.

Shimada, S., Kamada, A & Asano, S., (1980). The Cocoon Trehalase of the Silkworm, *Bombyx mori L Insect Biochem.* **10:** 49-52.

Shupe, J.L., Miner, M.L., Harris, L.F. and Green wood, D.A., 1962. Relative Effects of Feeding hay Atmospherically Contaminated by Fluoride residue, Normal hay plus Sodium Fluoride to Dairy Heifers. *Am. J. Vet. Res.* **23:** 777-787.

Shyamala, M.B., Venkatachalamurthy, M.R. and Bhatt, J.R., 1956. Effect of Chloromycetin of food Utilization by the Silkworm *Bombyx mori L. J. Ind. Inst. Sci.* **38:** 177-185.

Silva, G.M., Doyle. W.P. & Wang, C.H., 1959. Glucose Catabolism in the DDT treated American Cockroach (*Periplaneta americana*), *Arguirus Portugueses Biogriumica,* **3:** 298-305.

*Simmons *etal.,* 1989 (a,b). *Biochem. and Biophys. Res. Commun.,* **165:** 158-163.

Singaraju, R., Subramanian, M.A & Varadaraju, G. 1991., Sublethal Effects Malathion on the Protein Metabolism in the fresh water Field Crab *Paratelphusa Hydrodomus.* Eco toxicol. Environ. Monitor. **1 (1):** 41-44.

Singer, T.P., Kearney, E.B. & Ackrell, B.A.C., 1973. Newer Knowledge of the Regulatory Properties of Succinate Dehydrogenese. *Mech. Bioc energy. proc. invt. conf.,* 485-498.

*Smith M.I., Westfall B.V., Stonlmal E.F., 1938. *U.S. Public Health Rept.,* **53:** pp 1199.

Smitha, S., (2002). Impact of Selenium on some Physiological and Cocoon Commercial Characters of Silkworm *Bombyx mori L. M.Phil. Dissertation, S.K.University, Anantapur.*

Snyder, N.J., Walding, J.K. and Feyereisen, R. 1994. Metabolic fate of the Allelochemical nicotine in the Tobacco horn worm. *Manduca Sexta. Insect Biochemistry and Molecular biology,* **24:** 837-46.

Sondergaard L., (1993) Homology between the Mammalian Liver and the Drosophila Fat Body. *Trends Genet.;***9:** 193.

Spagnolo, A. Morsi, G. Marano, G., Righetti G., Maietta A. and Menothi A., 1991. Serum Selenium and Processors of Cardiovascular risk factors in Adolescent. *Eur. J. Epidimol.* **7:** 654 – 657.

Springe, J.H., 1990. Endocrine Regulation of Diuresis in Insects. *J. Insect. Physiol.,* **36:** 13-22.

Springthorpe, E.G., (1973). In: *An Introduction to Functional Systems in Animals.* Longman Group Ltd. Pp. 140-149.

Sridhara, S., 1981. In: *Metamorphosis, Problem in Developmental Biology (Gil-bert, L.I. and Frieden, E., eds)* pp.177-216 *Plenum Press, New York.*

Sridhara, S. & Bhatt, J.V., 1963. Alkaline and Acid Phosphotases of the Silkworm *Bombyx mori L. J. Insect. Physiol.* **9:** 693-701.

Srikantan J.N. & Krishnamoorthi, C. R., 1955. Tetrazolium test for Dehydrogenase. J. Sci. Industrial. Res., 14: 206-207.

Stagni, N. & Debenard, B., 1968. Lysosomal Enzyme Activity in rat and Beef Skelelal Muscle Biochem. *Biophys. Acts.,* 170(1): 129-139.

Steele, J.E., 1976. Hormonal Control of Metabolism in Insects. *Adv. Insect. Physiol.,* 12: 239-256.

Steele, J.E., 1980. Hormonal Correlation of Carbohydrate and lipid Metabolism in the Fat body. In: *Insect Biology in the Future, Academic Press inc.,* 253-271.

Steele, J.E., 1982. Glycogen Phosphorylase in Insects. *Insect Biochem.,* **12:** 131-147.

Steele, J. E., 1983. Endocrine Control of Carbohydrate Metabolism in Insects. In: *Endocrinology of Insects. Downer, R.G.H. and Lavfer, H.(Eds.). New York,* pp. 427-439.

Steele, J. E., 1985. Control of Metabolic Processes. In: *Comprehensive Insect Physiology, Biochemistry and Pharmacology,* **Vol.8:** ed. G.A. Kerkut and L.I. Gilbert, pp. 99-145, *Oxford; Pergman Press.*

*Steinhaver, A.L., & Stephen, W.P. 1959. *Ann. Entomol. Soc. Am.,* **52:** 733-738.

Steinz, G.H., Peneteton, G.W., Koynitsky, A.J. & Gold, L.G., 1990. Selenium Accumulation and Elimination in Mallards. *Archives of Environ. Contam. and Toxicol.,* **19:** 374-379.

Stevenson, E. & Wyatt, G.R., 1964. Glycogen Phosphorylase and its Activation in Silkmoth Fat Body. *Arch. Biochem. Biophys.* **108:** 420-429.

Stowe, H.D. & Brady, D.S. 1978. Effect of Copper Pretreatment on Selenium Toxicity in ponies, *Fed. Proc.* **37:** 324 (Abstr.).

Sutherland, E.W., 1955. Polysaccharide Phosphorylase, Liver. In: Methods in Enzymology, Vol.1 (Eds.) S.P. Colowick and N.O. Kaplan. *Academic Press, New York.* Pp. 215-225.

*Swaminathan, M., 1983. *Handbook of Food and Nutrition. 3rd edition;* pp.22.

Tae Won Goo, Eun Young Yun, Jae-Sam Hwang, Seok-Woo Kang, Kwan-Hee You and O – Yu Kwon., 2002. Molecular Characterization of a *Bombyx mori* Protein Isomerase (bPDI). Cell stress Chaperones., **7(1):** 118-125.

Tavill, A.S. & Cooksley, W.H.S., 1983. Bio Chemical Aspects of Livele Disense. In: Bio Chemical Aspects of Human Disease. *(Eds) R.S. Elkeles, A.S. Tavill, Black-weel Scientific Publications, Boston,* **22:** 1-12.

Terry N. & Zayed A.M., 1994. *Selenium Volatilization by Plants, New York,* pp 343-368.

*Theye, R.A. 1971., *Anasthesiology.,* **35:** 394.

Thompson, A.C. & Sikoroshiki, P.P., 1980. Fatty acid and Glycogen requirement of Heliothis Virescens infected with Cytoplasmic Polyhedrosis Virus. *Biochem. Physiol.,* **66B:** 93-97.

Tojo S. Kiguchi K. & Kimura S., 1980. Hormonal Control of Storage Protein Synthesis and obtake by the Fat Body in ths Silkworm *Bombyx mori.L., J. of Insect Physiology.* **27:** 491-7.

Tollersrud S., 1970. Studies on some Serum Enzyme assess and their Diagnostic value in Nutritional diseases of Ruminants and Pigs. Thesis. *Universitets for laget. Oslo.*

Tollersrud S., 1973. Changes in Enzymatic profile in blood and Tissues in Preclinical and clinical vitamin E deficiency in Pigs. *Acta. Agric. Scand.* **(Suppl., 19):** 124.

Tonge, C.H. and McCance R.A., (1965). Severe under Nutrition in Growing and Adult Animals: 15, the mouth, jaws And teeth of Pigs. *Brit. J. Nutrition,* **19:** 361-372.

Trelease, S.F. and Beath, O.A., 1949., *"Selenium" Published by the authors, New York.*

Tsen, C. Cand Collier., 1959. Selenite as a relatively weak Inhibitor of some Sulf Hyorye Enzymes. *Nature.* **183:** 1327-1328.

Turner, L.V. & Mancheslei., K.L., 1972. Effects of Denervation on the Glycogen context on the activities of Enzymes of Glucose and Glycogen Metabolism in Fat Diaphragm Muscle. *Biochem. J.,* **128:** 789-801.

Ursini, F. 1999. *Science,* **285:** 1393-1396.

Van Marrewijk, W. J.A. Vanden Broek, A. Th. M. and Beenakkers, A.M. Th., (1980). Regulation of Glycogenolysis in the locust Fat Body during Flight. *Insect Biochem.* **10:** 675-679.

Van Vleet, J.E. Ferrans, V.J. & Ruth, G.R., 1976. Ultra strucural Alterations in Skeletal Muscle of Pigs with Selenium – Vitamin E deficiency, *A. N. J. Vet. Res.* **37:** 911.

Van Vleet, J.E. Ferrans, V.J. & Ruth, G.R., 1977. Ultra structural Alterations in Nutritional Cardiomiopathy of Selenium- Vitamin E deficient Swine Vascular lesions. *Lab. Invest.* **37:** 201.

Venkat Reddy, S., Sivarami Reddy, N. & Ramamurthy, R., 1991. Effect of Carboryl on the Growth and Silk qualities of the Silkworm *Bombyx mori L. Ind. J. Seri.* **XXVIII (2):** 182-190.

Venkatarami Reddy, K., Rama Devi, O.K., Magadum, S.B., Benchamin, K.V & Datta, R.K. 1992. Uzi parasitization, Gluconeogenic precursor levels and related Enzyme activity profiles in Silkworm, *Bombyx mori L. Indian. J. Seric.* **31(2):** 123-129.

Venkatarami Reddy, K., Rama Devi, O.K. & Benchamin, K.V. 1991. Impact of Uzifly parasitization on the body growth, silkgland tissue Somatic index and naemolymph properties of silkworm *Bombyx mori L. Indian. J. Seric.,* **30 (2):** 113-120.

Venugopala Pillai, S., Krishnaswamy, S., & Kasi Viswanathan, K., 1987. Growth studies in Silkworm *Bombyx mori* L. under tropical conditions. Influence of Agronomical methods of mulberry on growth, Cocoon crop and Fecundity of Silkworm. *Indian J. Seric.,* **XXVI(1):** 32-45.

Vinson, S.B. & Dahlman, D.L., 1989. Physiological relationship between Braconid Endoparasites and their hosts. The Microplitus eroceipes (Hymenoptera Broconid) Heliothis Species (Lepidoptera: Noctuidae) System. *South Western Entomologist,* **12:** 17-37.

Waldbauer, 1964. The Consumption, Digestion and Utilization of Solanaceous and Non-solanaceous plants by the Larvae of the Tobacco Horn Worm, *Protoparce sexta* (Johan) (Lepidoptera: Sphingidea) *Entmol. Exp. Appl.* **7:** 253 – 269.

Waldbauer, G.P., 1968. The Consumption and Utilization of Food by Insects. *Advances in Insect Physiology* **5:** 229-288.

Wang, W-X., Fisher, N.S. Luoma, S.N., 1996, Kinetic Determinations of Trace Element Bioaccumulation in the Mussels. *Mytilus edulis. Mar. Ecol. Prog. Ser.* **140:** 91-113.

Wang, W-X., Stupakoff, I and Fisher, N.S., 1999. Bioavailability Dissolved and Sediment Bound Metals to a Marine deposit feeding Polychaete. *Mar. Ecol. Prog. Ser.* **178:** 281-293.

Wang, W-X., Reinfelder, J.R., Lee, B-G, Fisher, N.S., 1996. Assimilation and Regeneration of Trace Elements by Marine Copepods. *Limnol. Oceanogr.* **41:** 70-81.

Wang, W-X, Fisher, N.S., 1998. Accumulation of Trace Elements in a Marine Copepods. *Limnol. Oceangr.* **43:** 273- 283.

Wayne Chris Hawkes, Zeynep Alkan, Kar Lang, Janet C. King., 2004. "Plasma Se decrease during Pregnancy is Associated with Glucose Intolerance". *Biological Trace Element Research.* **Volume 100, Issue 1,** pps. 019-030.

Weis-Fogh, T., (1964). Diffusion in Insect Wing Muscle, the most Active Tissue known. *J. Expl. Biol.* **41:** 229-256.

Whanger, P.D., P.H. Weswig. J.A. Schmitz. & J.E. Old field, 1977. Effect of Selenium and Vitamin E on blood Selenium levels, Tissue Glutathione Peroxidak activities and White Muscle Disease in sheep fed purified or Hay Diets. *J. nutr.* **107:** 1298 – 1307.

Wheeler, C.H., (1989). Mobilization and Transport of Fuels to the Flight Muscles. In *Insect Flight,* ed. G.J. Goldsworthy and C.H. Wheeler, pp. 273-303. Boca Raton: CRC Press.

Whelan, B.R., Barrow, N.J. & Peter, D.W., 1994. Selenium Fertilizers for Pasteers Grazed by Sheep. 2. Wool and live weight Responses to Selenium. *Australian Journal of Agricultural Research,* **145:** 877-887.

Whelan, B.R., Barrow, N.J. & Peter, D.W., 1994. Selenium Fertilizers for Pasteurs Grazed by Sheep. 2. Wool and live weight Responses to Selenium. *Australian Journal of Agricultural Research;* **45:** 877-887.

Wiens, A.W. & Gillbert, L.I., 1967. The Phosphorylae System of the Silkmoth, *Hyalophora cecropia. comp. Biochem. Physiol,* **21:** 145-159.

Wigglesworth, U.B., 1939. *Principles of Insect Physiology. Methuen, London, E.P. Dutton, New York,* 1106-1123.

Wilkins, J.F., Kilgour, R.J., Gleeson, A.C., Cox, R.J., Geddes, S.K. and Simpson, I.A., 1982. Production responses in Selenium Supplemented Sheep in Northern New South Wales 2. Live weight gain, wool production and reproductive performance in young Merino ewes given Selenium and copper Supplements. *Australian Journal of Expl. Agriculture and Animal Husbandry,* **22:** 24-28.

Woodruff, I.O. and W.J. Gies., 1902. On the Toxicology of Selenium and its Compounds. *Am. J. Physiol.* **6:** XXIX-XXX.

Wolley, D.W., 1952. A Study of Antimetabolites. *Wiley, New York, Chapman and Hall, London.*

Worland, M.R. and Block, W., 2003. Desiccation Stress at sub-zero in polar Terrestrial Arthropods. *J. Insect. Physiol.* **49:** 193 – 203.

Worland, D.A., Wharton and Byars, S.G., 2004. Intracellular Freezing and Survival in the Freeze Tolerant Cockroach, *Celatoblatta quinquemaculata. J. Insect Physiol.* **50:** 225-235.

Wretlind, B. Ostradius, K. and Lindberg, P., 1959. Transaminase and Transferase Activities in Blood Plasma and in Tissues of Normal Pigs. *Zentralbl. Veterinae.med.* **6:** 963.

Wright, C.I., 1938. Effect of Sodium Selenite and Selenate on the Oxygen Consumption of Mammalian Tissues. *Public Health Rept. (U.S)* **53:** 1825-1836.

Wu, L., Guo, X. & Banvelos, G.S., 1997. Accumulation of seleno-amino acids in Legume and grass plant Sps. grown in Selenium-caden soils. Environ. *Toxicol. Chem.,* **16:** 491-497.

Wu, L., Van Mantgem, P.J., Guo, X., 1996. Effects of Forage Plant and Field Legume Species on soil Selenium Redistribution, Leaching and Bioextraction in soils contaminated by Agricultural drain water Sediment. *Archives of Environmental Contamination and Toxicology,* **31:** 329-338.

Wu.Y, Sun Z, Che S, Chang H, 2004. Effects of zinc and Selenium on the disorders of blood Glucose and lipid Metabolism and its Molecular Mechanism in Diabeticrats. 1: *Wei Sheng Yan Jiv.* **33(1):** 70-3.

Wyatt, G.R & Kalf, G.F., (1957). The Chemistry of Insect Haemolymph. I. Trehalose and other Carbohydrates, *J. Gen. Physiol.* **40:** 833-847.

Wyatt, G.R. & Kalf, G.F., (1956) Trehalase in Insects. *Fed. Proc.* **15:** 188.

Wyatt, G.R. & Kalf, G.F. (1956). Trehalose in Insects. *Fed. Proc.* **15:** 388.

Wyatt, G.R., Lougheed, T.C. & Wyatt, S.S., (1956). The Chemistry of Insect Haemolymph. Organic Compounds of the Haemolymph of the Silkworm, *B. mori* and two other species. *J. Gen. Physiol.,* **39:** 853-868.

Wyatt, G.R., Lougheed, T.C. & Wyatt, S.S., 1956. The Effect of External Calcium and Magnesium Depletion on single Nerve Fibres. *J. Gen. Physiol.,* **39:** pp. 853.

Wyatt, G.R., 1961. The Biochemistry of Insect Haemolymph. *Annual Review of Entomology,* **6:** 75-102.

Wyatt, G.R., 1967. The Biochemistry of Sugars and Polysaccharides in Insects. *Advance Insect. Physiol.,* **4:** 287-360.

Xeros, N., 1956. The Virogenic Stroma in Nuclear and Cytoplasmic Polyhedrosis. *Nature,* 412-413.

Yamashita, O. & Hasegawa, K., 1974. Mobilization of Carbohydrates in Tissues of Female Silkworms, *Bombyx mori L.* during Metamorphosis. J. *Insect Physiol.,* **20:** 1749-1760.

Yamashita, O., Hasegawa, K & Seki, M., 1972. Effect of Diapause Hormone on Trehalose activity in Pupal Ovaries of the Silkworm, *Bombyx mori L. Gen. Comp. Endocrinol.* **18:** 514-523.

*Yanagawa, H., 1971. *Insect Biochem.,* **1:** 102.

Yanagawa, H. & Horie, Y 1977. Studies on Phosphorylase in the Tissues of the Silk worm, *Bombyx mori L.* The activities of Phosphorylase 'a' and 'b' in various Tissues. *J. Sericult. Sci. Japan.* **46:** 130-138.

Yanagawa, H. & Horie, Y, 1977b. Studies on Phosphorylase in the Tissues of the Silkworm, *Bombyx mori* Purification and Properties of Phosphorylase b. *J. Sericult. Sci. Japan.* **46:** 139-146.

Yanagawa, H. & Horie, Y., 1978. Activating Enzyme of Phosphorylase b in the Fat Body of the Silkworm, *Bombyx mori* L. *Insect. Biochem.* **8:** 155-158.

*Yanagawa, H., 1973. *Bull. Seric. Exp. Sta.,* **25:** 267.

Yoneda, S., 1997. *Biochemical and Biophysical Research Communications,* **231(1):** 7-11.

Young, U.R., 1970. In: *Mammalian Protein Metabolism, Academic Press, New York, U.S.A.*

Zalkin, H., Tappel, A.L., Caldwell, K.A., Shillkos, M., Desai, I.D & Holliday, T.A., 1962. Increased Lysosomal Enzymes in Muscular Dystrophy of Vitamin E. Deficient rabbits. *J. Biol. Chem.,* **237(8):** 2678-2682.

Zeng, H. 2005. *J. of Inorganic Biochemistry,* **99(6):** 1269-1274.

Zhon, C.H., Iwashita, Y., Fukami & Kanke, E., 1995. Histopathological Observations on the Larval Midgut cells of Silkworm *Bomboyx mori* poisoned by NaF. *Journal of Sericultural Science, Japan,* **64:** 344-351.

Index